Economic forecasting: an introduction

Economic forecasting: an introduction

K. HOLDEN, D.A. PEEL
and J.L. THOMPSON

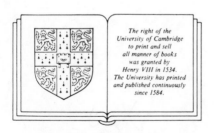

The right of the
University of Cambridge
to print and sell
all manner of books
was granted by
Henry VIII in 1534.
The University has printed
and published continuously
since 1584.

CAMBRIDGE UNIVERSITY PRESS

Cambridge

New York   Port Chester

Melbourne   Sydney

Published by the Press Syndicate of the University of Cambridge
The Pitt Building, Trumpington Street, Cambridge CB2 1RP
40 West 20th Street, New York, NY 10011, USA
10 Stamford Road, Oakleigh, Melbourne 3166, Australia

© Cambridge University Press 1990

First published 1990

Photoset and printed in Malta by Interprint Limited

British Library cataloguing in publication data

Holden, K. (Kenneth), *1943–*

  Economic forecasting: an introduction.
  1. Economic forecasting
  I. Title II. Peel, D. (David), *1950–*
  III. Thompson, John L., *1931–*
  338.5'44

Library of Congress cataloguing in publication data

CIP applied for

ISBN 0 521 35612 1   hard covers
ISBN 0 521 35692 x   paperback
IP

Contents

Figures

Tables

viii   **Figures and tables**

Preface

In recent years there have been extensive developments in the methods used in economic forecasting. This book presents an introduction to these methods for advanced undergraduate and postgraduate students of economics. We assume a background of intermediate economics and introductory econometrics. Part 1 is concerned with techniques. In chapter 1, a general introduction to forecasting methods is presented, and in chapter 2 recent advances in time-series methods are reviewed. Ways of combining forecasts are discussed in chapter 3. Part 2 is concerned with applications of these techniques in microeconomics (chapter 4), macroeconomics (chapter 5) and asset markets (chapter 6). The concluding chapter brings together some of the earlier results.

We are grateful to Peter Stoney, University of Liverpool, Paul de Grauwe, Catholic University of Leuven, David Byers, Michael Cain and David Law, University College, Aberystwyth for their comments on parts of the manuscript. Any errors and omissions are the responsibility of the authors. We acknowledge financial assistance from the Economic and Social Research Council (Grant B01250033) and Liverpool Polytechnic.

K. Holden
D. A. Peel
J. L. Thompson

PART 1

Techniques

CHAPTER 1

Introduction to forecasting methods

1.1 Why forecasts are needed

This book is concerned with forecasting. Forecasts are required for two basic reasons: the future is uncertain and the full impact of many decisions taken now is not felt until later. Consequently, accurate predictions of the future improve the efficiency of the decision-making process. For example, at the simplest level, in most countries weather forecasts are produced which are publicised by the media. These are of interest to the general public, farmers and travellers. If the weather was always the same from day to day, forecasts would not be produced. It is only because the weather changes that forecasting becomes relevant.

Most decisions are made with a view to influencing where one will be in the future: a firm builds a new factory to meet expected future demand for its product; workers decide to save part of their incomes in order to pay for holidays later in the year or to make provision for their retirement; a stock market investor buys some shares now in the hope of receiving a worthwhile return, in dividends and/or capital gains, in the future; a banker buys foreign currency on the forward market to reduce risks of losses from movements in exchange rates. All these activities require some idea or forecast of the future behaviour of key environmental variables so that an assessment can be made of what will happen if nothing is done now, and what is likely to happen if certain steps are taken.

Managers in firms use forecasts in their day-to-day planning and control of company operations. The success of a business depends on the ability of management to foresee and prepare for the future. Reliable forecasts enable timely decisions to be made which are based on sound plans. An assessment of the future, normally in the shape of a sales forecast, is an integral part of decisions on: company financial planning, investment in plant and machinery, the timing of the purchase of materials, manpower requirements, setting production and inventory levels, determining sales targets and deciding advertising expenditures. All firms are affected by three areas of activity: the macroeconomy, their industry and the firm itself. Usually, it is only the last of these that the firm can control, and so it is important it is well informed on outside trends. This means having forecasts about the economy and their industry.

3

Macroeconomic forecasts are needed by government, industry and financial agents. Governments use forecasts for macroeconomic policy making. The annual budget requires estimates of future revenues (income tax, profits tax, sales or value added tax, excise duties, etc.) and future expenditure (including unemployment benefit, index-linked state pensions, and central and local government expenditure on goods and services). While some of these are under the direct control of the government, it is obvious that, among other things, the government needs to take some view on future values of national output, unemployment, interest rates and price levels in planning the budget. The international sector is also important since imports and exports affect national income directly, and, together with monetary and fiscal policy, determine the value of the exchange rate.

As well as this direct requirement to formulate macroeconomic policy, governments need forecasts because of their responsibilities for the provision of the necessary infra-structure of the country. Thus, for example, the viability of major road and tunnel projects is assessed by cost/benefit techniques which involve projections of future traffic levels and these in turn are affected by future incomes. In the case of a major road project there may be a delay of up to ten years between the time the decision is made on whether the road is needed and its completion. The future level of traffic will be an important consideration in determining the capacity of the road, and this in turn will be affected by national and regional economic growth. Forecasts of the future state of the economy are therefore an essential input into the decision-making process. Similarly, with large investment projects such as electric power stations, there can be a long lag, possibly of ten or fifteen years, between the decision to go ahead with the project and the time it begins production. Since the demand for electricity depends on the level of industrial output and consumer prosperity, forecasts are needed to help to decide whether further investment in power stations is desirable. In this example, the problems are the same for governments and industrial companies. The rate of growth of the home and world economy, the amount of inflation, the price and availability of labour and capital, and the level of the exchange rate, all have important implications for planning for the future.

In financial markets the focus of activity is on the interactions between the present and future values of assets. The inter-relationships between short-term and long-term interest rates, current and future exchange rates, and government monetary and fiscal policy, affect agents' views of the market. Macroeconomic forecasts attempt to predict these and so can become an important factor in decision making.

It is usual to distinguish between short-term, medium-term and long-term forecasts. Short-term forecasts generally refer to the next few months.

Because of the delays which occur in producing data, it is frequently necessary to forecast the current situation. For example, sales data may be compiled for each month, but for a large organisation it may be the middle of the next month before the figures are ready. In the case of government statistics the delay may be several months. With short-term forecasts, the assumption usually made is that there will be little change in recent patterns of behaviour. For example, the market structure for a product or government policy would be expected to react to external influences, such as forecasts the period is the next few years (say one to three years ahead), when some changes in behaviour might be expected. In this case new firms may enter the market, new products might be developed and a simple extrapolation of past trends may give misleading forecasts. Similarly, government policy would be expected to react to external influences, such as a rapid change in the exchange rate. This is an example of the Lucas (1976) critique which states that the parameters of a model alter if the policy regime changes. An estimated model should not be used to predict behaviour beyond the current policy regime. See Minford and Peel (1983) for a detailed discussion. Long-term forecasts concern the period beyond about three years ahead, when much more dramatic changes may occur. For a firm, this may include new types of products, developments in international markets and possibly a re-organisation of the management following amalgamation with other firms. For the national economy, changes in population structure, in the relative sizes of industries and in the importance of trading partners could occur.

Part 1 of the book is mainly concerned with techniques of forecasting. This chapter provides an introduction to the concepts which are developed in the rest of the book. In section 1.2 below we discuss the ways of forecasting that are available and in section 1.3 we review the main techniques used by business enterprises. Econometric forecasting is considered in section 1.4, while section 1.5 introduces ways of evaluating forecasts. In chapter 2 we discuss in detail the methods used in time-series forecasting and ways of combining different forecasts are presented in chapter 3.

In part 2, the techniques of forecasting are applied in a number of different fields. The problems of microeconomic forecasting are reviewed in chapter 4, where, as well as the econometric approach, the other methods covered include using anticipations data, leading indicators and scenario analysis. Macroeconomic forecasting is the subject of chapter 5, with a discussion of the preparation and the analysis of forecasts. Chapter 6 examines the efficient markets hypothesis applied to foreign exchange markets, stock markets and commodity markets. The concluding chapter reviews when the different techniques can be used, examines some of the current developments in forecasting and considers the relationship between forecasting and the design of macroeconomic policy.

In writing this book we have made a conscious decision not to discuss the details of computer packages. This is for two reasons: the range of packages available for forecasting has expanded enormously in recent years so that any comprehensive review dates rapidly, and also, students generally have little choice over which package to use. Up-to-date information on software is available in the software review sections of journals such as the *Journal of Forecasting*, the *International Journal of Forecasting*, *Applied Statistics* and the *Economic Journal*.

1.2   Methods of forecasting

Given a need for forecasts in many areas of business and economic activity, the question arises as to how they should be obtained. While this book is mainly concerned with economic forecasting based on econometric models, it is worthwhile looking at what alternatives are available.

Forecasts can be classified as *subjective* or *model-based*. Subjective forecasts are based on guesses, experience or intuition. They do not follow clear rules and rely on processing information in an informal way, usually inside someone's head. It is possible for two people, given the same information, to end up with different subjective forecasts. For example, two stockbrokers may reach different conclusions when presented with the information that a particular share has reached an historically high value. While one of them may expect further rises, the other may expect a fall. Each of the stockbrokers is processing the available information in the light of their years of experience and their intuitive 'feel' for the market, but no formal structure or method is being used. Essentially their treatment of the information is *ad hoc* and subjective. This does not, of course, mean that their forecasts will necessarily be inaccurate, since in some circumstances experience can be the best source of information. However, it does mean that it is difficult to analyse why a particular forecast is good or bad and also to learn from past forecast errors. Dawes (1986) compares the results of making decisions based on (a) a subjective 'gut feeling' for the situation and (b) a rational consideration of the relevant positive and negative points. The conclusion is that while method (a) is popular (particularly with 'experts') there is strong evidence that the more formal approach of method (b) gives better results. Also, when method (a) is used, people are over confident in the correctness of their decisions.

Model-based forecasts arise from a rule or model which formalises the relationship between the variables of interest. In the literature on forecasting it is usual to distinguish between causal and non-causal models. The former utilise an explanation of how the values of variables are determined, while the latter are solely concerned with prediction rather than with understanding behaviour. That is, *non-causal models* do not present any explanation of the mechanism generating the variable but simply provide a method for projecting the historical data. The simplest example is the naive 'no-change' model. This predicts the future value of a variable, say inflation, to be the current value. If the rate of inflation for the past year is 4 per cent then the prediction for the next year would also be 4 per cent. This model does not tell us what variables affect inflation, but it simply extrapolates the recent pattern. It provides a rule which, once stated, allows anyone given the same information to arrive at the same forecast. While it may not seem to be a particularly useful model, the no-change model can be extended by adding a random term to give the random walk model. We discuss this in the next section and in chapter 2, and apply it in chapter 6 in connection with forecasting stock-market prices and foreign exchange rates.

Other types of more complex non-causal models are given the general title of 'time-series models', since they are used when data are available for a number of time periods in the past. Examples of such methods are trend extrapolation and decomposition analysis discussed in section 1.3 below. A further type of complex non-causal model which has many uses in economic forecasting is the Box–Jenkins univariate time-series model. In this, the current value of a variable is expressed as a function of a selection of past values of the same variable, so that given past observations it is possible to predict future values. This is a generalisation of the naive 'no-change' model and has been found to give good forecasts in a wide range of circumstances. It is particularly useful for predicting future values of the exogenous variables in an econometric model and is discussed in detail in chapter 2.

An alternative to mathematical non-causal forecasting methods is provided by 'chartism', where charts show the way prices of assets (usually shares) have changed in the past (see, for example, Levy 1971 for a detailed discussion). The aim of preparing the charts is to identify recurring patterns which will lead to predictions of future price changes. The only information used relates to past prices. A similar concept to chartism is the use of filter rules of the form 'buy if the price of the security rises x per cent above a recent trough and sell when the price falls y per cent below a recent peak'. The precise values of x and y are derived from historical data. The aim is to identify profitable opportunities by forecasting the general direction of future price movements. A feature of this approach is that precise quantitative forecasts are not made and in fact are not necessary. We consider filter rules further in chapter 6, section 4 in connection with forecasting foreign exchange and stock-market prices.

The main advantages of non-causal models are their cheapness and their relative simplicity. Where the benefits to be gained from accurate forecasts are low, a simple, low-cost method of obtaining forecasts may be optimal. Their disadvantage is that they do not explain behaviour and they imply that what has happened in the past will continue in the future. That is, when applied to economic and business situations, non-causal models require the *ceteris paribus* assumption to be valid. Therefore they cannot provide guidance on the likely effects of changes in government policy or in the institutional framework.

In contrast, *causal models* are intended to explain behaviour by identifying the links between different variables and so help us to understand the world. By implication, the correct causal model is expected to give better forecasts than a non-causal model. When causal models are used in forecasting they can be qualitative, which indicate the direction in which a variable is likely to change, or quantitative, which predict the size of movement in the variable of interest. An example of the former is the statement in elementary demand theory that if the price of a product rises then, *ceteris paribus*, the quantity demanded will fall. The corresponding quantitative statement might be that if the price of the product rises by 1 per cent the quantity demanded will fall by 1.5 per cent. In many situations, qualitative forecasts are not particularly useful because any indicated change resulting from the interaction of a number of variables may be so small as to be negligible. Also, interest usually focuses not only on the direction of change but on its numerical value. Thus it is not helpful to be told that a new policy will reduce unemployment unless there is also some idea of the quantitative effect of that policy. The result is that economists and politicians are interested in quantitative macroeconomic forecasts and these are generally produced by using econometric models. Before considering these in detail we first examine a number of other techniques which are commonly used in business and industrial forecasting.

1.3   A review of business forecasting techniques

The main techniques used in business and industrial forecasting are surveys, the Delphi method, various extrapolation methods and input–output analysis. They are useful in many areas of microeconomics and also give insights which are helpful for macroeconomic forecasting.

Surveys of customers are one method of obtaining information for predicting the future level of sales of a product. They are commonly used in market research (see, for example, Luck and Rubin 1987 or Chisnall 1986), particularly for industrial products, and rely on a questionnaire administered by mail, telephone or personal interview. The questions concern the respondent's expected future consumption of the product, either in general or for the particular brand under consideration. By attempting to cover a wide range of customers (and potential customers), a good indication of the future demand for the product may result. More generally, surveys can be used to find out the views of the target group – consumers, sales staff, businessmen or experts – on any aspect of the future.

The advantage of a survey is that information is obtained directly from agents about their future behaviour and hopefully this will be reliable. The main disadvantage is that its success depends on the judgement and cooperation of the respondents, some of whom may not give much thought to their answers, particularly if there is a guarantee of anonymity and there are no costs in getting a forecast wrong. There are frequently problems in identifying who the respondents should be, in framing the questions unambiguously and in getting a reasonable number of replies. The method implies that the agents have formed plans for the future and that nothing will happen which will change these plans. We will return to this topic in chapter 4, section 4 below.

A variation on surveying experts is to use the *Delphi* method, also referred to as the 'jury of executive opinion' method, which relies on combining together the views of a number of experts in a series of forecasting rounds. Several versions are discussed in the literature (see Parente and Anderson-Parente 1987, for example) but the basic idea is that initially perhaps a dozen experts are asked, independently, to forecast some particular event, such as the growth of total market for a product over the next five years. The experts may be from within or outside the company. The results from this exercise are then collected together and discussed by the experts. Those with the highest and lowest forecasts are asked to justify their views and, after further discussion, a second survey is conducted, a discussion follows and the process may be repeated until a consensus forecast emerges which is acceptable to everyone. In an alternative version, the experts never meet but their views are circulated by post (or by computer), together with a summary of their arguments. They are encouraged to revise their forecasts in the light of the other participants' views until a consensus is reached. This may not occur until after several such rounds.

The Delphi method has the advantages of combining the views of several experts, encouraging the participants to put some thought into forming their forecasts and iterating to a consensus result. The assumption is that the consensus view will be more accurate than any outlier, and that those making incorrect forecasts will change their opinion. The method has the disadvantage of being affected by the personalities of the experts, and, in particular, on how determined they are in holding their opinions. It can be costly to put into practice, and can end up with a forecast that no-one has a strong belief in. Also, according to Parente and Anderson-Parente (1987), there are many problems in implementing the method. There is no agreement as to whether experts should be used (Armstrong 1985 suggests using people with a minimal knowledge of the field), on how to define an 'expert') should the panel be from different specialisms?), or on how much information should be passed on from the first stage (medians can cause a bias towards the centre of the distribution). The Delphi method seems to be most appropriate for longer-term forecasting where past data may be misleading, and for qualitative forecasting, such as predicting what technological developments will occur and when.

The class of techniques using *extrapolation methods* is extremely varied. The basic idea is that past patterns in the data will be repeated in the future. Thus it is the time profile of the observations which is important, so that time-series rather than cross-section data are relevant. That is, the data are ordered by time, say in successive months or years. The problem is to identify the past patterns. We deal with this in some detail in chapter 2 where time-series methods are explained. For the present we will consider briefly three techniques: simple extrapolation, decomposition analysis and smoothing methods. We will assume that the data are observed at regular time intervals, say weekly, quarterly or annually. If this is not the case these techniques can still be applied with adjustments.

The simplest of the extrapolation methods is the naive 'no-change' model mentioned in the previous section in which, for some variable Y the forecast value for period t is the value of the variable in period $t-1$. That is

$$Y_t = Y_{t-1}$$

Since, if the values of the variables change, forecasts from this equation will be incorrect then a modification which takes account of the probabilistic nature of time series is to include a random or stochastic term u_t to give

$$Y_t = Y_{t-1} + u_t \tag{1.1}$$

This can also be written

$$Y_t - Y_{t-1} = u_t$$

so that the change in Y is random. This is known as the random walk model, since the best prediction of Y_t is its previous value, and it is important both in time-series models (see chapter 2) and in forecasting in asset markets (see chapter 6). In general we will assume that the random term u is a *white noise* or *classical* error and so has a mean of zero, a constant variance and is uncorrelated with other values of *u*. More formally

$$E(u_t) = 0 \tag{1.2}$$

$$E(u_t^2) = \sigma^2 \tag{1.3}$$

$$E(u_t u_s) = 0 \text{ for } t \neq s \tag{1.4}$$

where σ^2 is a constant. These are, of course, the standard assumptions made in least squares regression analysis in econometrics. The advantage of (1.1) is that the only information needed in order to make a forecast for the next period is the current value of the variable. It is therefore a *univariate* model in that data on other variables are ignored.

While the random walk model is useful as a starting point, more general extrapolation methods are available based on trends. A trend can be defined as 'the general movement of a series in a particular direction'. It reflects the underlying or long-term movement of the series, rather than temporary variations. For example, national income grows as a result of such factors as technical progress, population growth and infra-structure investment, while sales of a new product grow as customers become aware of its existence, through advertising and experiencing the product. Because these factors are difficult to measure reliably, they can be represented by a time-trend variable, *t*, which increases by one with each successive observation. In *trend extrapolation*, the type of trend observed in past values of the series is determined and this is then projected into the future. The trend may be linear or non-linear and can be measured by a regression method or by forming a moving average of the series. For a series of observations $Y_1, Y_2, Y_3, Y_4, Y_5,\ldots$ a linear trend can be estimated from the regression model.

$$Y_t = \alpha + \beta t + u_t \tag{1.5}$$

where α and β are the intercept and slope terms respectively and u_t is a random disturbance term. The disturbance term is needed because it represents all the factors (other than *t*) associated with *Y*, and also to account for the innate randomness of the series. That is, the linear relationship between *Y* and *t* to be estimated will be the average or typical one, around which the individual observations will be expected to vary. The estimate of β gives the average absolute increase in *Y* per unit of time. This corresponds to an arithmetic series, where there is a constant change each period. Non-linear trends can also be estimated. For geometric (compound) growth at a rate of ρ per unit of time

$$Y_t = A(1 + \rho)^t 10^u \tag{1.6}$$

where A is a constant. This can be transformed by taking logarithms to give

$$\log Y_t = \log A + t \log(1 + \rho) + u \tag{1.7}$$

which is linear in the parameters and so can be estimated by regressing log Y on t. For exponential (continuous) growth at a rate λ per unit of time

$$Y_t = A\, e^{\lambda t + u} \tag{1.8}$$

and taking natural logarithms gives

$$\ln Y_t = \ln A + \lambda t + u$$

which is basically the same as (1.7). We consider the more complex trends represented by the logistic and Gompertz growth curves in chapter 4, section 2 below (see (4.16) and (4.17)). Alternatively, a simple moving average might capture the characteristics of a varying trend. For example, given $Y_1, Y_2, \ldots, Y_n$ a fifth order moving average forecast for period $n + 1$ is obtained from

$$Y_{n+1} = (Y_n + Y_{n-1} + Y_{n-2} + Y_{n-3} + Y_{n-4})/5 \tag{1.9}$$

This is another illustration of a simple univariate model where a variable is explained purely in terms of its own past values.

To illustrate the use of trends we present in table 1.1 annual data for the UK on the index (1980 = 100) of the average estimate of gross domestic product (GDP) in 1980 prices for 1973–85. The data are from *Economic Trends Annual Supplement* 1988, table 4. We will use the data for 1973–83 to estimate the trends and then use the estimates to predict GDP for 1984 and 1985. The accuracy of the forecasts for these two years will be a guide to the usefulness of fitting trends. In a practical situation where forecasts are needed from using trends the general approach would be the same but perhaps one third of the data would be saved for testing the model (instead of just two observations), and, after a suitable model is found for the first two-thirds of the data, it would be re-estimated using all of the data as a check on its stability, before being used for forecasting.

In this example the time trend t can be defined as any series of consecutive integers such as 1973, 1974, 1975, ... but it is more convenient to use 1, 2, 3, ... which we adopt here. The estimates of (1.5) and (1.7) are

$$Y_t = 91.03 + 1.09t \tag{1.10}$$
$$(66.03) + (5.36)$$

$\bar{R}^2 = 0.74$ Durbin–Watson statistic $= 1.16$

$$\log Y_t = 1.96 + 0.0049t \tag{1.11}$$
$$(318.56) \quad (5.36)$$

$\bar{R}^2 = 0.74$ Durbin–Watson statistic $= 1.14$

Table 1.1. *Gross domestic product (1980 = 100)*

	(1)	(2)	(3)	(4)	(5)
1973	94.1	92.1	2.0	92.3	1.8
1974	92.3	93.2	−0.9	93.3	−1.0
1975	91.5	94.3	−2.8	94.2	−2.7
1976	94.1	95.4	−1.3	95.3	−1.2
1977	96.3	96.5	−0.2	96.4	−0.1
1978	99.7	97.6	2.1	97.5	2.2
1979	102.5	98.7	3.8	98.6	3.9
1980	100.0	99.8	0.2	99.8	0.2
1981	98.8	100.8	−2.0	100.9	−2.1
1982	100.3	101.9	−1.6	101.9	−1.6
1983	103.7	103.0	0.7	103.0	0.7
1984	106.4	104.1		104.4	
1985	110.3	105.2		105.6	
Accuracy for 1973–83:					
MSE		3.67		3.68	
RMSE		1.91		1.92	
MAE		1.60		1.59	
RMSPE		1.96		1.96	

Note:

(1) Actual values.

(2) Predictions from (1.10).

(3) Forecast errors from (1.10) = (1)–(2).

(4) Predictions from (1.11).

(5) Forecast errors from (1.11) = (1)–(4).

The numbers in brackets are t-values for the hypothesis that the coefficient is zero, so a high value (greater than 2.622 for 9 degrees of freedom in this example) implies that it is not zero. The fit is measured by the multiple correlation coefficient corrected for degrees of freedom, $\bar{R}^2$, for which a value near to one indicates a close association between the dependent and independent variables, which are Y and t respectively in (1.10). The Durbin–Watson statistic tests for the presence of first-order autocorrelation, a form of non-randomness of the residuals. A value near 2 indicates no autocorrelation, while a low (as here) or high value implies that there is a pattern in the residuals. When this occurs a standard assumption of least squares regression is not satisfied and in particular the t-values are misleading and forecasts will be inaccurate. Further details of the Durbin–Watson statistic and $\bar{R}^2$ are given in introductory econometrics books such as Kennedy (1985), Gujarati (1988) or Pokorny (1987). The linear equation (1.10) implies that the index of real GDP increases by an average of 1.09 units each year, while (1.11) gives an estimated growth rate of, from the anti-log of 0.0049, 1.13 per cent per annum. These equations can be used to give 'within sample predictions' which are the 'forecasts' from the equations for the period covered by the data used in estimation. These are included in table 1.1 column (2), from (1.10), and, from (1.11), after taking anti-logarithms, column (4). Also included are the prediction errors, the differences between the actual values, column (1) and the predictions, columns (2) and (4).

We have quoted the corrected multiple correlation coefficient as a measure of the fit of the equations. Several alternative measures of forecasting performance are used in the literature. Here we will briefly consider some simple descriptive measures and discuss alternatives in section 5 of this chapter.

The most popular of the descriptive measures is probably the mean square error or MSE. If we denote the forecasts by F_t and the outcomes or actuals by A_t, the mean square error for n forecasts and outcomes is defined as

$$MSE = \Sigma(F_t - A_t)^2/n \tag{1.12}$$

Because the errors are squared, large errors are given extra weight when the MSE is calculated. Thus the cost of making positive and negative errors is assumed to be the same and varies with the size of the error. This type of cost function is generally used in economic forecasting but it is important to realise that in some circumstances it may be inappropriate. For example, consider the decision to buy a share because of the forecast that the price will rise by 10 per cent. If the price subsequently rises by 20 per cent there is a forecast error but the decision will still be correct and, in fact, will benefit the forecaster. Conversely a forecast with a smaller average error but which is frequently incorrectly signed (e.g. a fall instead of a rise) imposes a cost. See chapter 6, section 3 for a discussion of scoring techniques and the 'right side of the market approach' designed to meet this caveat. Granger (1969a) discusses other forms of cost function.

An alternative way of expressing the MSE is to let e_t be the forecast error or $F_t - A_t$ then, suppressing the subscript t,

$$MSE = \frac{\Sigma e^2}{n} = \frac{\Sigma(e - \bar{e} + \bar{e})^2}{n}$$

$$= \frac{\Sigma(e - \bar{e})^2}{n} + \bar{e}^2 \tag{1.13}$$

The first term is the variance of the forecast error and the second is the square of the mean. Therefore MSE is an increasing function of the variance and mean of the error. Since, like the variance, the units of MSE are the squares of the units of F_t it is common to take its square root to give the root mean square error, defined by

$$\text{RMSE} = \sqrt{\frac{\Sigma(F_t - A_t)^2}{n}} \tag{1.14}$$

Other descriptive measures of forecast accuracy are the mean absolute error, MAE, defined by

$$\text{MAE} = \frac{\Sigma|F - A|}{n} \tag{1.15}$$

which measures the average absolute size of the error, and the root mean square percentage error, RMSPE, defined by

$$\text{RMSPE} = \sqrt{\frac{100}{n} \Sigma\left[\frac{F - A}{A}\right]^2} \tag{1.16}$$

which takes the error as a percentage of the actual value. For illustrative purposes these accuracy measures are included in table 1.1 and are seen to be almost identical for (1.10) and (1.11), showing there is little to choose between the fit of these equations for 1973–83. When the different accuracy measures are compared the RMSE and RMSPE are close together, since in this example the actual values are near 100, while the MAE is smaller, because it is not penalised by the effects of squaring large errors.

But even though the overall fit of each of (1.10) and (1.11) is relatively high, the low Durbin–Watson statistics show that the residuals are autocorrelated and not random and so forecasts from these equations will be misleading. For example, from columns (3) and (5) it can be seen that since 1981 the errors have been getting larger so that the errors in 1984 and 1985 are expected to be positive. The appropriate correcting action would be to try to remove this non-randomness by, for example, trying other non-linear forms of trend. However, for completeness we will use the equations for forecasting GDP in 1984 and 1985. From (1.10), remembering that the trend was defined as the year minus 1972 (so that $1973 = 1$), for 1984, $t = 12$, and the predicted value of Y is 104.1 with the actual value 106.4. When $t = 13$, the prediction is 105.2 and the actual 110.3. Thus the predicted changes are 1.09 each year while the actual changes were 2.7 and 3.9. Similarly, from (1.11), when $t = 12$, the predicted value of log Y is 2.0186 or 104.4 for Y (actual value 106.4), and when $t = 13$, the prediction is 2.0235, giving a Y value of 105.6 (actual value 110.3).

The conclusions from these results are that the simple trend models used for GDP do not forecast well and/or the growth of the UK economy in 1984 and 1985 was exceptional compared with the period 1973–83. As suggested earlier, if a satisfactory model had been obtained at this point, it would now be re-estimated using the full set of data (for 1973–85), and *ex ante* forecasts could then be made.

Decomposition analysis assumes that a series of data can be split up into four components: a trend term, a cyclical term, a seasonal factor and an irregular or residual element, and these can be related additively or multiplicatively. Initially, interest in the model arose because of the need to seasonally adjust data. More recently, it has been used as a forecasting technique. The assumption is that each of the components can be identified from past data and can then be projected into the future. As we have just seen, the trend term reflects the general tendency of a series to increase or decrease. Shorter-term fluctuations result in the actual values of variables differing from their trend values. The two types of fluctuations which are normally of interest are referred to as the cyclical term and seasonal variation.

The cyclical term occurs because of business cycles, building cycles, fluctuations in the number of births and natural cycles such as those between good harvests. In so far as a regular cycle, for example the four-year business cycle in the 1950s, can be identified, the cyclical term can be forecast. However, in practice for many series the length of the cycle can vary to such an extent that any identification of it is subjective.

Seasonal fluctuations are any regular variations that occur within a year. While they are primarily related to seasonal factors, such as the weather (so that unemployment is high in winter and low in summer), they can include man-made influences such as holidays (manufacturing output is low in the peak holiday season) and social patterns (retail sales are high on Saturdays and low on Mondays).

The remaining element in a time series is the irregular or residual term. This is the unexplained variation which remains when the other sources of variation are removed from the series. On average, the residual cancels out and so its forecast value is always zero in the additive model and one in the multiplicative model.

An illustration of the calculations required for the multiplicative model is given in table 1.2 where quarterly data on new car registrations for the UK are presented. The data are taken from *Economic Trends Annual Supplement* 1988, table 34. Since we are only taking data for five years we will assume that there is no cyclical component. If there was, for example, a five-year cycle then the first step would be to take a five-year moving average of the data to remove it. Estimates of the cyclical term can then be obtained, by subtraction in the case of an additive model and by division for

Table 1.2. *New car registrations in the UK*

		(1)	(2)	(3)	(4)	(5)	(6)	(7)
1981	1	139						
	2	124						
			498					
	3	138		124.500	1.108	1.164	128.351	149.4
			498					
	4	97		124.375	0.780	0.754	130.183	98.2
			497					
1982	1	139		126.750	1.097	1.120	132.016	147.9
			517					
	2	123		130.625	0.942	0.962	133.848	128.8
			528					
	3	158		135.375	1.167	1.164	135.681	157.9
			555					
	4	108		141.000	0.766	0.754	137.513	103.7
			573					
1983	1	166		146.375	1.134	1.120	139.345	156.1
			598					
	2	141		150.000	0.940	0.962	141.178	135.8
			602					
	3	183		150.625	1.215	1.164	143.010	166.5
			603					
	4	112		151.500	0.739	0.754	144.842	109.2
			609					
1984	1	167		150.375	1.111	1.120	146.675	164.3
			594					
	2	147		147.625	0.996	0.962	148.507	142.9
			587					
	3	168		146.750	1.145	1.164	150.339	175.0
			587					
	4	105		146.500	0.717	0.754	152.172	114.7
			585					
1985	1	167		148.750	1.123	1.120	154.004	172.5
			605					
	2	145		152.375	0.952	0.962	155.836	149.9
			614					
	3	188						
	4	144						

Note:

(1) Actual numbers of new car registrations.

(2) Four period moving total.

(3) Centred moving average.

(4) Raw seasonal factors (ratio of (1) to (3)).

(5) Mean seasonal factors (based on (4)).

(6) Predicted trend from (1.18).

(7) Forecast series (product of (5) and (6)).

a multiplicative model, and, when the other components are estimated, it can be used in forecasting. Without the cyclical term the additive model is

$$Y_t = T_t + S_t + I_t$$

and the multiplicative model is

$$Y_t = T_t \times S_t \times I_t \tag{1.17}$$

where Y is the series, T is the trend term, S is the seasonal effect and I is the irregular or residual term. Notice that each of the terms has a t subscript, indicating that it varies with t. Since the data are quarterly, the seasonal factor can be removed by forming a four period moving average of the series. In column (2) of table 1.2 the moving total of each block of four values is presented, so that 498 is the sum of 139, 124, 138 and 97, and is centred between 1981 (2) and 1981 (3). The second block of four is 124, 138, 97 and 139 which also gives a total of 498, now centred between 1981 (3) and 1981 (4). To get a moving average centred on the quarters, the sum of two successive terms in column (2) is found and then divided by 8, since there are four values of the series in each term in column (2). The result, in column (3), is the series with the seasonal effect (S) removed. That is, column (3) is $T_t I_t$. Assuming the multiplicative model, the seasonal effect can be estimated by dividing column (1) by column (3), or Y by TI, and this is given in column (4). However, as it stands column (4) cannot be used for predicting S since there is no obvious pattern in its values. Some assumption about the seasonal pattern is now needed. For some series it may be sensible to assume that the seasonal pattern is slowly changing over time. For example, the seasonal pattern of sales of ice-cream might be expected to change as the proportion of households owning freezers changes from zero to near 100 per cent. In this case it might be possible to estimate trends in the seasonal effects. For the data in table 1.3 we will assume that the seasonal effects are the same every year and that, as the variations between the years shown in column (4) are the result of random fluctuations, an average seasonal effect can be obtained. Details are given in table 1.3, where the values of S from column (4) are averaged for each quarter. The seasonal effects measure the relative importance of the different quarters in the annual total. Since the averages add up to 3.984, rather than 4, they are all multiplied by 4/3.984 to avoid understating the annual total. The result is the set of mean seasonal factors given in column (5) of table 1.2. The next step is to estimate the trend component by the method of least squares, using (1.5). Since the data for estimation start in 1983 quarter 3, we define t to be 1 then. The result is

$$TI = 126.5188 + 1.8324t \tag{1.18}$$
$$(43.65) \quad (6.11)$$

$$\bar{R}^2 = 0.71 \qquad \text{Durbin–Watson statistic} = 0.22.$$

Table 1.3. *Seasonal effects from table 1.2*

	Quarter				
	1	**2**	**3**	**4**	
1981			1.108	0.780	
1982	1.097	0.942	1.167	0.766	
1983	1.134	0.940	1.215	0.739	
1984	1.111	0.996	1.145	0.717	
1985	1.123	0.952			
Mean	1.159	0.751	1.116	0.958	Total = 3.984
Adjusted mean	1.164	0.754	1.120	0.962	Total = 4.000

Here TI, the dependent variable is the series in column (3). Again the Durbin–Watson statistic indicates non-random residuals so that the estimated equation is unreliable in that the t-values are over-estimates of the true values. To get over these problems an alternative way of modelling the trend, such as the non-linear model (1.6) or the moving average model (1.9) might be tried. For simplicity we will continue to use (1.18). The predictions from this equation are given in column (6) of table 1.2. These differ from column (3) because of the random error, so column (6) is the estimate of T_t, the trend component of Y. We can now use the estimate of the trend, column (6), and the estimated seasonal pattern, column (5), for forecasting the series, using (1.17) and assuming that the irregular component (I) always takes the value 1. The result is in column (7).

Forecasts for 1981(3)–1985(3) can be obtained in the same way, without taking the values 17, 18, ..., 25. Equation (1.18) is used to forecast T (see column (3) in table 1.4) and the seasonal factor is given in column (4). The product is in column (5), and the forecast error is found by subtracting the forecast from the actual. It is clear that there is a pattern in the forecast errors, which was to be expected from the non-randomness of the residuals in (1.18). Even so, the forecasts in table 1.4 are reasonably accurate, given the variability in the actuals series. The RMSE for these forecasts is 9.3, which compares with a value of 7.5 for the fit for 1981(3)–1985(2).

There are several variations possible in the way the decomposition method is applied. Apart from the multiplicative and additive versions, trends can be represented by moving averages which allow more flexibility than the linear or log-linear models, and special events, such as strikes, can be taken account of when seasonal factors are estimated. One well-known method for doing this is the X-11 version of the Census Method II Seasonal Adjustment Program, produced by the US Department of Commerce (1967). A detailed example is given by Jarrett (1987). Another variation,

Table 1.4. *Forecasts from table 1.2*

		(1)	(2)	(3)	(4)	(5)	(6)
1985	3	188	17	157.67	1.164	183.5	4.5
	4	114	18	159.50	0.754	120.3	−6.3
1986	1	167	19	161.33	1.120	180.7	−13.7
	2	151	20	163.17	0.962	157.0	−6.0
	3	193	21	165.00	1.164	192.1	0.9
	4	117	22	166.83	0.754	125.8	−8.8
1987	1	175	23	168.66	1.120	188.9	−13.9
	2	156	24	170.50	0.962	164.0	−8.0
	3	213	25	172.33	1.164	200.6	12.4
						RMSE	9.3

Note:

(1) Actual value.

(2) Trend value (t).

(3) Predicted trend from (1.18).

(4) Mean seasonal effect.

(5) Forecast (product of (3) and (4)).

(6) Forecast error = (1)−(5).

popular with econometricians, is to use multiple regression to estimate the trend and seasonal effects at the same time. For example, (1.17) could be written as

$$Y_t = [A \exp(\lambda t)][\exp(\alpha_1 Q_{1t} + \alpha_2 Q_{2t} + \alpha_3 Q_{3t})][\exp(u_t)] \tag{1.19}$$

where the term in the first square brackets is the trend component, in the second is the seasonal component and in the third is the irregular component. Here Q_{1t}, Q_{2t} and Q_{3t} are seasonal dummy variables, which take the value 1 in a particular quarter and zero in the other quarters. Taking natural logarithms of (1.19) gives

$$\ln Y_t = \alpha_0 + \lambda t + \alpha_1 Q_{1t} + \alpha_2 Q_{2t} + \alpha_3 Q_{3t} + u_t \tag{1.20}$$

and this can be estimated by multiple regression. For the data in table 1.2, we could estimate (1.20) for 1981(1)–1985(4), but for comparability with the previous results we use 1981(3)–1985(2). The result is

$$\ln Y_t = 4.5522 + 0.0131t + 0.4001Q_1 + 0.2484Q_2 + 0.4366Q_3 \tag{1.21}$$
$$(108.5) \quad (3.8) \quad\quad (9.0) \quad\quad\quad (5.5) \quad\quad\quad (9.8)$$

$\bar{R}^2 = 0.90$ Durbin–Watson statistic = 0.72

Table 1.5. *Forecasts from (1.21) and (1.23)*

		(1)	(2)	(3)	(4)	(5)
1985	3	188	183.4	4.6	180.5	7.5
	4	114	120.1	−6.1	124.3	−10.3
1986	1	167	181.5	−14.5	178.5	−11.5
	2	151	158.0	−7.0	157.8	−6.8
	3	193	193.2	−0.2	188.0	5.0
	4	117	126.5	−9.5	131.8	−14.8
1987	1	175	191.3	−16.3	186.0	−11.0
	2	156	166.5	−10.5	165.3	−9.3
	3	213	203.6	9.4	195.5	17.5
			RMSE	9.8		11.0

Note:

(1) Actual value.

(2) Forecast from (1.21).

(3) Forecast error $=(1)-(2)$.

(4) Forecast from (1.23).

(5) Forecast error $=(1)-(4)$.

The corresponding additive model is

$$Y_t = \alpha_0 + \lambda t + \alpha_1 Q_{1t} + \alpha_2 Q_{2t} + \alpha_3 Q_{3t} + u_t \qquad (1.22)$$

and the estimated equation is

$$Y_t = 90.50 + 1.875t + 52.375Q_{1t} - 29.7501Q_{2t} + 58.125Q_{3t} \qquad (1.23)$$
$$\quad\;\; (14.2) \quad (3.5) \qquad (7.7) \qquad\quad (4.4) \qquad\quad (8.6)$$

$\bar{R}^2 = 0.87$ Durbin–Watson statistic $= 1.05$

Both (1.21) and (1.23) suffer from autocorrelation and so are unsatisfactory, as was to be expected from our earlier results. Forecasts from these equations are given in table 1.5, and have RMSEs of 9.8 for (1.21) and 11.0 for (1.23), which are slightly larger than the 9.3 in table 1.4. The benefits of the multiple regression approach are that all the available data can be used in estimation; it is easy, given access to a multiple regression package, to try variations on the basic model and forecasting is straightforward.

In our earlier terminology, the decomposition method is a non-causal, univariate technique since the forecasts depend only on the past values of the variable and other influences are ignored. It has the advantage that regular patterns can be explicitly identified and used in forecasting, but there is no guarantee that those patterns will be unchanged in the future.

Smoothing methods are the third kind of extrapolation technique we consider and also fall into the class of univearaite models. For an excellent review of these methods, see Gardner (1985). In the classical decomposition method each observation is effectively given equal weight. With smoothing methods, averages are formed with the more recent observations being given higher weights than earlier ones. If the highest weight is given to the current observation and the weights given to the other observations decline geometrically as they become more distant, then the resulting average is known as the exponentially weighted average or the exponentially smoothed series. For example, suppose we require a smoothed forecast, F_{t+1}, for period $t+1$, for a series with observed actual values Y_t, Y_{t-1}, Y_{t-2}, etc. We will assume initially that there is no seasonal variation and that there is also no trend. Let β be the rate of decline of the weights on past actual values and α be the weight on Y_t, then

$$F_{t+1} = \alpha Y_t + \alpha\beta Y_{t-1} + \alpha\beta^2 Y_{t-2} + \alpha\beta^3 Y_{t-3} + \cdots \qquad (1.24)$$

Lagging (1.24) by one period gives

$$F_t = \alpha Y_{t-1} + \alpha\beta Y_{t-2} + \alpha\beta^2 Y_{t-3} + \alpha\beta^3 Y_{t-4} + \cdots \qquad (1.25)$$

Multiplying (1.25) by β and subtracting the result from (1.24) gives

$$F_{t+1} = \alpha Y_t + \beta F_t$$

That is, the forecast for $t+1$ is a weighted average of the current actual value and the current forecast. If the forecast is to be unbiased or correct on average then the sum of the weights α and β must be one so that $\beta = 1 - \alpha$ and

$$F_{t+1} = \alpha Y_t + (1 - \alpha)F_t \qquad (1.26)$$

This can also be re-arranged in a slightly different form as

$$F_{t+1} = F_t + \alpha(Y_t - F_t)$$

so that the forecast for period $t+1$ is the forecast for period t plus a term which is related to the forecast error in period t. In the statistical literature this is referred to as the 'error correction' term and α reflects the speed at which the new forecast adjusts to the error. If α is zero there is no adjustment while if α is one there is full adjustment. This method was developed by Holt (1957) and Brown (1959) and we discuss more recent developments in chapter 3, section 7.

Before (1.26) can be used for forecasting a value of α is needed and also an initial forecast F_1. The value of α can be obtained by trial and error by taking a number of values, for example 0.1, 0.3, 0.5, 0.7 and 0.9 and seeing how good the fit is to past data (that is, which gives the smallest RMSE or

Table 1.6. *Exponential smoothing: forecasts of real consumers' expenditure on coffee, tea and cocoa in the UK using (1.26) (£ million at 1985 prices)*

	(1)	(2)	(3)	(4)	(5)
1977	1084				
1978	1132				
1979	1195				
1980	1215	1137	1137	1215	1215
1981	1196	1192	1160	1215	1215
1982	1193	1195	1171	1202	1209
1983	1244	1194	1178	1196	1204
1984	1170	1229	1198	1230	1216
1985	1146	1188	1190	1188	1202
1986	1176	1159	1177	1159	1185
1987	1135	1171	1177	1171	1182
1988		1146	1164	1146	1168
RMSE		36.6	39.0	37.2	37.3

Note:

(1) Actual value.

(2) Smoothed series, 1980 forecast = 1137, $\alpha = 0.7$.

(3) Smoothed series, 1980 forecast = 1137, $\alpha = 0.3$.

(4) Smoothed series, 1980 forecast = 1215, $\alpha = 0.7$.

(5) Smoothed series, 1980 forecast = 1215, $\alpha = 0.3$.

other error measure). A suitable initial forecast might be the average of the first few values of the series or the most recent actual value. An example is given in table 1.6 where annual data for real consumers' expenditure on coffee, tea and cocoa in the UK are presented for 1977–87. There is no clear trend in the data and, being an annual series, there is obviously no seasonal variation. This variable is the total market for these beverages and forecasts are useful for producers of these products. In column (2), the initial forecast (for 1980) is taken as 1137, the average of the values for 1977–9, and $\alpha = 0.7$. The forecast for 1981 is from

$$F_{1981} = 0.7(1215) + 0.3(1137) = 1192$$

Forecasts for 1982–8 are obtained in the same way. Since (1.26) gives the one-step ahead forecast, and Y is unknown for 1988, all future forecasts are set equal to the 1988 forecast. Thus the exponential smoothing method is particularly suited to situations where a one-step ahead forecast is required in successive time periods.

There is a certain amount of arbitrariness about the choice of the initial forecast and the value of α. In table 1.6, column (3) shows the effect of changing α to 0.3, and keeping the initial forecast as 1137. Columns (4) and (5) take 1215, the 1980 actual value, as the 1980 forecast, and have α as 0.7 and 0.3 respectively. The forecasts have been rounded to the nearest whole number throughout the calculations, with the result that columns (2) and (4) are the same from 1985. Note that these each have $\alpha = 0.7$ but have different initial forecasts. The RMSEs for 1980–7 are very similar, showing a slight preference for a value of $\alpha = 0.7$ rather than 0.3. In general the choice of the initial value becomes less important the larger the number of observations available before forecasting commences.

This example of exponentially weighted moving averaging assumes that there was no trend and no seasonal variation. Following Holt (1957) and Winters (1960), these can be incorporated by writing the smoothing equation (1.26) as

$$F_{t+1} = \alpha(Y_{t+1}/S_{t+1-L}) + (1-\alpha)(F_t + T_t) \qquad (1.27)$$

where F is the current estimate of the smoothed series and L is the number of seasons per year. The updated trend term (T) is given by

$$T_{t+1} = \beta(F_{t+1} - F_t) + (1-\beta)T_t \qquad (1.28)$$

and the seasonal factor (S) is from

$$S_{t+1} = \gamma(Y_{t+1}/F_{t+1}) + (1-\gamma)S_{t+1-L} \qquad (1.29)$$

where β and γ are smoothing constants (like α) satisfying $0 \leqslant \beta \leqslant 1$ and $0 \leqslant \gamma \leqslant 1$. As previously, the forecaster has to select their values. To produce the forecast for period $t+j$, P_{t+j}, when the values at time t are known, the procedure is to use (1.27), (1.28) and (1.29) to give the current values of F, T and S, and substitute them into

$$P_{t+j} = [F_t + (j\,T_t)]S_{t+j-L} \qquad (1.30)$$

That is, the smoothed series F has to be adjusted for the change in the trend and seasonal components.

We discuss other variations on exponential smoothing in chapter 3, section 7 in relation to the Makridakis forecasting competition. Bowerman and O'Connell (1987) provide a comprehensive review, as does Gardner (1985). Smoothing methods generally require the user to choose the values for the parameters, such as α, and their value can have a big effect on the accuracy of the forecasts. A grid search can be used to see if the results are sensitive to the choice. In general, smoothing methods are particularly applicable when the patterns in the data are changing, so that the last few observations include important information. However, it is in these circumstances that a grid search is likely to give misleading results.

Input–output analysis is a method of examining the economy by focusing on the inter-relationships between industries. Introductions to the subject are given in many economics books, including Holden and Pearson (1983), and also in publications which include input–output data, such as Central Statistical Office (1988). More advanced treatments are given by Leontief (1986), who was awarded the Nobel prize for Economic Science in 1973 for his work in this area, and Hadley (1965).

To illustrate the principles, consider the example of producing motor vehicles. For the vehicle industry to produce its output (cars, lorries, etc.) it needs to purchase inputs (such as steel, glass, paint, upholstery, wiring, electricity, transport services) from other industries. In turn, these other industries require inputs before they can supply the vehicle industry. These requirements of inputs are known as intermediate demands, in contrast to final demands, which are the requirements for consumption by individuals, government and for export. In input–output analysis, the pattern of intermediate demands is the prime consideration. By examining the relationship between intermediate demand, industrial output and final demand, it is possible to predict the effects of a forecast change in the output of one industry on the rest of the economy, and also the effects on each industry of a change in national output. This means that input–output analysis is useful in centrally planned economies where the fact that the forecasts for different industries need to be compatible is important.

In table 1.7 we present a simplified input–output table for the UK economy in 1984. This is based on table 4A of Central Statistical Office (1988), which in turn is a summary of a 101 by 101 commodity matrix. The table refers to the sales and purchases of domestic goods, classified according to commodity groups which are basically industries. Reading

Table 1.7. *Simplified domestic use matrix for the UK, 1984*

| | | Purchases (£ millions) by | | | | | |
		Agri-culture	Energy	Manu-facture	Services	Final demand	Gross output
	Agriculture	2304	0	8713	376	3727	15119
Sales	Energy	611	17065	7108	6211	28686	59683
by	Manufacture	4251	2739	65182	20290	131854	224315
	Services	1980	4239	33391	39559	101316	180486
	Total inputs	15119	59682	224316	180486		

Note: Manufacture includes manufacturing industry and construction. Services includes distribution and transport.

Source: Based on tables 4A and 2A of Central Statistical Office (1988).

across the table gives the destinations of sales by the industries in the rows. Thus there were agricultural sales of £2304 millions to other firms in agriculture, £8713 millions to manufacturing, £376 millions to services and £3727 millions to final demand (mainly to consumers and exports), with total agricultural sales of £15119 millions. The columns list the purchases by each industry, so that agriculture purchased goods valued at £2304 millions from agriculture, £611 millions of energy and £4251 millions from manufacturing and so on. The total value of the inputs includes not only the intermediate goods shown but also imports, taxes, income from employment and profit. The minor discrepancies between total inputs and gross output are due to rounding errors.

As it stands, table 1.7 provides a useful way of describing the interdependencies between industries. If we let q_i denote the output of industry i, f_i be the final demand for industry i and s_{ij} be the sales of output of industry i bought by industry j, then table 1.7 can be represented by the equations

$$\begin{aligned}
q_1 &= s_{11} + s_{12} + s_{13} + s_{14} + f_1 \\
q_2 &= s_{21} + s_{22} + s_{23} + s_{24} + f_2 \\
q_3 &= s_{31} + s_{32} + s_{33} + s_{34} + f_3 \\
q_4 &= s_{41} + s_{42} + s_{43} + s_{44} + f_4
\end{aligned} \tag{1.31}$$

However, for forecasting purposes the next step is to form the technology matrix or matrix of input–output coefficients. This is obtained by dividing purchases of inputs by the gross output of the purchasing industry. For example, gross output of agriculture is £15119 millions and sales of energy to agriculture (the input into agriculture) are £611 millions, so the input–output coefficient is 611/15119 or 0.0404. That is, each £1 of agricultural output produced requires inputs of energy costing £0.0404. This is an average value and, for it to be useful, the assumption of a linear (proportional) relationship between inputs and output should be reasonable. That is, basic input–output analysis relies on the production function being linear. The matrix of input–output coefficients is presented in table 1.8. High coefficients indicate which inputs are important. Since a proportional relationship between each input and output is assumed, if we let a_{ij} be the input–output coefficient for input i into industry j, then

$$s_{ij} = a_{ij} q_j \tag{1.32}$$

and substituting into (1.31) gives

$$\begin{aligned}
q_1 &= a_{11} q_1 + a_{12} q_2 + a_{13} q_3 + a_{14} q_4 + f_1 \\
q_2 &= a_{21} q_1 + a_{22} q_2 + a_{23} q_3 + a_{24} q_4 + f_2 \\
q_3 &= a_{31} q_1 + a_{32} q_2 + a_{33} q_3 + a_{34} q_4 + f_3 \\
q_4 &= a_{41} q_1 + a_{42} q_2 + a_{43} q_3 + a_{44} q_4 + f_4
\end{aligned} \tag{1.33}$$

Table 1.8. *Input–output coefficients for table 1.7*

	Agriculture	Energy	Manufacture	Services
Agriculture	0.1524	0.0000	0.0388	0.0021
Energy	0.0404	0.2859	0.0317	0.0344
Manufacture	0.2812	0.0459	0.2906	0.1124
Services	0.1310	0.0710	0.1489	0.2192

In matrices, this is

$$q = Aq + f \qquad (1.34)$$

where q is (4×1), A is (4×4) and f is (4×1). By matrix manipulation we can get the solution of (1.34) as

$$q = (I - A)^{-1} f \qquad (1.35)$$

This equation relates the vector of gross outputs (q) and the vector of final demands (f) via the Leontief inverse $(I - A)^{-1}$. It allows forecasts of the level of gross output needed to satisfy given patterns of final demand, and in doing so takes account of the inter-relationships within the economy. The Leontief inverse of table 1.8 is given in table 1.9, and the ij-th element can be interpreted as the amount of gross output of commodity i needed to produce one unit of commodity j for final demand. For example, to produce one unit of final demand of agriculture requires 1.2050 units of gross output of agriculture (since some is used as inputs for other industries), 0.1070 units of energy, 0.5343 units of manufacture and 0.3138 units of services.

When using input–output analysis for forecasting, it is usually assumed that A changes only slowly and so can be taken as fixed. From (1.34) it is clear that given A and either q or f the other can be calculated. As an example, suppose that, relative to 1984, by 1990 final demand for energy is expected to increase by 10 per cent, and for services by 5 per cent, with agriculture and manufacturing unchanged. The final demand will be £3727 millions for agriculture, £31555 millions for energy, £131854 millions for

Table 1.9. *The Leontief inverse for table 1.8*

	Agriculture	Energy	Manufacture	Services
Agriculture	1.2050	0.0058	0.0690	0.0134
Energy	0.1070	1.4132	0.0847	0.0747
Manufacture	0.5343	0.1178	1.4906	0.2212
Services	0.3138	0.1519	0.3035	1.3320

Table 1.10. *Forecasts from* (1.35)

	Final Demands			Gross outputs		
	Original	New	% change	Original	New	% change
Agriculture	3727	3727	0.0	15119	15198	0.5
Energy	28686	31555	10.0	59683	64107	7.4
Manufacture	131854	131854	0.0	224315	225782	0.7
Services	101316	106382	5.0	180486	187681	4.0

manufacture and £106382 millions for services. The corresponding gross outputs, using (1.35), are given in table 1.10, where it can be seen that the gross outputs increase at different rates from the final demands. Alternatively, re-arranging (1.35)

$$f = (I - A)q \tag{1.36}$$

which can be used to forecast final demand given assumptions about future levels of gross output.

The detailed input–output tables which are available for many countries allow exercises such as these to provide useful forecasts at the industry level. These have the advantage of being mutually consistent so that potential shortages can be identified in advance and dealt with. In practice, published input–output tables are most useful to large companies (and their suppliers) who are mainly in one of the industries identified in the tables. Another use is in regional forecasting (see Hewings 1985 or Polenske 1980 for examples) where it may be possible to conduct a survey to get the cross-section data required for an input–output table but not the time-series data needed for econometric modelling. This point also applies to third world countries. References to applications to forecasting in marketing are given by Stoney and Davies (1980).

The weaknesses of the basic input–output model include the fact that the tables are generally several years out of date when they are published, the coefficients reported are averages which may not apply at the margin and the assumption that the production function is linear. Also, prices have no effect on the allocation of resources so, for example, a big increase in oil prices which leads to the substitution of other fuels for oil would not change the technological coefficients in an (historical) input–output table. The assumption of a fixed technology is also unsatisfactory when forecasting more than a few years into the future. In principle the way in which the input–output coefficients change should be discernible when tables are available for different years. However, it is rare that the definitions of industries and commodities are the same so comparisons are difficult. Leontief (1986) describes some of the recent developments which attempt to deal with these problems.

1.4 Econometric forecasting

The methods of business forecasting just described are rather different from the general approach used in economic modelling and forecasting, which we now consider briefly. The intention is to provide a background for the multivariate time-series models to be reviewed in chapter 2.

The starting point in econometric forecasting is the construction of an econometric model of the economy. While this use of econometric models will be emphasised in this book, it is important to realise that they can also be used for evaluating the impact of alternative economic policies and for testing economic theory. We do not pursue these further here since there are a number of textbooks, such as Thomas (1985) and Hebden (1983) dealing with them.

Turning now to the process of econometric modelling and forecasting, the essential difference between an econometric model and a non-causal model is in the way the former has economic theory as its foundation. In some cases, the two types of model can appear to be similar, particularly if the latter is a simple time-series model, but the interpretation is different. As we will see in chapter 2, the variables in a time-series model are included only because they have desirable statistical properties and not because of their economic relevance.

The main steps in constructing an econometric model and using it for forecasting can be summarised as:

1 Select the correct theory explaining economic behaviour and decide which variables are of interest: those to be explained are the endogenous variables and those which are taken as determined outside this model are the exogenous variables.

2 Write the theory as a series of equations linking together these variables, paying particular attention to the leads and lags in the equations and to expectations variables.

3 Find data on the variables, keeping as close as possible to the theoretical concepts.

4 Use the appropriate econometric techniques to estimate the numerical values of the unknown parameters of the equations.

5 Given the estimated equations, generate predictions of the future

values of the exogenous variables and use these to obtain the forecasts of interest, namely the future values of the endogenous variables.

To illustrate these steps we will consider a simple demand function for alcoholic drink in the UK. This is not intended to be a realistic explanation of consumer behaviour (see McGuiness 1980 for a more detailed approach) but is chosen as being an example within a field which will be familiar to readers and which allows important points to be made while avoiding some of the problems of simultaneous equation macroeconomic models (see chapter 5).

1 Select the correct theory. We will assume that the demand function can be written as

$$q = f(p, Y) \tag{1.37}$$

where q is the quantity of alcoholic drink demanded, p is the price of alcoholic drink relative to the general price level, Y is the level of consumers' real income, and the absence of subscripts indicates that there are no time lags. Here the endogenous variable is q and there are two exogenous variables, p and Y. That is, the intention is to explain variations in the quantity demanded, q, by variations in the relative price, p, and incomes, Y. Thus, values of p and Y will be used to predict q. As it stands, this equation is too general to estimate and so we need to move to the next stage of the procedure to make progress.

2 The particular form of the equation is now selected. From consideration of economic theory, we might argue that the correct functional form for a demand function is linear in logarithms of the variables, giving constant elasticities. That is

$$\log q = \alpha + \beta \log p + \lambda \log Y + u \tag{1.38}$$

where β is the price elasticity and λ is the income elasticity. Alternative forms which might also be plausible are the linear function and the semi-logarithmic function. Notice that we have included in the equation a constant term α and a disturbance term u. This is assumed to have the classical properties set out in (1.2)–(1.4) and so is a white noise variable. The justifications for including u are:

(a) that it represents all other variables which explain q but which are relatively unimportant and

(b) that it is needed since the equation is only able to explain average or typical behaviour and not every observed value.

More generally, econometric models can include mixtures of linear and non-linear functions, depending on the circumstances. The linear form has the attraction of simplicity, particularly when the estimation and forecasting stages are reached. However, the inclusion of variables such as the price level and its percentage rate of change (the rate of inflation) means that even simple models involve non-linearities.

A further point about equation (1.38) is that we have some ideas about the values of β and λ. From economic theory, we expect an increase in the relative price of an alcoholic drink to lead to a reduction in q so that β is expected to be negative. Also, an increase in income is expected to lead to an increase in q so λ is expected to be positive. We might also expect that λ will be fairly small because only a small proportion of an increase in real income will be spent on alcoholic drink.

3 Next we consider the data problems. Ideally we require accurate data on the variables of interest. However, published data are a compromise between the needs of the users – economists, civil servants, businessmen and industrialists – and the needs of the producers – usually government statisticians. For our demand example, the quantity of alcoholic drink sold could be measured in some units of volume or in equivalent units of pure alcohol but we know that changes in composition, between say sales of beer and sales of wine, could make such figures meaningless. Instead, real consumers' expenditure on alcohol, which is essentially a quantity index number with weights determined by base-year prices, could be used for q. In this case it is clear that the values are affected by the choice of base year. Similar problems occur with prices and incomes. This means that there is a difference between the theoretical concepts we are trying to measure and the data. Also, published data are to some extent inaccurate because of incomplete coverage (small firms are omitted from some enquiries), the 'hidden' economy, the use of sample estimates rather than census values, and data-processing errors.

4 Estimation of the parameters. This is the point where the data and the theoretical model are brought together and the parameters of the model (the unknown coefficients α, β and λ in equation (1.38)) are estimated. The usual method of estimation is some form of least squares regression and is achieved using a computer package. With simultaneous equation models ordinary least squares gives biased estimates of the parameters because of the presence of right-hand-side endogenous variables so some alternative is adopted, such as instrumental variables or a systems method (see Maddala 1988 or Johnston 1984 for an introduction to these methods).

For our demand example, if we assume that the variables p and Y are exogenous and also that there are no identification problems (so that we are sure that we do not have a supply curve), then we can use ordinary least squares to estimate the parameters.

Once the parameter estimates are obtained, they can be examined to see if they are consistent with our theory. That is, their size and signs are compared with what was expected. If they disagree with the theory we can either reject the results and maintain the theory or reject this particular version of the theory and accept the results. In the former case we might conclude that the data are unreliable or reflect unusual factors and try to remedy this. In the latter case we might try to improve the theory by considering alternative specifications of equations (1.37) and (1.38).

5 Forecasting. Once an acceptable model is obtained it can be used for forecasting. In our demand example, to forecast the value of q for next year we need to know the values of the exogenous variables p and Y, so our forecasts are conditional on these values. While this is an extra complication it is important to recognise that it arises because we have a causal model: we can explain how q is determined and we are not simply projecting past behaviour into the future. Also, the reason for making the forecast may be to see what the effects of different taxation levels on tax revenue are, so that p is treated as a variable which we control. If this is so we still need to predict the value of Y, the remaining exogenous variable, for next year. One method of doing this is to use a simple time-series model to project forward the historical time path of income. Another is to take a forecast of income from a different source – say a macroeconomic model. Given the values of p and Y we can then use the estimated equation to get the forecast of q. When forecasts are needed for a number of periods into the future they can be obtained as a sequence of one-step forecasts.

The methodology outlined above for making economic forecasts is frequently supplemented by what is referred to by Howrey, Klein and McCarthy (1974) as 'tender loving care'. This means that, rather than accepting the result of the forecasting procedure at face value, the forecasts are modified subjectively to take account of factors which are not incorporated in the model. For example, data revisions may mean that the data used to estimate the model are incorrect, or temporary events, such as a docks strike, may disturb the short-run time path of particular variables. While these adjustments introduce a subjective aspect into what is, in principle, an objective forecasting method, it is important to realise that many of the decisions made at earlier stages in the forecasting procedure are to some extent also subjective, as, for example, in the choice of functional form.

From our discussion of economic modelling and forecasting it should be clear that accurate forecasting requires not only the correct economic theory but also correct decisions at each of the remaining stages in the forecasting procedure. In other words, forecasts are a combination of economic theory and the judgement of the forecasters. The result is that an analysis of forecasts does not necessarily indicate which version of economic theory is correct nor tell us much about the differences between economic models. It may turn out that the most important determinant of forecasting accuracy is the prediction (or guess) of future government behaviour and the values of the exogenous variables.

1.5   Evaluating forecasts

We have reviewed several methods of forecasting in this chapter and have seen that forecast accuracy can be assessed by simple descriptive measures such as mean square error (1.12). We now consider the properties we expect good forecasts to have, and then look in more detail at ways of measuring forecast accuracy.

While it seems obvious that a good forecast should be close to the outcome, it is clear that some variables are easier to forecast than others. For example, for the UK, the current account of the balance of payments, being the difference between two large items, imports and exports, is regarded as being more difficult to forecast than a variable such as unemployment which changes relatively slowly. The result is that it is necessary to take the alternative approach of defining an optimal forecast as the best forecast that can be made in the circumstances. This is often referred to as the rational expectations forecast or the rational expectation of a variable. It is defined as the prediction from economic theory using all the relevant information that is available at the time the forecast is made. Strictly speaking, optimality should be defined with reference to the cost function of the user of the forecasts. That is, with reference to how positive and negative forecast errors are to be penalised, and also the value of the benefits, relative to the extra costs, which arise from improved forecasts. The optimal forecast is the one for which the marginal costs and marginal benefits are equal. Feige and Pearce (1976) call these forecasts the 'economically' rational expectations.

It is important to realise that the rational expectation can differ from the outcome, but any difference must be random and unpredictable. Since it is based on the correct economic theory, the rational expectation will have the properties of unbiasedness (assuming a quadratic cost function) and efficiency. Unbiasedness requires that the forecast error has an expected value of zero. Efficiency means that the available information has been fully exploited so that forecast errors are uncorrelated with this information.

There are a number of ways of testing whether a set of forecasts are rational. For a comprehensive review see Holden, Peel and Thompson (1985). The usual test for unbiasedness, which Holden and Peel (1990) show is strictly a test for inefficiency, involves estimating

$$A_t = \alpha + \beta F_t + u_t \tag{1.39}$$

where A is the actual or outcome series, F is the forecast series and u is a residual, and then testing the joint hypothesis $\alpha = 0$ and $\beta = 1$. An illustration of this test is given by Holden and Peel (1985) who apply it to quarterly UK forecasts from the National Institute of Economic and Social Research (NI). The forecasts are for six variables – the rates of change of real GDP, consumer prices, consumers' expenditure, investment, imports and exports – and have horizons of one to four quarters ahead. For forecasts j periods ahead, the residual term in (1.39) follows a moving average process of order $j-1$, so that generalised least squares should be used for estimation. Unbiasedness is rejected for only one of the series, four quarters ahead forecasts of inflation. McNees (1978) conducts the same test for US forecasts from the Chase, DRI and Wharton econometric models and finds evidence of bias, particularly in forecasts of the GNP deflator.

Testing for efficiency is more complicated since it is not possible to be sure of defining correctly the 'relevant' information set with which forecast errors are to be uncorrelated. In Holden and Peel (1985), the appropriate information set was chosen to be the four most recently observed actual values of the variables and the NI forecasts are found to be efficient with respect to this information. Thus, any information contained in these values is already incorporated in the forecasts. McNees (1978) finds that current forecast errors are related to previous forecast errors for the GNP deflator, showing that these forecasts could have been improved by using this information.

Turning now to the measurement of the accuracy of forecasts, from its definition, (1.12), the size of the mean square error (MSE) increases with the square of the error. That is, a quadratic cost function is assumed. We saw in (1.13) that the MSE could be decomposed into the variance of the forecast error and the square of the mean error so that it increased as the mean and variance of the forecast error increased. An optimal or rational expectations forecast will be unbiased and efficient. Thus, the mean error will be zero and the variance of the forecast error will be small, resulting in a small MSE.

The size of the MSE depends on both the accuracy of the forecasts and the units of measurement. The effects of the latter become important when forecasts of different variables are being compared. One method of dealing with this is to use a unitless measure such as Theil's inequality coefficient which is discussed below. Another method, used by Wallis *et al.* (1987) to compare forecasts for four variables from a number of macroeconomic models is, for each variable, to divide individual RMSEs by their average value. This gives a relative root mean square error which has a low value for accurate forecasts.

Like the mean absolute error (1.15) and the root mean square percentage error (1.16), the MSE is generally used as a purely descriptive statistic for summarising the characteristics of the sample evidence. However, Ashley, Granger and Schmalensee (1980) have proposed a statistical test by which two MSEs can be compared to see if one is significantly smaller than the other. Their starting point is (1.13), which we reproduce in slightly different notation as

$$MSE(e) = var(e) + mean(e)^2 \qquad (1.40)$$

where var(e) is the sample variance and mean(e) the sample mean of the forecast error e. Initially we will only consider the sample values of the various statistics, and defer reference to population values till later. For two sets of n forecasts with white noise errors e_{1t} and e_{2t} the difference between their MSEs is

$$MSE(e_1) - MSE(e_2) = var(e_1) - var(e_2) + (mean(e_1)^2 - mean(e_2)^2) \qquad (1.41)$$

Now let

$$s_t = e_{1t} + e_{2t}$$

and

$$d_t = e_{1t} - e_{2t}$$

be the sum and difference of the two forecast errors. We note that the covariance of s and d is

$$cov(s_t, d_t) = var(e_1) - var(e_2) \qquad (1.42)$$

Substituting in (1.41) gives

$$MSE(e_1) - MSE(e_2) = cov(s_t, d_t) + (mean(e_1)^2 - mean(e_2)^2) \qquad (1.43)$$

This relates the difference between two sample MSEs to the sample covariance of s and d, and the mean errors. If we now switch to the relationships between the population parameters, then by analogy with (1.43), if the forecasts F_{2t} are more accurate than F_{1t}, the MSE will be smaller so that the terms on the right-hand side will be positive. Therefore a test of whether the MSE is smaller for F_{2t} can be based on whether the combination of the covariance and the difference between the squares of the mean errors is positive. This can be done by estimating the regression equation

$$d_t = \beta_1 + \beta_2(s_t - \bar{s}) + u_t \tag{1.44}$$

where u_t is an error term with a mean of zero. Ashley, Granger and Schmalensee point out (in their footnote 13) that u is correlated with s but they argue that the resulting bias in β_2 is likely to be negligible in moderate sized samples. The least squares estimators of the parameters are

$$\beta_1 = \bar{d} \quad \text{and} \quad \beta_2 = \frac{\text{est.cov}(s, d)}{\text{est.var}(s - \bar{s})}$$

where est. indicates an estimated term. If we consider (1.43) again, the hypothesis that there is no difference in the MSEs implies that β_1 and β_2 will be close to zero, and can be tested by setting up the joint hypothesis $\beta_1 = 0$ and $\beta_2 = 0$. The alternative hypothesis, that (say) the forecasts F_2 have a smaller MSE, implies that either or both of β_1 and β_2 will be positive. Should the estimated coefficients in (1.44) be significantly negative, the forecasts F_2 are not more accurate than F_1. The individual coefficients can be tested by the standard t-test for regression, where, for $j = 1, 2$

$$t_0 = \frac{\beta_j}{\text{s.e.}}$$

and the degrees of freedom are $n - 2$, where there are n observations and s.e. is the square root of the estimated variance of β_j. A one-tailed test is used when the alternative hypothesis is that F_2 has a smaller MSE than F_1. The joint test that both population values are zero is an F-test with

$$F_0 = \frac{(\Sigma d_t^2 - \Sigma e_t^2)/2}{\Sigma e_t^2/(n-2)} \tag{1.45}$$

where e_t is the observed residual in the estimate of (1.44). This has an F-distribution with 2 and $n - 2$ degrees of freedom, and for the one-tailed alternative the significance level is half the value given in the tables. The standard assumptions required for these tests are that the residual u in (1.44) has a mean of zero, constant variance, no autocorrelation, is uncorrelated with s_t and, if the value of n is small, is normally distributed. Of these, the constant variance and no autocorrelation assumptions are unlikely to be valid with economic forecasts if there are large (sustained) external shocks. We discuss the use of non-parametric tests which avoid these assumptions below.

An illustration of these calculations is given in table 1.11 for two series of forecasts of the growth of GNP in constant dollars in the USA. The forecasts are both from the American Statistical Association–National Bureau of Economic Research (ASA–NBER) quarterly business outlook

Table 1.11 *Accuracy of ASA–NBER forecasts of growth of US GNP*

	Actual	e_1	e_2	s	d
1969	2.8	0.5	0.7	1.2	−0.2
1970	−0.4	1.5	1.1	2.6	0.4
1971	2.7	0.1	0.0	0.1	0.1
1972	6.5	−1.0	−0.8	−1.8	−0.2
1973	5.9	0.2	0.2	0.4	0.0
1974	−2.2	3.3	2.8	6.1	0.5
1975	−2.0	1.2	−1.0	0.2	2.2
1976	6.2	−0.3	−0.1	−0.4	−0.2
1977	4.9	0.1	−0.1	0.0	0.2
1978	3.9	0.4	0.4	0.8	0.0
1979	2.3	0.1	0.3	0.4	−0.2
1980	−0.2	−1.1	0.2	−0.9	−1.3
1981	2.0	−0.8	−0.5	−1.3	−0.3
1982	−1.5	2.0	1.1	3.1	0.9
RMSE		1.25	1.00		

Estimate of (1.44) is $d = 0.1357 + 0.1403(s - \bar{s})$
t-values (0.68) (1.38)

From (1.45), $F_0 = 0.95$ with (2, 12) degrees of freedom, so there is no difference in the accuracy of these forecasts.

Source: Forecast errors are from Moore (1983), tables 26.3 and 26.4.

survey of about 50 economists in business, government and academic institutions. The first series, giving errors e_1, is from the November surveys, with forecasts for the next calendar year, and the second, with errors e_2, is from the February surveys, with forecasts for the current years. From table 1.11 the two RMSEs are 1.25 and 1.00, based on fourteen observations, and are not significantly different.

Another measure of forecast accuracy is the mean absolute percentage error (MAPE) defined by

$$\text{MAPE} = \sum \frac{100|A - F|}{n|A|} \tag{1.46}$$

This differs from the MSE in that, like the MAE, it does not give extra weight to large errors, and so corresponds to a linear (in proportionate errors) loss function. A variation on the MAPE is the median of the absolute percentage errors (MdAPE). This is simply the median value of the absolute percentage errors and it is preferred when these errors have a skewed distribution so that the mean is distorted by a few extreme values.

A problem with the measures of forecast accuracy we have discussed so far is that they are affected by the units of measurement of the data. It would be useful to have a unitless measure, equivalent to, say, the correlation coefficient, as an accuracy measure. One such measure is the inequality coefficient of Theil (1961), defined by

$$U1 = \frac{(\Sigma(F_t - A_t)^2/n)^{1/2}}{(\Sigma F_t^2/n)^{1/2} + (\Sigma A_t^2/n)^{1/2}} \tag{1.47}$$

so the numerator is the RMSE and the denominator is the sum of the root mean squares of the forecasts and actuals. The advantage of $U1$ is that it lies between zero and one. If all the forecasts are correct, the value is zero, while, if the forecasts are always zero, and the actual values are non-zero, or *vice-versa*, $U1$ will be one. Thus a low value of $U1$ indicates accurate forecasts. However, it is not easy to interpret the denominator and Theil (1966) proposed using $U2$, defined by

$$U2^2 = \frac{\text{MSE}}{\Sigma A^2/n} \tag{1.48}$$

in which the MSE is scaled by the mean squares of the forecasts. Theil proposed using (1.48) for forecast *changes*, but it is commonly used for forecasts of levels also. Again the minimum value is zero (for perfect forecasts), but, there is no maximum value. The value one corresponds to the case of all the forecasts being zero. This has no relevance for levels variables, where forecasts of zero are unlikely to be plausible, but for forecasts of changes it is the value given by no-change forecasts. That is, a value greater than one indicates that the forecasts are worse than a no-change forecast. Theil (1961) proposed two ways of decomposing the MSE and, following Granger and Newbold (1973) we use

$$\text{MSE} = (\bar{A} - \bar{F})^2 + (S_F - rS_A)^2 + (1 - r^2)S_A^2 \tag{1.49}$$

where $\bar{A}$ and $\bar{F}$ are the means of A and F, S_A and S_F are their sample standard deviations and r is the simple correlation of A and F. Dividing throughout by MSE gives

$$1 = UM + UR + UD \tag{1.50}$$

where $\quad UM = \dfrac{(\bar{A} - \bar{F})^2}{\text{MSE}}, \quad UR = \dfrac{(S_F - rS_A)^2}{\text{MSE}}$

and $\quad UD = \dfrac{(1 - r^2)S_A^2}{\text{MSE}} \tag{1.51}$

and UM is the proportion of MSE due to the mean error or bias of the forecasts. The interpretation of UR and UM is helped by considering the relationship

$$A_t = \alpha + \beta F_t + v_t \tag{1.52}$$

for which the least squares estimators are

$$\beta = \frac{S_{AF}}{S_F^2} \quad \text{and} \quad \hat{\alpha} = \bar{A} - \beta \bar{F} \tag{1.53}$$

where S_{AF} is the sample covariance of A and F. For UR notice that

$$S_F - r S_A = S_F(1 - \beta)$$

and so UR is the proportion of MSE due to the regression coefficient β differing from one. Finally, since UD would be zero if (1.52) has a perfect fit, UD can be interpreted as the disturbance proportion of MSE or that part of the forecasting error which is unexplained by mean or slope error. Since (1.50) holds, good forecasts will have a low mean error (UM), a low regression error (UR) and a high disturbance or unexplained error (UD).

The accuracy measures described above are all parametric in the sense that they rely on the desirable properties of means and variances which occur when the underlying distributions are normal. For example the use of the MSE implicitly assumes that each of the forecast errors has the same mean and variance and that these are constants. It can be argued that each time a forecast is made there is a new situation and that comparisons of the numerical accuracy of forecasts made at different times are misleading. For an organisation producing economic forecasts each quarter, as time passes there are developments in the modelling techniques used, changes in the personnel producing the forecasts and new information becomes available about the past accuracy of the forecasts which should enable persistent errors to be recognised. The result is that it is unlikely that the distribution of forecast errors will have a constant mean and variance. Such considerations have led to the use of *non-parametric* methods of analysing forecast accuracy. These are generally 'distribution free' in that they do not assume a normally distributed population, and so can be used when this assumption would be invalid. They are particularly relevant for ordinal data, where a numerical scale has not been used. We will consider two types of nonparametric tests, the sign test and the rank tests.

To compare the accuracy of two sets of forecasts, say A and B, the sign test (see, for example, Mendenhall and Reinmuth 1982) is based on the percentage of times that forecasting method A is better than forecasting method B. This is done by comparing individual forecasts of the same event. For example, in table 1.12 the forecast errors from (1.21) and (1.23) (see table 1.5) are reproduced, and the answers to the question 'is (1.21) better than

Table 1.12. *Example of a sign test*

		Error from (1.21)	Error from (1.23)	Is (1.21) better?
1985	3	4.6	7.5	yes
	4	−6.1	−10.3	yes
1986	1	−14.5	−11.5	no
	2	−7.0	−6.8	no
	3	−0.2	5.0	yes
	4	−9.5	−14.8	yes
1987	1	−16.3	−11.0	no
	2	−10.5	−9.3	no
	3	9.4	17.5	yes
			Number of 'yes' 5	

Note: 'yes' indicates that (1.21) is more accurate than (1.23).

(1.23)?' are included. If there is a tie, that observation is ignored. It can be seen that (1.21) gives the smaller error in 5 out of 9 forecasts or 56 per cent of cases. If both methods are equally accurate, the probability of 'yes' is 0.5 for each of the nine forecasts and the probability distribution of P, the number of times (1.21) is better, is given by the binomial distribution

$$p(P = x) = {}^9C_x 0.5^x 0.5^{9-x}$$

so the probability of observing $x = 5$ or more can be evaluated, and is found to be 0.5000. That is, there is a 50 per cent chance of observing smaller errors for (1.21) in at least 5 out of 9 forecasts if both methods are equally accurate. The conclusion here is that the evidence suggests that (1.21) and (1.23) are equally accurate. If the number of forecasts (9 in this example) was large, the normal approximation to the binomial distribution could be used to evaluate the probability of the result.

The sign test can also be used to test the significance of the descriptive statistic known as 'the percentage better', which is simply the percentage of times one method of forecasting is better than another. Flores (1986) applies this method to the Makridakis competition results (see chapter 3, section 7 for a discussion), where the test is applied not to the individual forecasts but to the percentage better statistics from a number of series.

In rank tests the original numerical measure of accuracy, which might be the absolute error for individual forecasts or the MSE for a number of forecasts, is replaced by a ranking which is then tested for significance. For example if forecasts of two series, say A and B, are obtained using k different methods and the MSEs are obtained, their size could be ranked from 1 (smallest MSE) to k (largest MSE) for each series, giving ranks R_{Ai} and

R_{Bi}, for $i = 1$ to k. The difference (d_i) between the ranks is obtained and Spearman's rank correlation coefficient

$$r_s = 1 - \frac{6\Sigma_i^2 d}{n(n^2 - 1)} \tag{1.54}$$

is calculated. Special tables of critical values are published (see for example, Mendenhall and Reinmuth, 1982, p. 854). The hypothesis that there is no association between the ranks, so that no forecasting method is consistently better or worse than the others, is rejected if r_s is sufficiently large.

While these non-parametric tests have attractions, it is important to realise that they ignore some of the information which is available. Thus the sign and rank tests ignore the numerical size of the errors. Whether this is desirable depends on the circumstances.

1.6   Conclusions

In this chapter we have reviewed the various approaches to forecasting. It should be clear that there are important differences between the methods used in business, generally based on surveys or a range of extrapolation techniques, and the model-based approach of economic forecasting. We will see in chapter 2 that there are in fact links between univariate time-series models and structural economic models, and that there is some evidence that these two approaches are converging. Also, each of the methods of forecasting we have covered requires the forecaster to use judgement, both in selecting a method and in implementing it. Each method is expected to produce different results. This raises two questions: does any one method dominate the others, and can the forecasts from different methods be combined in some way to give a composite forecast which is more accurate than any of the individual forecasts?

Taking the first of these questions, there is no general agreement amongst forecasters as to which method is the best. In so far as comparisons of different techniques have been made (see chapter 5, section 8 for details), there is a consensus that extrapolation methods are preferred for short-run forecasting, and econometric models for long-run forecasting. However, much of this evidence is based on particular case-studies and it is not clear that the results are generally valid. When different versions of the same technique are compared, such as the forecasts from different econometric models, the evidence is that, while one organisation may give the best forecasts for a particular variable over a given horizon and for a certain historical period, changing any of these factors results in an alternative forecaster being preferred. Similar evidence occurs for time-series methods (see chapter 3, section 7).

The question of whether forecasts from alternative techniques should be combined together has been considered by a number of researchers. Bates and Granger (1969) pointed out that different forecasts can be expected to embody useful information because they rely on different information sets or different assumed relationships between the variables. Therefore gains are to be expected from combining forecasts. Various methods of combination have been suggested. We review them in detail in chapter 3 below. However, at this point it is worth noting that there is some evidence in favour of a simple averaging of the available forecasts as a reliable method of forming a combination.

CHAPTER 2

Time-series methods

2.1 Introduction

Other things being equal, the best method for forecasting the future values of a given variable would be to build a structural econometric model employing the correct theory, estimate its parameters from an accurate data base, and employ this model to predict the future values of the variable of interest. Since, by construction, such a model embodies the correct economic theory, it must produce forecasts which are, *a priori*, superior to those derived from other methods. However, the practitioner is seldom in this ideal situation and it is not always possible to construct an econometric model. This is because first, the practitioner may be unclear as to what constitutes the appropriate economic theory. Thus, for example while the theory of the consumption function is relatively uncontroversial, the role of money is not. Second, reliable data on the values of the variables believed to be relevant for the model may not exist. For example, monthly wealth and national income figures are not published in the UK. Third, the cost of constructing and estimating an econometric model may be greater than the perceived benefits from such an exercise, so that a cheaper method of forecasting is sought.

In chapter 1 we discussed some extrapolation methods in which past values of a single series were smoothed to give forecasts. Here we outline some of the more complex procedures, generally known as time-series methods, for univariate forecasting and then discuss multivariate forecasting methods. We start by linking econometric models and univariate models.

Our discussion of the univariate models such as (1.26) for exponential smoothing saw that they are essentially statistical models of the data and are not based on any economic theory. In contrast, our discussion of econometric modelling and forecasting emphasised the role of economic theory, with statistical aspects of the data being regarded as relatively unimportant. To show how these rather different approaches might be linked let us take the example of a simple model of an economy given by the following equations:

$$Y_t = C_t + I_t + G_t \tag{2.1}$$

$$C_t = \alpha + \beta Y_t + \varepsilon_t \tag{2.2}$$

$$I_t = \delta(Y_t - Y_{t-1}) \tag{2.3}$$

$$G_t = \rho Y_{t-1} + G' \tag{2.4}$$

where the endogenous variables Y_t, C_t, I_t and G_t are, respectively, real income, consumption, investment and government expenditure at time t. There is one lagged endogenous variable, Y_{t-1}, the value of real income at time $t-1$, and $\alpha, \beta, \delta, \rho$ and G' are positive constants. The term ε_t is a white noise disturbance term so that $E(\varepsilon_t) = 0$ for all t and $E(\varepsilon_t \varepsilon_s) = 0$ for $t \neq s$, and $E(\varepsilon_t^2) = \sigma^2$ which is a constant.

In general we can solve the system of equations to obtain the reduced form equations in which each endogenous variable is written as a function of all the exogenous and lagged endogenous variables in the system. Here, by substitution of (2.2), (2.3) and (2.4) into (2.1) we obtain the reduced form equation for income as

$$Y_t = \lambda + \pi Y_{t-1} + u_t \tag{2.5}$$

where $\lambda = (\alpha + G')/(1 - \beta - \delta)$, $\pi = (\rho - \delta)/(1 - \beta - \delta)$, and $u_t = \varepsilon_t/(1 - \beta - \delta)$. In (2.5) Y is expressed in terms of its lagged value, a constant and a disturbance. That is, (2.5) is a particular univariate representation of Y known as a *first-order autoregressive* or AR(1) process since Y is regressed on itself lagged one period. Thus we have demonstrated that an economic model can lead to a simple univariate model. Also, if we employ the lag operator, L, which is defined by

$$L Y_t = Y_{t-1} \tag{2.6}$$

$$L^n Y_t = Y_{t-n} \tag{2.7}$$

we can write (2.5) as

$$Y_t = \lambda + \pi L Y_t + u_t \tag{2.8}$$

Or, $(1 - \pi L)Y_t = \lambda + u_t$

$$Y_t = (1 - \pi L)^{-1}\lambda + (1 - \pi L)^{-1}u_t \tag{2.9}$$

Now if $-1 < \pi < 1$ then, from expanding the sum of a geometric series,

$$(1 - \pi L)^{-1} = 1 + \pi L + \pi^2 L^2 + \pi^3 L^3 + \cdots$$

and substituting into (2.9) gives

$$Y_t = (1 - \pi L)^{-1}\lambda + u_t + \pi u_{t-1} + \pi^2 u_{t-2} + \pi^3 u_{t-3} + \cdots \tag{2.10}$$

In (2.10) we have expressed Y solely as a function of a constant and an infinite number of white noise errors. If a series can be expressed in this way, it is said to be a *moving average process*. Since there are an infinite number of terms here, (2.10) is said to be an infinite moving average process or MA(∞). Finally, we can re-arrange (2.2) to express Y in terms of C and then substitute for Y_t and Y_{t-1} in (2.5) to give, after some manipulation,

$$C_t = (\alpha - \alpha\pi + \beta\lambda) + \pi C_{t-1} + \varepsilon_t - \pi\varepsilon_{t-1} + \beta u_t \qquad (2.11)$$

Here C is expressed in terms of both its own lagged value (and so is first-order autoregressive or AR(1)) and current and lagged residuals (and so is first-order moving average or MA(1)). The resulting process is known as a mixed *autoregressive moving average* or ARMA(1, 1). Using this notation, AR(1) and ARMA(1, 0) models are the same, as are MA(1) and ARMA(0, 1) models.

This simple example illustrates how two of the endogenous variables from this structural model, Y and C, can be given a univariate time-series representation and can be expressed solely in terms of their own past values and/or random errors. This also applies to the remaining endogenous variables, I and G. Of course if the model is changed to include extra exogenous variables or other lagged variables then the particular univariate representations will also change. Now the true model for any economy is generally unknown but, whatever the model, if certain conditions, such as the equations are linear, are satisfied then each endogenous variable has a univariate representation. Therefore one justification for using a univariate model is that it could come from a structural model. If this can be found by statistical techniques then the resulting estimated univariate model may provide high quality forecasts at a relatively low cost.

The early development of AR, MA and ARMA models was by Box and Jenkins (1976) who unified several strands in the literature and proposed a method of starting with the data, identifying a suitable ARMA model and then estimating the parameters. In the next section we provide the background material for this and then discuss the details in section 2.3 and an example in section 2.4. The univariate technique is extended in section 2.5 to include other variables. Next, in section 2.6, we examine the recently developed theory of cointegration and its relevance to modelling and forecasting. The final sections briefly review the different types of trend and non-linear forecasting methods.

2.2   Stochastic models of time series

In this section we commence by setting out the various properties of time series which are an essential prerequisite for the discussion of forecasting methods contained in the rest of the chapter. The starting point in modelling a series of observations arranged in time order, say $Y_1, Y_2, \ldots, Y_n$ is to assume that these values have been generated by a random or stochastic process. If the process generating the series can be assumed to have finite parameters and to be invariant with respect to time then the series is said to be *stationary*. This results in the mean, variance and the (auto) covariances of the series being constants. Thus for Y_t to be stationary, for all values of t,

$$E(Y_t) = \mu \tag{2.12}$$

$$\text{Var}(Y_t) = E(Y_t - \mu)^2 = \sigma^2 < \infty \tag{2.13}$$

$$\text{Cov}(Y_t Y_{t+s}) = E[(Y_t - \mu)(Y_{t+s} - \mu)] = \gamma_s \tag{2.14}$$

Notice in particular that the covariance between Y_t and Y_{t+s} depends only on s, the lead or lag between the two Y values, and it is a measure of whether they move together. From the definition, γ_s is equal to γ_{-s}. Also, the covariance for lag zero is the variance. It is frequently more convenient to use autocorrelations rather than covariances since autocorrelations vary between -1 and $+1$. They are simply the correlations between Y_t and Y_{t+s}, and are defined by

$$\rho_s = \gamma_s / \gamma_0 \tag{2.15}$$

As s varies, the values of ρ_s trace out the *autocorrelation function* or ACF. The sizes of the autocorrelations indicate the strength of the pattern between past values of the variable. For a white noise series, ε_t, since each value is uncorrelated with every other value, all the autocorrelations, $E(\varepsilon_t \varepsilon_{t+s})$, are zero for $s \neq 0$, and as the mean and variance are constants, the series is stationary.

More generally, in the regression framework the autocorrelations are given by the coefficient in

$$Y_t = \rho_s Y_{t-s} + \varepsilon_t \tag{2.16}$$

Another characteristic of a time-series variable is its *partial autocorrelation* function or PACF. This is best explained in the context of regression. Consider the regression of Y_t on Y_{t-1} and Y_{t-2}

$$Y_t = \phi_{12} Y_{t-1} + \phi_{22} Y_{t-2} + \varepsilon_t \tag{2.17}$$

where the first subscript on ϕ indicates the lag of the variable concerned (1 for Y_{t-1}) and the second the maximum order of the regression (2 in this case). Here the coefficient on Y_{t-2} is the partial autocorrelation coefficient since it indicates the partial or extra effect of adding Y_{t-2} to the equation when Y_{t-1} is already there. In this particular case it is the partial autocorrelation coefficient (PAC) of order 2 which is given by (2.17). The first order PAC, ϕ_{11}, is given by

$$Y_t = \phi_{11} Y_{t-1} + \varepsilon_t \qquad (2.18)$$

and by comparison with (2.16) for $s = 1$ it should be clear that ϕ_{11} and ρ_1 are identical. More generally, the PAC of order p is ϕ_{pp} in

$$Y_t = \phi_{1p} Y_{t-1} + \phi_{2p} Y_{t-2} + \cdots + \phi_{pp} Y_{t-p} + \varepsilon_t \qquad (2.19)$$

If Y is a white noise series, since each value is uncorrelated with the other values, all the coefficients in (2.19) will be zero, resulting in the PACs all being zero. For other series, while it is possible to estimate the PACs by repeated regressions as above, it is more convenient to relate them to the autocorrelations. We have already shown that

$$\phi_{11} = \rho_1 \qquad (2.20)$$

For the second PAC, multiplying (2.17) by Y_{t-1} and taking expected values

$$E(Y_t Y_{t-1}) = \phi_{12} E(Y_{t-1}^2) + \phi_{22} E(Y_{t-2} Y_{t-1}) + E(\varepsilon_t Y_{t-1}) \qquad (2.21)$$

Dividing through by γ_0 and using (2.14) and (2.15) gives

$$\rho_1 = \phi_{12} + \phi_{22} \rho_1$$

or $\quad \phi_{12} = \rho_1 (1 - \phi_{22}) \qquad (2.22)$

Similarly, multiplying (2.17) by Y_{t-2} and proceeding as above,

$$\phi_{22} = \rho_2 - \phi_{12} \rho_1 \qquad (2.23)$$

which, using (2.22), can be written

$$\phi_{22} = (\rho_2 - \rho_1^2)/(1 - \rho_1^2) \qquad (2.24)$$

The expressions for the other PACs can be obtained following the same steps, of writing out (2.19) for the particular value of p, multiplying this equation by $Y_{t-1}, Y_{t-2}, \ldots, Y_{t-p}$ in turn, taking expectations and finally solving for ϕ_{pp}.

The properties of the ACF and PACF are important guides to determining the generation process for a series. If a variable is stationary the data can be regarded as a sample of n observations from the underlying probability distribution of the random variable Y. This means that we can use the data to estimate these parameters. The estimates based on a sample of n observations $Y_1, Y_2, \ldots, Y_n$ are

$$\hat{\mu} = \Sigma Y_t / n \qquad (2.25)$$

$$\hat{\sigma}^2 = \Sigma (Y_t - \hat{\mu})^2 / (n-1) \qquad (2.26)$$

$$\hat{\gamma}_s = \Sigma (Y_t - \hat{\mu})(Y_{t+s} - \hat{\mu})/(n-s) \qquad (2.27)$$

where the first two summations are from 1 to n and the third from 1 to $n-s$.

We have seen that a white noise series has a constant mean (of zero), a constant variance and zero covariances and so is stationary. If additionally the variable has a normal distribution it is called a Gaussian white noise variable. The best prediction or forecast of a white noise variable is its mean of zero. While white noise series do not occur frequently in practice many other series can be transformed into white noise. An example of this is the random walk model (1.1)

$$Y_t = Y_{t-1} + \varepsilon_t \tag{2.28}$$

where ε is a white noise disturbance. This can be written

$$Y_t - Y_{t-1} = \varepsilon_t$$

to give a white noise process. With this model the expected value of Y for period $t+1$, namely the forecast for $t+1$, is

$$E(Y_{t+1}) = E(Y_1) + E(\varepsilon_{t+1})$$

and if Y_t is known, then since $E(\varepsilon_t) = 0$ for all t

$$E(Y_{t+1}) = Y_t$$

and in fact all the forecasts of future values of Y equal Y_t. In this model the variable Y is not stationary since repeated substitution into (2.28) for the lagged variable gives

$$Y_t = \varepsilon_t + \varepsilon_{t-1} + \cdots$$
$$= \Sigma \varepsilon_i \text{ for } i = 1, 2, \ldots, t$$

which, as t tends to infinity, will include an infinite number of terms, each of which has a non-zero variance σ^2. The variance of Y will therefore be infinite.

We now consider how to test whether a variable is stationary. This is both an art and a science. The starting point is to graph the data to get an overall impression of its variability. A stationary series has no trend or pattern in the mean or variance, and if there does appear to be some pattern a more objective check is needed. This might be done by estimating the mean, variance and autocorrelations for particular groups of observations. For example the values for the first one third and last one third of the data could be obtained. For the two means, a normal distribution z-test could be used to check if they are significantly different. For the variance, if the assumption of normality is valid, an F-test, as proposed by Goldfeld and Quandt (1965), could be used. There is no easy test for the significance of differences between autocorrelations but a simple comparison might indicate changing values. A more useful property of the autocorrelations is that for a stationary series there is some value S, say, for which if $s > S$, γ_s is approximately zero. Therefore if the autocorrelations tend to zero as the lag increases this suggests the series is stationary.

A formal test of whether a series is stationary has been proposed by Sargan and Bhargava (1983) who use a variation on the Durbin–Watson test. In this case consider the series

$$Y_t = \alpha + u_t \tag{2.29}$$

where u follows a Gaussian random walk, so that

$$u_t = u_{t-1} + \varepsilon_t \tag{2.30}$$

and the differenced equation

$$\Delta Y_t = \Delta u_t = \varepsilon_t \tag{2.31}$$

We are interested in determining whether the specification $(2.29)-(2.30)$ is correct. This implies that since ε_t is white noise then ΔY_t is stationary while Y is not. If this was the case we would say that ΔY_t is *integrated of order zero* (or is $I(0)$) and Y_t is integrated of order one (or is $I(1)$). That is, Y needs to be differenced once to become stationary. In general, the order of integration indicates how many times a variable needs to be differenced to become stationary. Sargan and Bhargava propose estimating (2.29) and calculating the Durbin–Watson statistic. This is given by

$$\text{DW} = \Sigma(\hat{u}_t - \hat{u}_{t-1})^2 / \Sigma \hat{u}_t^2$$

where the hat indicates an estimated value, and the summations are from 2 to n in the numerator and 1 to n in the denominator. If the proposed model $(2.29)-(2.30)$ is correct, it is clear that from (2.31) the numerator of DW is the sum of squares of $n-1$ white noise terms and the denominator is the square of n terms, each of which (by repeated substitution for u_{t-1} into (2.30)) can be written as an infinite number of white noise terms. Hence the Durbin–Watson statistic will be close to zero, and so the test is to see whether it is significantly different from zero. This statistic is called the *cointegrating regression Durbin–Watson (CRDW) statistic* and Sargan and Bhargava give a table of critical values. If the CRDW statistic for (2.29) is not significantly different from zero then the conclusion is that ΔY_t is stationary and Y is $I(1)$.

Engle and Granger (1987) suggest using a test for stationarity first proposed by Dickey and Fuller (1981) and based on the residuals from estimating (2.29). Consider the equation

$$\Delta \hat{u}_t = \beta \hat{u}_{t-1} + \varepsilon_t \tag{2.32}$$

where Δ indicates a first difference and ε_t is a white noise disturbance. This equation can also be written

$$\hat{u}_t = (1 + \beta)\hat{u}_{t-1} + \varepsilon_t \tag{2.33}$$

Now if β is zero then from (2.32), $\Delta\hat{u}_t$ is white noise and hence stationary, which means that Y_t is not stationary. But if β is negative, and $(1 + \beta)$ is between -1 and $+1$, then (2.33) is an AR(1) model and Y_t is stationary. Finally if β is positive then (2.33) will be explosive with $\hat{u}_t$ tending to infinity and so u and Y_t are not stationary. Engle and Granger propose estimating (2.32) and testing if β is zero against the alternative that β is negative. The test statistic, which is the ratio of the estimate of β to its standard error, is compared with the values in table I of Dickey and Fuller (1981). At the 5 per cent level of significance the critical value is -2.56 for 50 observations, compared with the conventional t-value of -1.68. An alternative form of this test, known as the augmented Dickey–Fuller test, includes lagged values of $\Delta\hat{u}$ in (2.32) in order to make the disturbance white noise.

If the conclusion from these tests is that the variable is not stationary it may be possible to transform it in some way, for example by differencing as in (2.31), to make it stationary. We will return to a discussion of tests for stationarity in section 2.6 in connection with cointegration.

2.3   Box–Jenkins modelling

We saw in section 2.1 that an endogenous variable from a structural economic model could have a univariate time-series representation, and that it might take the form of an autoregressive (AR) model, a moving average (MA) model or a mixed autoregressive moving average (ARMA) model. However, the original development of ARMA models was as a generalisation of simple non-causal models, such as exponential smoothing. Their application to economic forecasting followed from the availability of computer packages which in turn resulted in the production of forecasts at a low cost. Feige and Pearce (1976), for example, point out that ARMA models are likely to be an optimal method of forecasting since they have a low marginal cost and in many situations their marginal benefits would appear to be high. In this section we will examine in more detail the properties of these models and will outline the procedure proposed by Box and Jenkins (1976) for specifying and estimating such models. More rigorous expositions are provided by Harvey (1981) and Judge et al. (1985) and (1988). Initially we will determine the form of the autocorrelation function (ACF) and partial autocorrelation function (PACF) of some simple models which are also those most commonly occurring in practice. These will then allow us to attempt to identify a possible model when given information about the sample ACF and PACF for a set of observations on a variable. The reader who wishes to omit our derivation of the ACF and PACF can, without loss of continuity, proceed to page 56.

We start with the first order moving average or MA(1) model. This can be written as

$$Y_t = \mu + \varepsilon_t - \theta_1 \varepsilon_{t-1} \tag{2.34}$$

where Y_t is the variable of interest, μ is a constant and ε_t is a white noise error. We notice that this equation cannot be estimated by the usual ordinary least squares regression since ε_t and ε_{t-1} are only observable once the two parameters μ and θ_1 are estimated. This problem will be considered later in this section. Also, the process in (2.34) has a one-period 'memory' in that Y_t is affected by ε_t and ε_{t-1}, Y_{t-1} by ε_{t-1} and ε_{t-2} and Y_{t-2} by ε_{t-2} and ε_{t-3}, etc. Therefore Y_t is independent of Y_{t-2}. Taking expectations of (2.34) it can be seen that the mean of Y is μ. The range within which θ_1 lies can be determined by writing (2.34) as

$$\varepsilon_t = (Y_t - \mu) + \theta_1 \varepsilon_{t-1}$$

and repeatedly substituting for the lagged disturbance gives

$$\varepsilon_t = [1 + \theta_1 L + \theta_1^2 L^2 + \cdots][Y_t - \mu] + \theta_1^t$$

For ε to be finite, as t increases the right-hand side must converge, so that $-1 < \theta_1 < 1$. This is the condition for the MA(1) model to be *invertible*, that is, for the MA model to have an autoregressive (AR) representation. If θ_1 lies outside the required range then the variable Y will not be stationary. The variance of Y is given by

$$\begin{aligned}
\gamma_0 &= E(Y_t - \mu)^2 \\
&= E(\varepsilon_t - \theta_1 \varepsilon_{t-1})^2 \\
&= E(\varepsilon_t^2 + \theta_1^2 \varepsilon_{t-1}^2 - 2\theta_1 \varepsilon_t \varepsilon_{t-1}) \\
&= \sigma^2 + \theta_1^2 \sigma^2 \\
&= \sigma^2 (1 + \theta_1^2) \tag{2.35}
\end{aligned}$$

since ε is a white noise disturbance with a mean of zero, a variance σ^2 for all t and zero covariances. Similarly, the first autocovariance is

$$\begin{aligned}
\gamma_1 &= E(Y_t - \mu)(Y_{t-1} - \mu) \\
&= E\{(\varepsilon_t - \theta_1 \varepsilon_{t-1})(\varepsilon_{t-1} - \theta_1 \varepsilon_{t-2})\} \\
&= E(\varepsilon_t \varepsilon_{t-1} - \theta_1 \varepsilon_{t-1}^2 - \theta_1 \varepsilon_t \varepsilon_{t-2} + \theta_1^2 \varepsilon_{t-1} \varepsilon_{t-2}) \\
&= -\theta_1 \sigma^2 \tag{2.36}
\end{aligned}$$

again using the result that cross-products of ε have an expectation of zero.

The second autocovariance is

$$
\begin{aligned}
\gamma_2 &= E(Y_t - \mu)(Y_{t-2} - \mu) \\
&= E\{(\varepsilon_t - \theta_1 \varepsilon_{t-1})(\varepsilon_{t-2} - \theta_1 \varepsilon_{t-3})\} \\
&= 0
\end{aligned}
\tag{2.37}
$$

since only cross-products of ε occur. In general, γ_s is zero for $s > 1$. The autocorrelations (ACs) are

$$
\begin{aligned}
\rho_1 &= \gamma_1 / \gamma_0 \\
&= -\theta_1 / (1 + \theta_1^2)
\end{aligned}
\tag{2.38}
$$

and $\rho_s = 0$ for $s > 1$.

The first two partial autocorrelations (PACs) can be found from the ACs using (2.20) and (2.24):

$$
\begin{aligned}
\phi_{11} &= \rho_1 \\
&= -\theta_1 / (1 + \theta_1^2) \tag{2.39} \\
\phi_{22} &= (\rho_2 - \rho_1^2)/(1 - \rho_1^2) \\
&= -\theta_1^2 / (1 + \theta_1^2 + \theta_1^4) \tag{2.40}
\end{aligned}
$$

The other PACs can be found by the same method. The result of all this is that for the MA(1) process the ACF has the value zero after the first AC while the PACF is more complex but approximately declines geometrically.

The MA(2) process can be written

$$
Y_t = \mu + \varepsilon_t - \theta_1 \varepsilon_{t-1} - \theta_2 \varepsilon_{t-2}
\tag{2.41}
$$

where μ is the mean and $-1 < \theta_1, \theta_2 < 1$ and, by a similar argument to that above the autocovariances are

$$
\gamma_0 = (1 + \theta_1^2 + \theta_2^2)\sigma^2
\tag{2.42}
$$

$$
\gamma_1 = -\theta_1(1 - \theta_2)\sigma^2
\tag{2.43}
$$

$$
\gamma_2 = -\theta_2 \sigma^2
\tag{2.44}
$$

$$
\gamma_s = 0 \text{ for } s > 2
$$

Thus the ACs are

$$
\rho_1 = -\theta_1(1 - \theta_2)/(1 + \theta_1^2 + \theta_2^2)
\tag{2.45}
$$

$$
\rho_2 = -\theta_2/(1 + \theta_1^2 + \theta_2^2)
\tag{2.46}
$$

$$
\rho_s = 0 \text{ for } s > 2
$$

Hence the PACs are found by substitution into

$$\phi_{11} = \rho_1$$
$$\phi_{22} = (\rho_2 - \rho_1^2)/(1 - \rho_1^2)$$

Thus an MA(2) model is characterised by an ACF with a value of zero after the second AC and a rather complex PACF which tends to decline.

More generally, an MA(q) model takes the form

$$Y_t = \mu + \varepsilon_t - \theta_1 \varepsilon_{t-1} - \theta_2 \varepsilon_{t-2} - \cdots \theta_q \varepsilon_{t-q}$$
$$= \mu + \theta(L)\varepsilon_t \tag{2.47}$$

and μ is the mean, the θ_s lie between -1 and $+1$ and $\theta(L)$ is a polynomial in the lag operator L, and q is a positive integer. By the same methods as were used above it can be shown that ρ_s is zero for $s > q$ and that the PACF declines. Thus a general characteristic of an MA process is that, beyond a particular point, corresponding to the order of the process and so the length of the memory, the autocorrelations are zero.

Next we consider the properties of various autoregressive (AR) models. The general AR(p) process can be written

$$Y_t = \delta + \phi_1 Y_{t-1} + \phi_2 Y_{t-2} + \cdots + \phi_p Y_{t-p} + \varepsilon_t \tag{2.48}$$

where δ is a constant (and is not the mean), ε is a white noise disturbance and p is a positive integer. Notice that here ϕ_1 is not the same as the ϕ_{11} in the PACF formula (2.18). Also, since Y_t is related to Y_{t-1} and, by lagging (2.48), Y_{t-1} is related to Y_{t-2} and so on then the AR process has an infinite memory in that the current value depends on all past values. For future reference it is convenient to write (2.48) as

$$\varepsilon_t + \delta = (1 - \phi_1 L - \phi_2 L^2 \ldots - \phi_p L^p) Y_t$$
$$= \phi(L) Y_t \tag{2.49}$$

where $\phi(L)$ is a polynomial in the lag operator L. If μ is the mean of Y then taking expected values of (2.48) gives

$$\mu = \delta + \phi_1 \mu + \phi_2 \mu + \cdots + \phi_p \mu$$

and solving for μ,

$$\mu = \delta/(1 - \phi_1 - \phi_2 - \cdots - \phi_p) \tag{2.50}$$

For a stationary process the mean is finite which requires the sum of the ϕ_s to be not equal to one, and in fact consideration of the variance (below) requires this sum to be less than one.

The AR(1) model is

$$Y_t = \delta + \phi_1 Y_{t-1} + \varepsilon_t \tag{2.51}$$

and from (2.50) the mean is

$$\mu = \delta/(1 - \phi_1)$$

and so for a finite mean ϕ_1, is not one. Determination of the variance is helped by noting that

$$Y_t - \mu = \delta + \phi_1 Y_{t-1} + \varepsilon_t - \delta/(1 - \phi_1)$$
$$= \phi_1(Y_{t-1} - \mu) + \varepsilon_t \tag{2.52}$$

Hence the variance is

$$\gamma_0 = E(Y_t - \mu)^2$$
$$= \phi_1^2 \text{var}(Y_{t-1}) + \text{var}(\varepsilon_t)$$
$$= \phi_1^2 \gamma_0 + \sigma^2$$

and solving for γ_0,

$$\gamma_0 = \sigma^2/(1 - \phi_1^2) \tag{2.53}$$

For the variance to be positive $-1 < \phi_1 < 1$.

The first covariance is from

$$\gamma_1 = E\{(Y_t - \mu)(Y_{t-1} - \mu)\}$$

and using (2.52),

$$\gamma_1 = \phi_1 E(Y_{t-1} - \mu)^2 + E(Y_{t-1} - \mu)\varepsilon_t$$
$$= \phi_1 \gamma_0$$
$$= \phi_1 \sigma^2/(1 - \phi_1^2) \tag{2.54}$$

Similarly,

$$\gamma_2 = \phi_1 \gamma_1$$

and in general,

$$\gamma_s = \phi_1^s \gamma_0 \tag{2.55}$$

for $s > 0$. The autocorrelations follow directly from (2.55) and are

$$\rho_s = \phi_1^s \tag{2.56}$$

Since $-1 < \phi_1 < 1$ the autocorrelations decline geometrically for the AR(1) model. The partial autocorrelations, from (2.20) and (2.24), with (2.56) are

$$\phi_{11} = \phi_1 \tag{2.57}$$
$$\phi_{22} = 0 \tag{2.58}$$

and in general

$$\phi_{ss} = 0 \tag{2.59}$$

for $s > 1$. Thus the AR(1) process is characterised by a geometrically declining ACF and a PACF which, after the first, takes the value zero.

The general form of the AR(2) model is

$$Y_t = \delta + \phi_1 Y_{t-1} + \phi_2 Y_{t-2} + \varepsilon_t \tag{2.60}$$

By the same methods as used above, the mean and variance are

$$\mu = \delta/(1 - \phi_1 - \phi_2) \tag{2.61}$$

$$\gamma_0 = (1 - \phi_2)\sigma^2/(1 - \phi_2 - \phi_1^2 - \phi_2\phi_1^2 - \phi_2^2 + \phi_2^3) \tag{2.62}$$

and the autocorrelations are

$$\rho_1 = \phi_1/(1 - \phi_2) \tag{2.63}$$

$$\rho_2 = \phi_2 + [\phi_1^2/(1 - \phi_2)] \tag{2.64}$$

$$\rho_s = \phi_1\rho_{s-1} + \phi_2\rho_{s-2} \tag{2.65}$$

for $s > 1$. The partial autocorrelations are

$$\phi_{11} = \phi_1/(1 - \phi_2) \tag{2.66}$$

$$\phi_{22} = \phi_2 \tag{2.67}$$

$$\phi_{33} = 0 \tag{2.68}$$

$$\phi_{ss} = 0 \tag{2.69}$$

for $s > 2$. Therefore the PACF for the AR(2) process is zero after the second value. Similar results apply for the AR(p) process, where the ACF declines geometrically from ρ_p and the PACF is zero after ϕ_{pp}.

Finally we examine the characteristics of the mixed autoregressive – moving average (ARMA) model. The general form has an AR of order p and a MA of order q giving the ARMA(p, q) model as

$$Y_t = \delta + \phi_1 Y_{t-1} + \phi_2 Y_{t-2} + \cdots + \phi_p Y_{t-p} + \varepsilon_t - \theta_1\varepsilon_{t-1}$$
$$- \theta_2\varepsilon_{t-2} - \cdots - \theta_q\varepsilon_{t-q} \tag{2.70}$$

and using the polynomials in the lag operators defined in (2.47) and (2.49) we have

$$\phi(L)Y_t = \theta(L)\varepsilon_t + \delta \tag{2.71}$$

As might be expected, the properties of ARMA models are a mixture of those of AR and MA models. In fact, if an ARMA (p, q) process is stationary, then it can be written as either a pure autoregressive or moving two lag polynomials $\phi(L)$ and $\theta(L)$ both exist, so that (2.71) can be multiplied by $\phi(L)^{-1}$ to give an infinite MA representation, and similarly, multiplying (2.71) by $\theta(L)^{-1}$ gives an infinite AR representation.

Turning now to the properties of the ARMA(1, 1) model, this can be written

$$Y_t = \delta + \phi_1 Y_{t-1} + \varepsilon_t - \theta_1 \varepsilon_{t-1} \tag{2.72}$$

The mean and variance are

$$\mu = \delta/(1 - \phi_1) \tag{2.73}$$

$$\gamma_0 = (1 + \theta_1^2 - 2\theta_1\phi_1)\sigma^2/(1 - \phi_1^2) \tag{2.74}$$

and the autocorrelations are

$$\rho_1 = \phi_1 - (\theta_1\sigma^2/\gamma_0) \tag{2.75}$$

$$\rho_2 = \phi_1\rho_1 \tag{2.76}$$

$$\rho_s = \phi_1\rho_{s-1} \tag{2.77}$$

for $s > 1$. Therefore the autocorrelations decline as the lag increases. The partial autocorrelations are

$$\phi_{11} = \rho_1 \tag{2.78}$$

$$\phi_{22} = \rho_1(\phi_1 - \rho_1)/(1 - \rho_1^2) \tag{2.79}$$

and generally decline as the lag increases. These results also extend to the ARMA(p, q) model, where the ACF declines after lag p and the PACF declines after lag q.

The characteristics of the different models are summarised in table 2.1 and these can be used to identify the type of process that might have generated a particular set of data, which is the next thing we consider.

We have shown that the variables from a structural economic model can have a univariate time-series representation, and it should also be clear that a modification of the equations of the model can change the corresponding univariate model. We now turn to the problem of deciding, from the evidence of a sample of n observations $Y_1, Y_2, \ldots, Y_n$ what the appropriate ARMA model might be. This is the identification stage in the method proposed by Box and Jenkins (1976). The other stages are estimating its coefficients, checking the adequacy of the fitted model and using it for forecasting.

A model is identified by comparing the estimates of the ACF and PACF from the sample with various theoretical models in the hope of finding similar patterns. The first step is to examine the data and check to see if the series is stationary, using the methods outlined in section 2.2 above. In

Table 2.1. *The characteristics of ARMA models*

Model	ACF	PACF
White noise	all zero	all zero
MA(1)	zero after ρ_1	declines from ϕ_{11}
MA(2)	zero after ρ_2	declines from ϕ_{22}
MA(q)	zero after ρ_q	declines from ϕ_{qq}
AR(1)	geometric decline from ρ_1	zero after ϕ_{11}
AR(2)	geometric decline from ρ_2	zero after ϕ_{22}
AR(p)	geometric decline from ρ_p	zero after ϕ_{pp}
ARMA(1, 1)	geometric decline from ρ_1	decline from ϕ_{11}
ARMA(p, q)	geometric decline from ρ_p	decline from ϕ_{qq}

order to do this with any confidence a reasonable number of observations (say more than 50) is needed. If the series is not stationary then Box and Jenkins suggest differencing it until it is stationary. This is because first-differencing a series removes a linear trend, second-differencing removes a quadratic trend and so on. In general, we may have to difference a series d times in order to ensure stationarity. Let $X_1, X_2, \ldots, X_n$ be the original series and $Y_1, Y_2, \ldots, Y_n$ be the transformed series then first-differencing sets

$$
\begin{aligned}
Y_t &= X_t - X_{t-1} \\
&= (1 - L)X_t
\end{aligned}
\tag{2.80}
$$

and if Y has an ARMA(p, q) representation then X is said to have an ARIMA($p, 1, q$) or *autoregressive integrated moving average* $p, 1, q$ representation. More generally, if X has to be differenced d times to become stationary, so that

$$
Y_t = (1 - L)^d X_t
\tag{2.81}
$$

then X has an ARIMA(p, d, q) representation, where d is a positive integer or is zero if X is stationary. X_t is said to have a *stochastic trend* and we shall discuss this aspect in section 2.7.

When transforming a variable to make it stationary it is important to beware of over-differencing. This occurs when a stationary series is differenced. Fortunately, a simple indication of whether this has happened is gained by checking whether the variance of the series has increased. For example, suppose a series is white noise with variance σ^2, then differencing this series results in a variance of $2\sigma^2$. In contrast, for a simple linear time trend (which is non stationary) the differenced series (which is stationary) has a zero variance. More generally, differencing a non-stationary series usually results in a series with a smaller variance.

Once a stationary series is obtained the autocorrelations and partial autocorrelations are computed, using (2.25)–(2.27). The resulting patterns are compared with those listed in table 2.1 to see if there are similarities. In general, since we are using a sample of observations and frequently the sample size is relatively small, we expect sampling fluctuations to occur and there will not be an exact correspondence between the data and a theoretical model. This might lead to two or three tentative models (that is pairs of values of p and q) being selected at this stage.

The next step is to estimate each of the tentative models and select the best one. While an AR model can be estimated by ordinary least squares this cannot be used for MA or ARMA models. For example, for the MA(1) model

$$Y_t = \mu + \varepsilon_t - \theta_1 \varepsilon_{t-1} \tag{2.82}$$

data on Y alone do not allow the parameters to be estimated since it is only when the parameters are known that ε can be estimated. The procedure suggested by Box and Jenkins (1976) is to use an iterative method whereby the parameter estimates minimise the residual sum of squares. Now (2.82) can be written

$$\varepsilon_t = Y_t - \mu + \theta_1 \varepsilon_{t-1} \tag{2.83}$$

From the estimated ACF and PACF, initial guesses of the values of the parameters are made. Here we might use the sample mean (for μ) and the first autocorrelation (for θ_1). Suppose these are 100 and 0.2. Then (2.83) is

$$\varepsilon_t = Y_t - 100 + 0.2\varepsilon_{t-1} \tag{2.84}$$

and, setting ε_0 to zero, estimates of ε_t can be obtained for $t=1$ to n, and the resulting sum of squares of residuals, S_1, say, is calculated. New starting values for μ and θ_1 are selected and the steps repeated to give a new residual sum of squares, S_2. Other starting values are tried and the ones giving the minimum value of S are the final estimates. There are a number of computer packages, including TSP, RATS and MINITAB which include such an optimisation procedure, and also compute the standard errors and other relevant statistics.

Once a model is estimated it has to be checked to see if it is satisfactory. Four types of test can be used, covering the significance and stability of the parameters, the properties of the residuals and the forecasting ability of the model. The test of whether the parameter estimates are significantly different from zero is the standard z-test (or t-test for small samples) and for an acceptable model the parameters should all be significant. If they are not it suggests that the parameter(s) concerned should be set to zero and the model re-estimated. The stability of the parameters can be tested by re-estimating the model using sub-sets of the data to see if the parameters change. The conventional Chow test (see Johnston 1984 or Kmenta 1986, p. 420) is not valid for dyamic models and instead a likelihood-ratio test (see Kmenta 1986, p. 492) can be used to test the restrictions that all the parameters are constant over the sub-periods. If the unrestricted residual sum of squares is S_u and the restricted residual sum of squares is S_r, then the hypothesis that the restrictions are valid is tested by

$$\chi^2(k) = n \log(S_r/S_u) \tag{2.85}$$

which has a chi-squared distribution with k degrees of freedom where k is the number of restrictions. The hypothesis is accepted if the chi-squared value is low and the conclusion would be that the parameters are stable.

The next tests concern the residuals. If the correct model is estimated then the residuals should be white noise. Therefore the ACF and PACF of the residuals are calculated. If the sample size (n) is large, the individual autocorrelations and partial autocorrelations have a standard error of approximately $1/\sqrt{n}$ so that their significance can be tested using a normal distribution. Any significant values lead to a rejection of the model. However, it is important to realise that if 20 values are calculated for the ACF and PACF then at the 5 per cent level we expect one of each to be significant. This, together with the relatively small sample sizes that occur in practice, mean that tests based on individual coefficients can be unreliable. An alternative is to use a 'portmanteau' test in which all the estimated coefficients are included. Box and Pierce (1970) propose using

$$BP = n\Sigma r_i^2 \tag{2.86}$$

where r_i is the estimated autocorrelation of order i and the summation is for 1 to K. If the autocorrelations up to order K are all zero then BP has approximately a chi-squared distribution with $K - p - q$ degrees of freedom, where p and q are the order of the fitted ARMA model. A large value of BP, compared with the critical value, leads to a rejection of the hypothesis of white noise. Several modifications have been proposed, the most popular one being by Ljung and Box (1978) who use

$$LB = n(n+2)\Sigma(n-i)^{-1}r_i^2 \tag{2.87}$$

where again the summation is for $i = 1$ to K, and the degrees of freedom are $K - p - q$. These tests have also been applied to the partial autocorrelations. Another test concerns the distribution of the residuals, which is assumed to be normal if the sample is small. This is a standard goodness-of-fit test (see, for example, Kmenta 1986, p. 149).

average process. This is because stationarity ensures that the inverses of the

The final group of tests concerns the forecasting ability of the model. Ideally, when the data are collected, instead of using all the observations for selecting and fitting a model, some (say ten) might be saved for evaluating the model. These would then be used to check the forecasting accuracy of the estimated model. In the example in (2.82) the estimated model might be

$$Y_t = 100 + e_t - 0.3e_{t-1} \qquad (2.88)$$

where e_t is the estimated value of ε_t. The forecast for period $n+1$ is

$$F_{n+1} = 100 + e_{n+1} - 0.3e_n \qquad (2.89)$$

and here e_n is known while the expected value of e_{n+1} is zero. Therefore a forecast for $n+1$ can be found. If the residuals are normally distributed and forecasts for observations $n+1$ to $n+m$ are made, giving forecast errors f_t (defined as $Y_t - F_t$), the size of the errors can be tested by the statistic

$$\chi^2(m) = \Sigma(f_t/s)^2 \qquad (2.90)$$

which has a chi-squared distribution with m degrees of freedom, where the summation is for $t = n+1$ to $n+m$ and s is the estimated standard deviation of the residuals. If the model is satisfactory the chi-squared value will be small. Another test would be to see if there is any pattern in the forecast errors, since generally under- or over-predicting the outcomes indicates an unsatisfactory model. Once a model is accepted it is re-estimated using all the available data.

If a particular estimated model is found to be unsatisfactory it must be rejected, and an alternative one specified and estimated. Eventually, one or more models will be accepted. When there are several acceptable models some means of discriminating between them is needed. One obvious criterion is to select the model with the smallest sum of squares of residuals, since this has been used to fit the model. This is equivalent to maximising R^2. However, it is clear that adding extra terms to an ARMA model will, in general, reduce the residual sum of squares, even if the new parameter is not significantly different from zero, and in fact the residual sum of squares can be reduced to zero by using a model with n parameters. Unfortunately, such a model is likely to give poor forecasts since it ignores the stochastic nature of the series.

Box and Jenkins (1976) propose the principle of parsimony, which states that, given several adequate models, the one with the smallest possible number of parameters should be selected. To be useful, this principle has to be formalised as a rule, in which the closeness of the fit is traded-off against the number of parameters. One suggestion is to calculate $\bar{R}^2$, the coefficient of multiple correlation corrected for degrees of freedom, as used in chapter

1, section 3 and defined by

$$\bar{R}^2 = 1 - \frac{s^2}{(\Sigma(Y-\bar{Y})^2/(n-1))}$$

where s^2 is the estimate of the residuals variance. However, this is not really appropriate when the variable Y may be differenced in some models. In the time-series literature several information criteria have been proposed, with the model which is selected being the one for which the criterion is minimised. If n is the number of observations used in estimating an ARMA model, s^2 is the estimate of the variance of the residuals and k is the total number of estimated parameters, then the Akaike (1973) information criterion (AIC) is

$$\text{AIC} = n\log(s^2) + 2k \tag{2.91}$$

where natural logarithms are used. This gives a non-linear trade-off between the residuals variance and the value of k, since a model with a higher k value will only be preferred if there is a proportionately large fall in s^2. Geweke and Meese (1981) have suggested a Bayesian information criterion (BIC) defined by

$$\text{BIC} = n\log(s^2) + k\log(n) \tag{2.92}$$

This gives more weight to k than AIC if $n > 7$, so that an increase in k requires a larger reduction in s^2 under BIC than under AIC. Another alternative, suggested by Hannan and Quinn (1979) is

$$\text{HQ} = n\log(s^2) + 2k\log(\log n) \tag{2.93}$$

Here the weight on k is greater than 2 if $n > 15$. Akaike (1970) has also proposed a final prediction error (FPE), defined by

$$\text{FPE} = \{(n+k)/(n-k)\} - \{(n-k)s^2/n\} \tag{2.94}$$

To some extent the choice between these is arbitrary since they all move in the same direction as k increases. In practice, just one of these would be used.

Once an adequate model has been selected it can be used for forecasting. We saw how this is done for one-period ahead forecasts for the MA(1) model in (2.89), and the same method is used for AR and ARIMA models, and generalises to other horizons. Remember that an MA(q) process has a memory of q periods and the best forecast beyond this horizon is the mean of the series. This is easily demonstrated for (2.88) where for period $n + 2$ the forecast is

$$F_{n+2} = 100 + \varepsilon_{n+2} - 0.3\varepsilon_{n+1} \tag{2.95}$$

but the expected values of ε_{n+2} and ε_{n+1} are both zero so that the forecast for period $n+2$ is the mean, 100. It is also relatively straight-forward to work out the variances of forecasts, allowing confidence intervals to be estimated. Taking the MA(1) model (2.82), the forecast for $n+1$ is (2.89) so that the one-period ahead forecast error is

$$
\begin{aligned}
f_{n+1} &= Y_{n+1} - F_{n+1} \\
&= (\delta + \varepsilon_{n+1} - \theta_1 \varepsilon_n) - (\delta + E(\varepsilon_{n+1}) - \theta_1 \varepsilon_n) \\
&= \varepsilon_{n+1}
\end{aligned}
\tag{2.96}
$$

which has an expected value of zero and so the variance is σ^2, the variance of ε. For two (or more) periods ahead the forecast error is

$$
\begin{aligned}
f_{n+2} &= Y_{n+2} - F_{n+2} \\
&= (\delta + \varepsilon_{n+2} - \theta_1 \varepsilon_{n+1}) - \delta \\
&= \varepsilon_{n+2} - \theta_1 \varepsilon_{n+1}
\end{aligned}
\tag{2.97}
$$

and again the mean error is zero and the variance is

$$
E(f_{n+2})^2 = (1 + \theta_1^2)\sigma^2
\tag{2.98}
$$

As this applies for any horizon more than one period ahead, the width of a confidence interval for these forecasts is constant. In contrast, for AR models the variance of the forecast error increases as the horizon lengthens. For example, the AR(1) model

$$
Y_t = \delta + \phi_1 Y_{t-1} + \varepsilon_t
\tag{2.99}
$$

gives forecasts

$$
F_{n+1} = \delta + \phi_1 Y_n
\tag{2.100}
$$

$$
F_{n+2} = \delta + \phi_1 F_{n+1}
\tag{2.101}
$$

and substitution from (2.100) gives

$$
F_{n+2} = \delta(1 + \phi_1) + \phi_1^2 Y_n
\tag{2.102}
$$

In general, for forecasts L periods ahead,

$$
F_{n+L} = \delta(1 + \phi_1 + \phi_1^2 + \cdots + \phi_1^{L-1}) + \phi_1^L Y_n
\tag{2.103}
$$

Here, as L tends to infinity, the forecast tends to the mean of the series since the term in brackets is the sum of a geometric series which converges. By the same method as above, the forecast error is

$$
f_{n+L} = \varepsilon_{n+L} + \phi_1 \varepsilon_{n+L-1} + \ldots \phi_1^{L-1} \varepsilon_{n+1}
\tag{2.104}
$$

and the variance is

$$
E(f_{n+L})^2 = (1 + \phi_1^2 + \phi_1^4 + \ldots \phi_1^{2L-2})\sigma^2
\tag{2.105}
$$

As L increases, the variance increases and any confidence intervals widen. This is also the case with forecasts from ARMA models, which are a combination of the results for their components.

Our discussion has ignored the possibility of seasonal variation which is indicated by a high correlation between variables observed during the same season in consecutive years. For example, in quarterly series, consumers' expenditure is generally higher in the fourth quarter of each year because of Christmas, than in the third or first quarters. This results in the ACF and/or PACF having peaks at lags 4, 8, 12, ... There are three approaches to dealing with this. The first is to use seasonally adjusted data. This removes the problem and has the advantage, when the data have been seasonally adjusted by the producers, of the experts taking account of relevant special factors. The second method is to add extra parameters to the ARMA model to allow for the seasonal variation. The third method, suggested by Box and Jenkins (1976), is to use seasonal differencing (such as $Y_t - Y_{t-4}$) to take account of this effect. Bowerman and O'Connell (1987) present a detailed discussion of seasonal models.

We conclude our discussion of ARMA models with some comments on their theoretical limitations. The first of these is that the underlying (true) data generating process for the series under consideration may not be linear in the parameters and variables, so that the ARMA method, which assumes linearity, will be inappropriate. In recent years a number of non-linear time-series models have been proposed and we will review them in section 2.8.

The second limitation of ARMA methods concerns their ability to deal with a change in the structure of the underlying model generating the variable of interest. For example, in our illustrative economic model defined by (2.1) to (2.4), suppose the authorities change their behaviour so that, instead of being described by (2.4), it is now described by

$$G_t = \rho_1 Y_{t-1} + \rho_2 Y_{t-2} + G'$$

This changes the ARMA representation of each variable in the model. For instance, real output now becomes

$$Y_t = ((\alpha + G') + (\rho_1 - \delta)Y_{t-1} + \rho_2 Y_{t-2})/(1 - \beta - \delta) + (\varepsilon_t/(1 - \beta - \delta))$$

is now described by an ARMA(2, 0) process instead of being an ARMA(1, 0) process. Clearly, inefficient forecasts will result if we continue to employ an ARMA (1, 0) process when the true process is an ARMA (2, 0) one. In fact, matters may not be quite as bad as this example seems to indicate. The question arises as to why the switch in policy regime takes place. It is hard to think of an exogenous switch in regime. If, in the true model, policy switches are endogenous (for example, due to a change in the party in power), then ultimately each of the variables in the 'true' model will have a time-series representation. This process could well be non-linear, but at least in principle, as a first order approximation, ARMA representations of the variables will exist. In practice, the difficulty may be having sufficient observations to identify the appropriate model. Consequently, it is frequently suggested in the literature that the parameter estimates of ARMA models should be updated as new observations become available. We shall see in section 2.5 that this idea of parameter updating has been formalised in the Kalman filter. However, before discussing this, we extend the univariate ARMA framework to include other variables.

We now present a worked example of ARMA modelling.

2.4   A worked example

To help to clarify the Box-Jenkins approach to modelling a time series we now consider a particular example. The series is the quarterly level of consumers' expenditure in the UK, measured at 1980 prices in £ millions and seasonally adjusted for 1960(1)–1987(2), and can be interpreted as real consumption. The data are taken from *Economic Trends Annual Supplement* 1988, table 21 where they are coded CAAB. Following our earlier suggestion of reserving some observations to test the forecasting performance, we will save the last ten observations and so only use data for 1960(1)–1984(4) for model selection and estimation. When a model is finally selected it will be re-estimated using all the data.

A quick look at the data confirms that the series is not stationary. The values for 1960 are 18968, 19120, 19319 and 19271, while those for 1984 are 36375, 36880, 36628 and 37173, and there is a strong upward trend throughout the period. We must therefore consider how to transform the data to remove this trend. Several possibilities occur, including subtracting a linear or non-linear trend, first differencing and taking the proportional rate of change. While we discuss the different types of trend in section 2.8 below, here it seems sensible to take a proportionate rate of change for real consumption. The particular form adopted is to define DC by

$$DC = \log(C_t/C_{t-1})$$

where C_t is the level of real consumption. The one-period change is taken since the data are seasonally adjusted, whereas for unadjusted data a four-period change might have been more appropriate. A logarithmic change is preferred to simple differencing because this is expected to reduce the effects of a changing variance. Next, the resulting series, DC, is to be checked to see if it is stationary. Recall that a stationary variable has a constant mean, a constant variance and constant covariances. Here we

Table 2.2. *Testing whether DC is stationary*

Statistic		1960(1)–1968(4)	1976(1)–1984(4)
Mean		0.00609	0.00502
Variance		0.00014	0.00025
Autocorrelations:	lag 1	−0.28	−0.36*
	lag 2	0.07	0.04
	lag 3	−0.24	0.29
	lag 4	−0.10	−0.39*
Partial ACs:	lag 1	−0.28	−0.36*
	lag 2	−0.01	−0.11
	lag 3	0.24	0.32*
	lag 4	−0.26	−0.22

Note:
* significant at the 5 per cent level.

have 100 observations and so we will compare these statistics, based on (2.25)–(2.27), for the first 36 and last 36 observations. This choice is somewhat arbitrary, but in general each of the sub-sample sizes should be reasonably large and there should be a central band of observations omitted. Here we have roughly split the data into three. The sample values are given in table 2.2. To test for equality of the means a test based on the normal distribution (assuming we can take 36 as being a large sample) is used with

$$z = (m_1 - m_2)/\text{s.e.}$$

where the sample means are m_1 and m_2, and s.e. is the standard error which is given by

$$\text{s.e.}^2 = \frac{s_1^2}{n_1} + \frac{s_2^2}{n_2}$$

Here $z = 0.33$ which is small enough for us to accept the hypothesis that the means are equal. For the two variances, if we assume they are independent normal variables then their ratio as an F-distribution with $n_1 - 1$ and $n_2 - 1$ degrees of freedom. Here the observed F-value is 1.79 with 35 and 35 degrees of freedom. At the 5 per cent level the critical value is approximately 1.77 and so the observed value is just above this. However, at the 1 per cent level the critical value is about 2.25. In view of the closeness to the 5 per cent critical value we will accept the hypothesis of equal variances.

Also included in table 2.2 are the first four autocorrelations and partial autocorrelations. While the numerical values for the two periods differ, they are reasonably close together, with the exception of the ACs with lag 3, but each of these is not significantly different from zero. Bearing in mind the sample sizes of 36, we accept the tentative conclusion that there is no change in the ACs or PACs between these periods.

Next, for the full data, we perform the Dickey–Fuller and Sargan–Bhargava tests to see if DC is stationary. While these tests are alternatives, we include them both to show how they are used. The Sargan–Bhargava test is from estimating (2.29) for the levels variable, $\log(C)$, which gives

$$\log(C_t) = 10.28 \quad \text{Durbin–Watson statistic} = 0.0085$$
$$(659)$$

where the number in parentheses is the t-value and the 5 per cent bounds for the cointegrating-regression Durbin–Watson statistic, from Sargan and Bhargava (1983, table 1), are both 0.259. Thus we accept the hypothesis that $\log C$ is $I(1)$ and so DC is stationary. If this hypothesis had been rejected we would conclude that $\log C$ is $I(0)$.

The Dickey–Fuller test, from (2.32), uses the residuals, $\hat{u}_t$, from the above equation and the result is

$$\Delta \hat{u}_t = -0.008199 \, \hat{u}_{t-1}$$
$$(0.87)$$

where the number in parentheses is the t-value. From the tables in Dickey and Fuller (1981) the 5 per cent critical value for 100 observations is -2.54 so the hypothesis that DC is stationary is accepted. From the evidence so far we accept the hypothesis that the DC series is stationary and move on to examining the autocorrelations and partial autocorrelations for 1960(1)–1984(4). These are given in table 2.3, along with the Box–Pierce statistic, which indicates that the series is not white noise. The low values of the ACF and PACF make it difficult to identify a pattern. The only significant autocorrelations, at the 5 per cent level, are at lags 1 and 4 for the ACF and at lag 1 for the PACF. Referring to table 2.1 this is consistent with an MA(4) model (assuming all the autocorrelations at lags greater than 4 are zero) or possibly an AR(1) or MA(1) model if the autocorrelation of lag 4 is regarded as spurious. Estimating the MA(4) model

$$DC = \delta + \varepsilon_t + \theta_1 \varepsilon_{t-1} + \theta_2 \varepsilon_{t-2} + \theta_3 \varepsilon_{t-3} + \theta_4 \varepsilon_{t-4} \tag{2.106}$$

which gives

$$DC = 0.0054 - 0.0419 e_{t-1} + 0.0028 e_{t-2} + 0.2006 e_{t-3} - 0.4499 e_{t-4}$$
$$\quad (5.93) \qquad (0.46) \qquad (0.31) \qquad (2.29) \qquad (4.99) \qquad (2.107)$$

where t-values are in parentheses. The residual sum of squares is 0.01498 and the Box–Pierce statistic for 10 lags (and so 6 degrees of freedom) is 8.41,

Table 2.3. *Autocorrelations and partial autocorrelations of DC 1960(1)–1984(4)*

Lag	Autocorrelations	Partial autocorrelations
1	−0.233*	−0.223*
2	0.064	0.152
3	0.162	0.189
4	−0.239*	−0.180
5	0.193	0.099
6	−0.081	−0.031
7	0.121	0.168
8	−0.113	0.170
9	−0.174	−0.188
10	0.037	−0.103
Box–Pierce statistic for the ACF with 10 lags is 27.3*		

Note:
* significant at the 5 per cent level.

which is not significant. Thus the residuals appear to be white noise, the constant and the coefficients on e_{t-3} and e_{t-4} are significant and the only problem is whether the values of θ_1 and θ_2 are zero. If this is the case then the model would be

$$DC = \delta + \varepsilon_t + \theta_3 \varepsilon_{t-3} + \theta_4 \varepsilon_{t-4} \tag{2.108}$$

This is easily shown to have a variance of $\sigma^2(1 + \theta_3^2 + \theta_4^2)$ where σ^2 is the variance of ε_t, and the first four covariances are $\theta_3\theta_4\sigma^2$, zero, $\theta_3\sigma^2$ and $\theta_4\sigma^2$. Dividing the covariances by the variance gives the autocorrelations. It would be possible to try to unscramble the values of the θ_i by relating the theoretical and estimated values, but we know that sampling fluctuations result in these differing, even if the model is correctly specified. However, notice that the second theoretical autocorrelation is zero while its estimated value is 0.064 and is not significant, so this provides some support for the new model. We therefore estimate (2.108) which gives

$$DC = 0.0054 + 0.2035 e_{t-3} - 0.4522 e_{t-4} \tag{2.109}$$
$$(5.68) \qquad (2.36) \qquad (5.23)$$

with a residual sum of squares of 0.0150 and a Box–Pierce statistic of 8.29 for 10 lags (and so 8 degrees of freedom), which is not significant. Thus (2.109) is acceptable as a model, as is (2.107). Comparing these models using the AIC (see (2.91)), the value for (2.107) is −865.49 while for (2.110) it is −871.44, showing that the latter is preferred.

In table 2.4 we present forecasts using the estimated equations for the ten

Table 2.4. *Forecasts from (2.107) and (2.109)*

Quarter	Actual	Forecast from (2.107)	Error	Forecast from (2.109)	Error
1985(1)	0.01097	0.00958	0.00139	0.01014	0.00083
1985(2)	0.00189	0.00104	0.00085	0.00068	0.00121
1985(3)	0.02204	0.01027	0.01177	0.01051	0.01153
1985(4)	0.00720	0.00105	0.00614	0.00096	0.00623
1986(1)	0.01853	0.00542	0.01311	0.00542	0.01311
1986(2)	0.01637	0.00542	0.01096	0.00542	0.01096
1986(3)	0.01388	0.00542	0.00846	0.00542	0.00846
1986(4)	0.00527	0.00542	−0.00015	0.00542	−0.00015
1987(1)	0.00497	0.00542	−0.00044	0.00542	−0.00044
1987(2)	0.01702	0.00542	0.01160	0.00542	0.01160
Sum of squares of errors			0.00068		0.00067
Root mean square error			0.00825		0.00819

observations saved for testing the models. Actual values up to 1984(4) are used and the forecasts have an horizon varying from 1 to 10 periods. As pointed out above, forecasts from an MA(4) model equal the mean beyond a forecast horizon of four periods, and this occurs after 1985. The errors are shown as actuals minus the forecast values and the small difference between the sums of squares of the errors (and the root mean square error, from (1.14)) indicates that (2.109) gives slightly better forecasts than (2.107). However, we notice that the errors seem to be non-random, implying that we can get better forecasts by exploiting this. Rather than do this, we will accept (2.108) as the preferred model and move to the final step in the forecasting exercise which is to re-estimate this using the full set of data for 1960(1)–1987(2). The result is

$$DC = 0.0060 + 0.2409e_{t-3} - 0.4207e_{t-4} \qquad (2.110)$$
$$(6.24) \qquad (2.93) \qquad (5.10)$$

with a residual sum of squares of 0.0157 and a Box–Pierce statistic of 9.15 for 10 lags (and so 8 degrees of freedom), which is not significant. Comparing this equation with (2.109), the extra ten observations have resulted in slightly different coefficients, but the model is still satisfactory. Forecasts from (2.110), using information up to 1987(2), for the next six quarters are presented in table 2.5, along with the outcomes, as measured in April 1989. The errors are generally larger than those in table 2.4 and this is reflected in the larger root mean square error.

Table 2.5. *Forecasts from (2.110) for 1987(3)–1988(4)*

Quarter	Actual	Forecast	Error
1987(3)	0.02260	0.00099	0.02161
1987(4)	0.01971	0.00721	0.01250
1988(1)	0.01777	0.00786	0.00991
1988(2)	−0.00030	0.00106	−0.00136
1988(3)	0.02127	0.00600	0.01527
1988(4)	0.01805	0.00600	0.01205
Sum of squares of errors			0.00110
Root mean square error			0.01355

2.5 Vector autoregression models

We saw in section 2.1 how each of the endogenous variables in a simple economic model can be given a univariate ARMA representation, and this led on to the Box–Jenkins approach to modelling and forecasting. In this section we consider some multivariate generalisations of the ARMA model. We will take three alternative starting points: standard simultaneous equation systems, Sims's criticisms of econometric models and multivariate ARMA models, each of which can lead to vector autoregression (VAR) models. Then we will examine some practical problems with VAR models and consider an example.

The first equation in a dynamic simultaneous econometric model can be written

$$a_{11}(L)y_{1t} + a_{12}(L)y_{2t} + \cdots + a_{1m}(L)y_{mt} + b_{11}(L)x_{1t}$$
$$+ \ldots b_{1k}(L)x_{kt} = e_{1t} \tag{2.111}$$

where the $a_{ij}(L)$ and $b_{ij}(L)$ are polynomials in the lag operator, the y_{it} are the endogenous variables, the x_{it} are exogenous variables and the e_{it} are white noise error terms. It is assumed that any expectational variables have been substituted out. In matrix form this becomes

$$AY + BX = E \tag{2.112}$$

where the matrices are defined in an appropriate way. In particular, A and B involve lag operators. Now we have seen that any stationary variable, or variable that can be made stationary, can be represented by an ARMA (or ARIMA) model. We have also suggested that ARMA models can be used to forecast exogenous variables. Suppose then that X can be represented by the ARMA model

$$FX = GE \tag{2.113}$$

where F includes lag operators and is invertible so that

$$X = F^{-1}GE \tag{2.114}$$

Substituting from (2.114) into (2.112) gives

$$AY + BF^{-1}GE = E$$

and re-arranging,

$$AY = -(BF^{-1}G)E + IE = HE$$

Assuming the inverse of H exists, and multiplying by it gives

$$H^{-1}AY = E$$

or $$JY = E \tag{2.115}$$

Here we have a system in which all the variables are endogenous, are inter-related and have white noise error terms. This is known as a *vector autoregression* (VAR) and the first equation can be written

$$j_{11}(L)y_{1t} + \cdots + j_{1m}(L)y_{mt} = e_{1t} \tag{2.116}$$

where only $j_{11}(L)$ includes a constant so that y_{1t} is the only current variable present. Thus one argument for adopting a VAR model relies on starting with a dynamic, linear model and assuming that exogenous variables can be represented by ARMA models.

The second approach leading to VAR models is proposed by Sims (1980). He starts by reviewing the standard procedures in economic modelling and states that the restrictions arising from economic theory which are imposed on models are incredible and cannot be taken seriously. This is because they involve (a) an arbitrary normalisation of each equation, (b) aggregation problems, (c) the choice of arbitrary lag lengths and (d) assumptions about expectational variables. Taking each of these in turn, an example of arbitrary normalisation occurs when an equation involving two or more endogenous variables, such as consumption and income, is called a 'consumption function' and is interpreted as such, when it could equally be called an 'income function'. Strictly, all the endogenous variables are jointly determined by the system of equations so that caution is needed when a particular equation is considered in isolation. Aggregation problems occur because economic theory is usually developed as a series of restrictions in a partial-equilibrium model for some particular area or market. The model is then aggregated across the economy, resulting in the restrictions being invalid. Arbitrary lag lengths are usually chosen when the dynamic properties of models are considered, since economic theory says little about the precise timing of events. Finally, in the past, expectations were frequently modelled in an arbitrary manner as a distributed lag of selected variables. While this method has, in the main, been replaced by the rational (or consistent) expectations approach, there is still a requirement that the investigator knows the appropriate restrictions on the serial correlation of the exogenous variables. Sims's conclusion is that the assertion that macroeconomic models are identified is invalid. He also points out that if policy-makers have particular aims in mind then macroeconomic policy will be endogenous, and, since policies affect expectations, models change when policy-rules change. The Lucas (1976) critique of economic policy is also relevant here.

In an attempt to deal with these points, Sims suggests estimating unrestricted reduced forms in which all the variables are treated as being endogenous. The forecaster has to choose the variables to be included, and because only a limited number of observations are available some limit on the length of lags has to be imposed. However, the particular length chosen can be tested. The result is that the system of equations takes the form

$$y_{1t} = f(y_{1t-1}, y_{1t-2}, \ldots, y_{1t-L}, y_{2t-1}, \ldots, y_{2t-L}, \ldots, y_{kt-L})$$
$$y_{2t} = f(y_{1t-1}, y_{1t-2}, \ldots, y_{1t-L}, y_{2t-1}, \ldots, y_{2t-L}, \ldots, y_{kt-L})$$
$$y_{kt} = f(y_{1t-1}, y_{1t-2}, \ldots, y_{1t-L}, y_{2t-1}, \ldots, y_{2t-L}, \ldots, y_{kt-L})$$

$$(2.117)$$

where there are k variables and the common lag length is L. Notice that the right-hand side variables are the same in every equation and do not include any current values. In these circumstances ordinary least squares is a suitable estimation method. These equations can be rearranged to take the form (2.115) or (2.116) above.

The third approach leading to VAR models takes the univariate ARMA model (2.71) and, for convenience, sets δ to zero to give

$$\phi(L)Y_t = \theta(L)\varepsilon_t \qquad (2.118)$$

We have seen that if both $\phi(L)$ and $\theta(L)$ are invertible then multiplying (2.118) by the inverse of $\phi(L)$ results in

$$Y_t = \phi^{-1}(L)\theta(L)\varepsilon_t \qquad (2.119)$$

which is an MA(∞) representation of Y, while multiplying by the inverse of $\theta(L)$ gives

$$\theta^{-1}(L)\phi(L)Y_t = \varepsilon_t \qquad (2.120)$$

which is an AR(∞) representation. Thus the invertible univariate ARMA model has both an MA and AR representation. A natural extension is to form a multivariate generalisation of these various forms. For ease of exposition we will use the example of two variables, Y_{1t} and Y_{2t}. The vector ARMA (or VARMA) model is

$$\phi_{11}(L)Y_{1t} + \phi_{12}(L)Y_{2t} = \theta_{11}(L)\varepsilon_{1t} + \theta_{12}(L)\varepsilon_{2t} \tag{2.121}$$

$$\phi_{21}(L)Y_{1t} + \phi_{22}(L)Y_{2t} = \theta_{21}(L)\varepsilon_{1t} + \theta_{22}(L)\varepsilon_{2t} \tag{2.122}$$

where ε is white noise, and this can be written in matrix form as

$$\phi(L)Y = \theta(L)\varepsilon \tag{2.123}$$

If the vector ARMA model is completely unrestricted, it is difficult to determine the orders of the autoregressive and moving average processes. However, in some circumstances, a formal underlying structure can be postulated so that the system of equations will contain explicit non-linear cross-equation restrictions on the parameters of the model. Examples are given by Baillie, Lippens and McMahon (1983) and Canarella and Pollard (1988). More generally, a VARMA representation may not be unique (see, for example, Judge *et al.* 1985, 1988), so that two different VARMA processes can represent the same autocovariance structure of the variables. The obvious special cases, where the matrices $\phi(L)$ and $\theta(L)$ are the unit matrix, give vector MA and VAR models. As we saw above, a VAR model can be estimated by ordinary least squares. This does not apply to vector MA models and in fact it is the estimation difficulties which have caused vector MA models to be neglected.

We have seen three different approaches which lead to VAR models with (2.117) being the resulting system of equations. In practice the forecaster has to make two important decisions in forming a VAR model. First, the variables of interest have to be selected. Sims does not discuss how they are chosen, but it is clear that a general knowledge of economic theory indicates that, in macroeconomics, variables such as national income, consumption and investment are contenders. However, it is not possible to carry this process too far before controversy occurs as to what 'theory' tells us. Another method of selection is to check likely variables to see if they are exogenous, and if so, reject them. This can be done by the Granger (1969b) causality test, which, in the case of the two variables x and y, involves regressing each of them on past values of both variables

$$y_t = \Sigma \alpha_i y_{t-i} + \Sigma \beta_i x_{t-i} + \varepsilon_{1t}$$

$$x_t = \Sigma \gamma_i y_{t-i} + \Sigma \delta_i x_{t-i} + \varepsilon_{2t}$$

where the summations are for some lag length k for which the ε_{it} are white noise, and testing (by a standard F-test of zero restrictions) whether the β_i and γ_i are zero. If the β_i are zero then past values of x do not help to predict

y and so x does not Granger-cause y. In this case y is exogenous with respect to x. Similarly if the γ_i are zero, y does not Granger-cause x and x is exogenous with respect to y. More generally, variables which are not found to be exogenous will be included in the VAR model. Maddala (1988) provides a detailed discussion of defining and testing for exogeneity.

It is also necessary to decide how to measure the chosen variables. Sims prefers to take logarithms of the levels of variables such as the price level and wages and include a time trend and seasonal dummies in each equation. Others, for example Lupoletti and Webb (1986), prefer to use percentage rates of change for variables which have a trend, since this will make them stationary. We will discuss these alternatives in sections 2.6 and 2.7 below.

Second, as mentioned above, the lag length has to be chosen. In (2.117) it is assumed that a common lag length, L, is adopted for every variable in every equation. A test to see whether the empirical value of L is correct can be carried out as a test of restrictions. Suppose a model has k equations, each with kL lagged variables, giving $k^2 L$ variables in total, and also including constants and possibly time trends. The model is first estimated with the lag length set at L_1, say, and the determinant of the contemporaneous covariance matrix of the errors, D_1, say, is calculated. The lag length is then reduced to L_2, the model re-estimated and the corresponding value of D_2 is found. The hypothesis that the $k^2(L_1 - L_2)$ restrictions are valid is tested by

$$\chi^2 = (n - k)\log(D_1/D_2) \tag{2.124}$$

which has a chi-squared distribution with $k^2(L_1 - L_2)$ degrees of freedom if the hypothesis is true. If the observed chi-squared value is small, the restrictions are accepted and the smaller model is preferred. Gordon and King (1982) raise some of the problems with this test, such as where particular lags are important in only one equation.

We now illustrate these points by presenting a simple two-variable VAR model for the UK using quarterly data. We do not claim that this is a realistic model of the UK. The variables are the annual rate of growth of real gross domestic product (g) and the annual rate of inflation (p), for 1961 (1)–1987(2). These variables are chosen as being the most interesting ones from the viewpoint of forecasting. Since quarterly data are used, lag lengths of 8 and 4 are tried as being sensible starting values, and estimation is by ordinary least squares. The results are presented in table 2.6 where (1) and (2) are the equations with a lag of 8 and (3) and (4) have a lag of 4. The Durbin–Watson statistics are quoted as indicators of first-order autocorrelation because Durbin's h-statistic for autocorrelation when a lagged dependent variable is present cannot be calculated. We will assume autocorrelation is not a problem. The $\bar{R}^2$ values fall when the lag length is

Table 2.6. *A simple VAR model for the UK 1961(1)–1987(2)*

Independent variables	Dependent variables			
	p_t (1)	g_t (2)	p_t (3)	g_t (4)
Constant	−0.697*	2.293*	−0.129	2.133*
p_{t-1}	1.560*	0.095	1.559*	0.101
p_{t-2}	−0.593*	−0.289	−0.583*	−0.275
p_{t-3}	0.078	−0.063	−0.071	−0.204
p_{t-4}	−0.526*	0.276	0.082	0.259
p_{t-5}	−0.781*	−0.467		
p_{t-6}	−0.290	0.386		
p_{t-7}	−0.083	0.126		
p_{t-8}	0.091	−0.186		
g_{t-1}	0.115	0.755*	0.130*	0.723*
g_{t-2}	−0.119	−0.065	−0.105	−0.129
g_{t-3}	0.143	0.042	0.044	0.080
g_{t-4}	−0.043	−0.500*	0.036	−0.244*
g_{t-5}	0.070	0.250		
g_{t-6}	−0.845	0.210		
g_{t-7}	0.093	−0.140		
g_{t-8}	0.076	−0.187		
$\bar{R}^2$	0.97	0.71	0.96	0.64
DW	2.01	1.96	2.04	1.83
Covariances	0.535	−0.098	0.721	−0.263
of residuals	−0.098	1.292	−0.263	1.778

Note:*significantly different from zero at the 5 per cent level.

reduced, but notice that, of the variables omitted in (3) and (4), only the coefficient on p_{t-5} in (1) is significant. To test the restrictions in moving from 8 lags to 4 lags we use (2.124). Here, n is 106, L_1 is 8, L_2 is 4, k is 2, D_1, from the variances and covariances of the residuals, is 0.68 while D_2 is 1.21. The chi-squared value is 51.3 with 16 restrictions, which is highly significant (the 5 per cent critical value is 26.30). The conclusion is that the equations with a lag length of 8 are preferred to those with a value of 4. For completeness our next step would be to re-estimate the model with other lag lengths, say 12, to see whether this is preferred to the lag of 8, and, if not, compare lags of 8 with 5 or 6. Finally the accepted equations would be used for forecasting. Since this is straightforward for VAR models we do not pursue it here.

A problem with the unrestricted VAR modelling procedure is the danger of including a large number of parameters in the model. For example, Litterman (1986a) reports that unrestricted VARs tend to produce very good in-sample fits to the data but produce very poor out-of-sample forecasts. This is because there are frequently relatively few observations for estimation. For our example we had 106 observations, but if the model was made more realistic, by increasing the number of variables to six and the lag length to 12, each equation would have 72 lagged variables, reducing the degrees of freedom to 34 (before allowing for constants, seasonal dummies, etc.) and the resulting parameter estimates are likely to be imprecise due to multicollinearity.

One solution to this problem is to use economic theory to decide which parameters to set to zero. However, this is against the spirit of VAR modelling and so will be ignored. A second method is to carry out a grid search, as suggested by Webb (1988), in which a range of lag patterns are tried and a criterion such as Akaike's (2.91) is used to select the best one. In this approach each equation can have different lag structures. A third method is to adopt a Bayesian framework in which the forecaster starts with some prior ideas about the values of the parameters, and then uses the data to modify these ideas. This is called the *Bayesian vector autoregression* (BVAR) model, as discussed by Doan, Litterman and Sims (1984). They assume a prior equation for each variable which is a random walk with drift, for example

$$x_t = x_{t-1} + c + \varepsilon_t \tag{2.125}$$

where c is a constant and ε is a white noise disturbance. Also, rather than simply setting all other coefficients on lagged variables to zero, they assume that the mean value of each parameter is zero but has a nonzero variance. This variance is assumed to decline with the length of lag. The result is that if a particular lagged variable has an effect in the data, there is the possibility that its coefficient will change from zero and it will contribute to the model. Another ingredient of the BVAR approach is that coefficients are re-estimated, period by period, employing the Kalman filter (see for example, Harvey 1981). This allows the underlying process to evolve over time, say in response to probabilities of regime changes. For a number of years Litterman (1986b) has produced forecasts for the US economy using a BVAR model, estimated on the RATS package. We discuss the accuracy of his results, as reported by McNees (1986) in chapter 5, section 8 below.

Our discussion of VAR models has shown that there are good reasons for using them for forecasting. They avoid the arbitrary restrictions of economic theory and, by including several variables, are expected to overcome the limitations of univariate models. However, one problem we mentioned above, of whether to use levels variables with a time trend or to only use stationary variables in VAR models, requires further discussion. Essentially, we have only considered stationarity in the context of a single series. Next we extend the idea to combinations of series in our discussion of cointegration.

2.6   Cointegration

In our discussion of non-stationary variables in section 2.3 above we introduced the idea of an integrated series as being one which, after differencing, becomes stationary. If a stationary series is defined to be integrated of order zero, or $I(0)$, following (2.81), a series X_t is said to be integrated of order d if it becomes stationary after differencing d times or

$$(1 - L)^d X_t = Y_t$$

where L is the lag operator and Y_t is stationary. The reason stationarity is important is because it is one of the basic assumptions made in modelling and forecasting. If a series is not stationary, then its mean, variance and covariances are changing so that models which assume these are constants will be misleading. For example, the random walk series, y_t, given by

$$y_t = y_{t-1} + \varepsilon_t \tag{2.126}$$

where ε is a white noise disturbance, has an infinite variance. Any estimated variance will be finite and so must be an under-estimate of the true value. It is also easily seen that y_t is $I(1)$, and we note that if we add another $I(0)$ variable to (2.126) the result will also be an $I(1)$ process.

These considerations are also important where relationships between different series are concerned. For example, Phillips (1987a,b) has demonstrated that the standard t-tests in regression are not valid when the variables are non-stationary. More generally, Engle and Granger (1987) discuss the joint properties of integrated series. While the results apply for any number of series, we will limit consideration to just two. Suppose two series x_t and y_t are both $I(1)$, then in general any linear combination of them will also be $I(1)$. A simple example of this is given by consumption and income. Over a long period, data on these variables exhibit strong upward trends, and their difference (saving) also has an upward trend. However, it sometimes occurs that a combination of two $I(1)$ variables is in fact $I(0)$. More formally, if a new variable, u_t can be defined by

$$u_t = y_t - \lambda x_t \tag{2.127}$$

where u is $I(0)$ then x and y are said to be *cointegrated* and λ is called the *constant of cointegration* or, in the case of more than two variables, the set of λ values is the *cointegrating vector*. The variable u can be interpreted as an error term and a constant can be included in (2.127) to make its mean zero so that it becomes the cointegrating regression equation. This links with the cointegrating regression Dubin-Watson statistic of section 2.2, which we return to below. Continuing with the example of consumption and income, a linear consumption function, which consists of $I(1)$ variables, may have stationary residuals, so that consumption and income are cointegrated.

We now consider some of the properties of cointegrated variables. First, including a constant in (2.127) does not have any effect. Second, if two variables are cointegrated then the constant of cointegration is unique. This can be shown by replacing λ in (1.127) by a new constant k which equals $\lambda + g$. This gives

$$
\begin{aligned}
u_t &= y_t - kx_t \\
&= [y_t - \lambda x_t] - gx_t
\end{aligned}
\tag{2.128}
$$

where the first term is $I(0)$ and the second is $I(1)$. The result is that (2.128) is $I(1)$, so that only if g is zero and the constant of cointegration is λ, is u an $I(0)$ variable. Third, it has been proved that cointegration in levels of variables implies cointegration in their logarithms, while cointegration in logarithms of variables does not imply cointegration in levels. This point suggests that unless there are strong theoretical reasons for choosing a particular functional form then some experimentation with non-linear transformations of the variables in the cointegrating relationship is desirable. Fourth, cointegration implies the two variables will not drift apart, since u, which measures the gap between y and x, and can be regarded as the 'error', is stationary with a mean of zero. This results in the interpretation of

$$
y_t - \lambda x_t = 0
\tag{2.129}
$$

as the long-run or equilibrium relationship between x and y. Fifth, Granger (1983) and Engle and Granger (1987) have proved that if x and y are both $I(1)$, have constant means and are cointegrated, then an 'error-correcting' data generating mechanism or *error correction model* (ECM) exists which takes the form

$$
\Delta y_t = -\rho_1 u_{t-1} + \text{lagged } (\Delta y, \Delta x) + d(L)\varepsilon_{1t}
\tag{2.130}
$$

$$
\Delta x_t = -\rho_2 u_{t-1} + \text{lagged } (\Delta y, \Delta x) + d(L)\varepsilon_{2t}
\tag{2.131}
$$

where u_t is given by (2.127) above, $d(L)$ is a finite polynomial in the lag operator L, ε_{1t} and ε_{2t} are joint white noise error processes which are possibly contemporaneously correlated and, finally

$$
|\rho_1| + |\rho_2| \neq 0
$$

This last condition ensures that u occurs in at least one of the equations. The validity of (2.130) and (2.131) follows from x and y being $I(1)$, so their differences are $I(0)$ and each term is therefore $I(0)$. It is also the case that, not only must cointegrated variables obey such a model, but the reverse is true: data generated by an ECM must also be cointegrated.

This result is of great importance because it links two previously separate areas: time-series models and ECMs. Error correction models have been widely used in economics (see, for example, Sargan 1964 and Davidson, Hendry, Srba and Yeo 1978). They require that the economic system has a well-defined equilibrium and that the speed of movement of variables towards the equilibrium will reflect the distance the system is away from that equilibrium. Consequently, (2.127), the cointegrating equation, reflects the specification of the equilibrium of the system. The absolute value of u_{t-1} measures the distance from the equilibrium in the previous period. Another interpretation is provided by Campbell and Shiller (1987, 1988) who demonstrate how the error correction mechanism can occur in asset markets in which agents' expectations of future variables are embodied in a current variable.

These results also have implications for modelling and forecasting since if two variables x and y are believed to be related, where x is $I(1)$, and y is $I(0)$, then in the regression

$$y_t = \alpha + \beta x_t + u_t \tag{2.132}$$

where u_t is the $I(0)$ error, the theoretical value of β will be zero. More generally, for equations to have $I(0)$ errors, the variables must also be $I(0)$ or, if $I(1)$, they must be cointegrated. This illustrates the need to examine the degree of integration of each candidate variable in a proposed model prior to estimation.

We now review some tests for the degree of integration of a series and also for cointegration. In section 2.2 we saw how the cointegrating regression Durbin–Watson (CRDW) test (2.29) and the Dickey–Fuller test (2.32) can be used to test the order of integration of a single series. Here we consider their more general use. For recent summaries of the literature see Granger (1986) and Perron (1988). First, to test whether two series are cointegrated (2.127) is written as

$$y_t = \alpha + \lambda x_t + u_t \tag{2.133}$$

The equation is estimated by ordinary least squares and the Durbin–Watson statistic is calculated. Following our discussion of (2.29), if the CRDW exceeds the critical value given by Sargan and Bhargava (1983) then u is $I(0)$ and x and y are cointegrated. We would also expect the R^2 value to be reasonably high for cointegrated variables. An alternative test, as in (2.32), proposed by Dickey and Fuller (1981), takes the residuals, $\hat{u}_t$ from (2.133) to estimate

$$\Delta \hat{u}_t = \rho \hat{u}_{t-1} + \varepsilon_t \tag{2.134}$$

and then test if ρ is significantly negative. The tables in Dickey and Fuller (1981) are used and if ρ is significant, then u is $I(0)$ so x and y are cointegrated. When the residual in (2.134) is not white noise the equation can be modified by including a constant and extra lagged values of $\Delta \hat{u}$ until it appears to be white noise. In this case different tables, from Dickey and Fuller (1979), are used. If ρ is zero u is said to have a *unit root*.

Once the fact has been established that two (or more) variables are cointegrated, an error correction model can be specified and estimated. Engle and Granger (1987) suggest a two-step procedure in which the cointegrating regression (2.133) is estimated by ordinary least squares at the first stage to give the estimated residuals $\hat{u}_t$. Where more than two variables appear to be cointegrated, it is important to check that they are all needed. The second stage of the procedure is to substitute the estimated residuals from (2.133) for u_{t-1} in the general error correction model (2.130) and (2.131) and estimate these equations. Finally, these are used for forecasting.

The methods outlined in the cointegration literature are valuable additions to the range of modelling procedures used by forecasters. Economic theory, however vague, can suggest the variables to be included in a model and the equilibrium relationships. If the tests show that the variables are not cointegrated, this implies that the theoretical model is incorrect and, in particular, important variables have been omitted. New variables may be added until cointegration is achieved. However, as pointed out by Dolado and Jenkinson (1987), the discovery of variables which appear cointegrated should signal the start of a further series of cointegration tests amongst sub-sets of these variables. The resulting model to be used for forecasting will generally be relatively simple, avoiding the need to build a large structural model.

There are three difficulties with employing the cointegration method which should be noted. The first is a statistical one. It has been demonstrated that the power of the tests for unit roots against alternatives of roots close to unity is often very low (see Evans and Savin 1984 and Nankervis and Savin 1985), unless the number of observations is high. In such situations the hypothesis of a unit root is likely to be accepted when the true value is, say, 0.96. However, in this case, further information on whether series are cointegrated or not can be gleaned by examining the significance of the coefficients on u_{t-1}, in the error correction equations.

The second point concerns the appropriate direction to regress the variables in the cointegrating regression. If y_t and x_t are two cointegrated variables then $y_t - \lambda x_t$ and $x_t - (1/\lambda)y_t$ are equally valid representations, so that using either y or x as the dependent variable should, in this bivariate context, yield identical estimates of λ, if the R^2 is high. Engle and Granger (1987) demonstrate that this result tends to hold in practice. More generally, if there are k variables in the cointegrating regression, the cointegrating vector will not be unique. This leads to some problems in interpreting the error correction model (see Johansen 1988 for a further analysis).

The third point is that, although the equilibrium relationships in a structural model will, *a priori*, be most unlikely to change in response to regime changes, this will not, in general, be the case for the adjustment towards the equilibrium. Therefore, the error correction model will vary with the policy regime. However, the same observations concerning the probabilities of regime changes, as were made for ARMAs (at the end of section 2.3) should be borne in mind here. In addition, the within sample constancy of the parameters, which is a useful guide to the underlying stability of a relationship, can readily be checked by the usual method of re-estimation for sub-periods.

We now consider the relationship between cointegrated variables and VAR models. Engle and Granger (1987) have proved that if several variables are cointegrated then a vector ARMA representation exists. This will include variables in both levels and difference form. However, in VAR modelling it is common to use only differenced variables, so that a VAR model for cointegrated variables will be misspecified. Alternatively, if the VAR model includes levels variables, it is not exploiting the restrictions from cointegration and so will be inefficient. Campbell and Shiller (1987) discuss the links between these models in detail.

2.7 Deterministic and stochastic trends

One topic that has arisen in several places, both in this chapter and in chapter 1, is how to model a trend. We now examine this in detail. We saw in (1.5) that a simple linear trend can be estimated from the regression model

$$Y_t = \alpha + \beta t + u_t \tag{2.135}$$

where α and β are the intercept and slope terms and u is a random disturbance which we assume to be white noise but can be any stationary process. Here the non-stationary variable Y is represented by what is known as a *deterministic* trend, that is, the trend itself is perfectly predictable and is non-stochastic. Of course the addition of the stationary variable u_t results in variation about the trend so that Y is stochastic, but in the long run the only information we have about Y_t is its mean, $(\alpha + \beta t)$.

Consequently, neither current or past events alter long-term forecasts for this process. It is this feature which makes the trend deterministic. It also follows that the long-term forecast error will have finite variance and therefore, as pointed out by Nelson and Plosser (1982) uncertainty is bounded even in the indefinitely distant future.

An alternative approach to dealing with trends was discussed earlier in this chapter (see (2.81) in section 2.3) where we saw that an integrated process, which has a *stochastic* trend, can be made stationary by differencing. While the effect, as with (2.135), is to model the general movement of a series, there is, however, a crucial difference between the two methods. To illustrate this difference, suppose Y is $I(1)$ and is given by

$$(1-L)Y_t = \beta + u_t \tag{2.136}$$

where u is white noise. This can be written as

$$Y_t = Y_{t-1} + \beta + u_t \tag{2.137}$$

and by repeating lagging this one period and substituting for the lagged Y values we get

$$Y_t = Y_0 + \beta t + u_t + u_{t-1} + u_{t-2} + \cdots + u_1 \tag{2.138}$$

where Y_0 is some starting value in the past and the errors run back to this point. By comparison with (2.135), in (2.138) instead of α there is Y_0, and instead of the single disturbance u there is the sum of t disturbances. This illustrates that the two types of non-stationary process, namely the deterministic trend and the integrated process, have similar forms. However, (2.138) is crucially different from (2.135). In (2.135) α is a fixed parameter whilst in (2.138) it is given by a past historical event, the starting point. In (2.135) the deviations from the trend are stationary whilst in (2.138) the error variance increases without bound as time passes. Consequently, the long-term forecast of Y_t from (2.138) will be influenced by the starting value and the variance of the forecast error will increase without bound.

Given these rather different properties, it is important to know for any particular non-stationary series whether it is described by a deterministic trend or whether it is an integrated process described by a stochastic trend. With a deterministic trend, variables can be made stationary by including a time trend in any regression or by doing a preliminary regression on time and subtracting the estimated trend. With a stochastic trend, tests for cointegration and non-stationarity are needed. Nelson and Kang (1984) investigate the implications of making the wrong choice. They show that, if a random walk variable with drift (as in (2.137)) is regressed on time, the R^2 value will approach one as the sample size increases. Also, if a random walk series is detrended, the autocorrelation function is determined entirely by the sample size, exhibiting high positive autocorrelation at low lags and spurious cyclical patterns at long lags.

One area where these problems are unresolved is in the current debate as to whether real output is more appropriately described by a deterministic or integrated process (see Perron and Phillips 1987, Campbell and Mankiw 1987). If output is a deterministic process then random shocks to output will have a finite impact on future output. Conversely, if it is an integrated process, shocks will have an indefinite impact, and forecasting will be more difficult.

Statistical tests to determine whether a non-stationary series is best described by a deterministic or integrated process have been developed by Perron and Phillips (1987) and Perron (1988). Currently, the available empirical evidence supports the view that many nonstationary economic time series appear to be generated by integrated processes (see Nelson and Plosser 1982 and Perron and Phillips 1987).

2.8   Non-linear time series

So far we have assumed that the underlying data generating process can be adequately captured by linear models. Of course there is no theoretical reason why the underlying data generating process must be linear. It is quite feasible for either the properties of the data or *a priori* theory to suggest that a linear model will be unsatisfactory. However, while in principle an infinite number of alternatives to linear models are possible, the recent literature has focused on four particular classes of non-linear models. These are bilinear models (see Granger and Anderson 1978), threshold autoregressive models (see Tong 1983), exponential autoregressive models (see Ozaki 1980), and state dependent models (see Priestley 1980) which include the previous three as special cases. We will not discuss these here but will provide one illustration, the bilinear model, and then discuss ways of testing for non-linearity. More general discussions of non-linear time-series analysis are given by Newbold (1984), Tsay (1988) and Maravall (1983).

The general bilinear model is a generalisation of the univariate ARMA model to include cross-product terms of lagged variables and errors. It has the form

$$Y_t = \Sigma \alpha_i Y_{t-i} + \Sigma \beta_j \varepsilon_{t-j} + \Sigma\Sigma \gamma_{kl} Y_{t-k} \varepsilon_{t-l} \tag{2.139}$$

where ε_i is Gaussian white noise, α_i, β_j and γ_{kl} are parameters and the summations are from 1 to p, 0 to q, 1 to r and 1 to s, respectively, with p, q, r

and s being different. In the special case where the γ_{kl} are all zero (2.139) reduces to an ARMA (p, q) model. Maravall (1983) estimates a bilinear process on Spanish money supply data and demonstrates that improved forecasts, with a decrease of mean square error of 13 per cent, were obtained over ARMA forecasts. From Maravall's results it appears that bilinear models capture 'outliers' in the data sequence better than ARMA models.

Turning now to testing for non-linearity, it appears that there is no general test for the 'global' non-linearity of a time series, since the test statistics are formed in relation to a particular type of non-linearity. Various tests are proposed by Keenan (1985), Petruccelli and Davies (1986), Maravall (1983) and Subba Rao and Gabr (1980). One of the simpler tests, suggested by Granger and Newbold (1976), and employed by Maravall (1983), is based on the autocorrelation function. Granger and Newbold show that for a series Y_t which is linear

$$\rho_k(Y_t^2) = [\rho_k(Y_t)]^2 \tag{2.140}$$

where $k = 0, \pm 1, \ldots$ and ρ_k denotes the lag k autocorrelaton. That is, the autocorrelations of Y^2 are the squares of the autocorrelations of Y. Any departure from this result indicates a degree of non-linearity (see also Granger and Anderson 1978). Maravall demonstrates why it is preferable to use the above test on the white noise residuals obtained after first fitting an ARIMA process to the Y_t series. The autocorrelation function of the residuals squared is compared with the squared autocorrelations of the residuals.

Recently, some new tests for non-linearity have been suggested which have arisen from the interest in chaotic dynamics in a number of different disciplines (see Brock and Sayers 1988, Brock, Dechert and Scheinkman 1987, Brock 1986, Scheinkman and LeBaron 1986, Frank and Stengos 1988 and Grassberger and Prococcia 1983). From one perspective any system is ultimately deterministic and modelling it as if it were the outcome of a random process is possibly a convenient simplification. Deterministic processes which look random are called *deterministic chaos* in non-linear science. It is well known that very simple deterministic non-linear difference equations can generate exceedingly complex time paths, which appear to be random. A simple example is the non-linear difference equation which can occur in the analysis of asset markets (see Van der Ploeg 1986)

$$Y_{t+1} = \alpha Y_t (1 - Y_t)$$

where Y is the price of bonds. For many economic applications the parameter α is restricted to lie between 1 and 4, thus excluding a negative equilibrium value for Y and also avoiding Y_t approaching infinity as t approaches infinity. As α varies between 1 and 4, the systems dynamics undergo radical changes. For instance for $1 < \alpha < 3$, the dynamics of the system are simple with the system tending to the equilibrium $Y_t = 1 - 1/\alpha$, for any deviation form $Y_t = 0$. On the other hand for $3.57 < \alpha < 4$ an infinite number of cycles occur with differing periodicity as well as an infinite number of equilibria with the precise evolution of the system depending critically on the starting value of the system. This type of behaviour is called 'chaos'. The other fascinating feature of the system is that, although the system is deterministic, a random walk can give a good description of the data generating mechanism (see Frank and Stengos 1988). Consequently in this case, although the changes in Y would exhibit no predictability, in principle the complete path is totally predictable.

Statistical tests for the detection of deterministic chaos have been suggested by Brock and Sayers (1988), and Scheinkman and LeBaron (1986). These can indicate not only the presence (or absence) of deterministic chaos but also non-linearity. Brock and Sayers (1988) for instance, examine a number of series and while they find no evidence of deterministic chaos there is evidence of non-linearities.

As the software for these tests, becomes more widely available we confidently expect that testing for deterministic chaos and nonlinearity will become standard practice in time-series analysis. The empirical results generated so far suggest that non-linearities may occur in many economic series. Consequently, the potential benefits for forecasting of using non-linear rather than linear methods are large.

In this chapter we have reviewed some of the important issues that arise in the use of time-series methods for modelling and forecasting. Our approach has been to start with simple univariate models and to generalise these to include other variables. While historically time-series models and econometric models have developed independently, there are many points of contact between the two, and this is an area where current research is making much progress.

CHAPTER 3

Combining forecasts

3.1 Introduction

We have seen that there are several different methods of producing forecasts and also that, even when a particular method is selected, a forecaster still has to choose such things as the variables of interest, the functional form and the estimation procedure. As a result, we frequently have several, generally different, forecasts available for the same outcome. The question then is should just one particular forecast be chosen or should some form of average be taken? This has received much attention in the academic literature over the last few years. In this chapter we consider the main themes of this literature as well as reviewing some of the empirical contributions. In section 3.2 we determine the optimal way in which two unbiased forecasts can be combined. The weights are shown to depend on the variances and covariances of the forecast errors. A generalisation of this, which extends to include biased forecasts, is presented in section 3.3, and the problems caused by serially correlated errors are discussed in section 3.4. Other approaches to combining forecasts, including the use of the simple average are considered in section 3.5. The empirical evidence on how different combinations perform is reviewed in section 3.6 and some practical suggestions for deciding how to choose an appropriate combination are offered. We then consider the results of the Makridakis forecasting competition which compares a wide range of time-series forecasts, as well as some simple combinations.

3.2 The variance-covariance method

In an innovative paper, Bates and Granger (1969) demonstrate how, in general, two unbiased forecasts can be combined to produce a new forecast which is more accurate than either of its components. They assume that the decision maker wishes to minimise the variance of the forecast errors, and so has a quadratic loss function. Let the variable being forecast be y, and the two unbiased forecasts be F_1 and F_2. Then for forecasts made at time $t-1$

$$y_t = F_{1t} + u_{1t} \tag{3.1}$$

$$y_t = F_{2t} + u_{2t} \tag{3.2}$$

where u_1 and u_2 are the forecast errors, which have means of zero, variances σ_1^2 and σ_2^2, and covariance σ_{12}. The problem is to determine the (constant) weights, λ_1 and λ_2, which give the optimal combined forecast c_t, where

$$c_t = \lambda_1 F_{1t} + \lambda_2 F_{2t} \tag{3.3}$$

Now the error of the combined forecast is

$$
\begin{aligned}
y_t - c_t &= y_t - \lambda_1(y_t - u_{1t}) - \lambda_2(y_t - u_{2t}) \\
&= (1 - \lambda_1 - \lambda_2)y_t + \lambda_1 u_{1t} + \lambda_2 u_{2t}
\end{aligned} \tag{3.4}
$$

For the combined forecast to be unbiased, the expectation of (3.4) must be zero. This is true if

$$1 = \lambda_1 + \lambda_2 \tag{3.5}$$

since $E(u_{1t}) = E(u_{2t}) = 0$. The variance of the forecast error, from (3.4) and (3.5) is

$$
\begin{aligned}
\sigma_c^2 &= E(y_t - c_t)^2 \\
&= E[(1 - \lambda_1 - \lambda_2)y_t + \lambda_1 u_{1t} + \lambda_2 u_{2t}]^2 \\
&= E[\lambda_1 u_{1t} + (1 - \lambda_1)u_{2t}]^2 \\
&= \lambda_1^2 \sigma_1^2 + 2\lambda_1(1 - \lambda_1)\sigma_{12} + (1 - \lambda_1)^2 \sigma_2^2 \\
&= \lambda_1^2(\sigma_1^2 + \sigma_2^2 - 2\sigma_{12}) - 2\lambda_1(\sigma_2^2 - \sigma_{12}) + \sigma_2^2
\end{aligned} \tag{3.6}
$$

since $\sigma_1^2 = E(u_{1t}^2)$, $\sigma_2^2 = E(u_{2t}^2)$ and $\sigma_{12} = E(u_{1t}u_{2t})$. Minimising this with respect to λ_1 gives

$$\lambda_1 = (\sigma_2^2 - \sigma_{12})/D \tag{3.7}$$

where $D = \delta_1^2 + \sigma_2^2 - 2\sigma_{12}$.

Similarly,

$$\lambda_2 = 1 - \lambda_1 = (\sigma_1^2 - \sigma_{12})/D.$$

Thus the optimal linear combination has weights which depend on the variances and covariances of the forecast errors, resulting in the name 'the variance-covariance method'. An explicit equation for σ_c^2 can be found by substituting (3.7) into (3.6)

$$
\begin{aligned}
\sigma_c^2 &= [(\sigma_2^2 - \sigma_{12})^2 - 2(\sigma_2^2 - \sigma_{12})^2 + \sigma_2^2 D]/D \\
&= (\sigma_1^2 \sigma_2^2 - \sigma_{12}^2)/D
\end{aligned}
$$

Now the correlation of u_1 and u_2 is $\rho = \sigma_{12}/\sigma_1\sigma_2$ and substituting for σ_{12} and re-arranging gives

$$\sigma_c^2 = \frac{\sigma_1^2\sigma_2^2(1-\rho^2)}{(\sigma_1-\rho\sigma_2)^2+\sigma_2^2(1-\rho^2)}$$

From this it can be shown that $(\sigma_1^2-\sigma_c^2)$ and $(\sigma_2^2-\sigma_c^2)$ are either zero or positive and therefore σ_c^2 is equal to or less than the minimum of σ_1^2 and σ_2^2. Thus the combined forecast is at least as accurate as the better of the two component forecasts.

While this appears to be an overwhelming argument for combining forecasts it has to be remembered that in practice the values of the variances and covariance of the forecast errors are unknown and have to be estimated. With a sample of T observations the estimators are

$$\hat{\sigma}_1^2 = \frac{\Sigma u_{1t}^2}{T} \quad \hat{\sigma}_2^2 = \frac{\Sigma u_{2t}^2}{T} \quad \hat{\sigma}_{12} = \frac{\Sigma u_{1t}u_{2t}}{T}$$

The result is that the estimated values of λ_1 and λ_2, from (3.7) are

$$\hat{\lambda}_1 = \frac{\Sigma u_{2t}^2 - \Sigma u_{1t}u_{2t}}{\Sigma u_{1t}^2 + \Sigma u_{2t}^2 - 2\Sigma u_{1t}u_{2t}} \tag{3.8}$$

$$\hat{\lambda}_1 = \frac{\Sigma u_{1t}^2 - \Sigma u_{1t}u_{2t}}{\Sigma u_{1t}^2 + \Sigma u_{2t}^2 - 2\Sigma u_{1t}u_{2t}}$$

Both Reid (1969) and Newbold and Granger (1974) have generalised this analysis to include N forecasts in the combination. In this case the $(N \times 1)$ vector of optimal weights, Z, is given by

$$Z = V^{-1}i/i'V^{-1}i$$

where V is the $(N \times N)$ covariance matrix of forecast errors and i is the $(N \times 1)$ column vector of ones.

The optimal weights derived above raise some interesting points. First, it is clear that the intuitively attractive idea of simply selecting the best (smallest error variance) forecast and using that one, is seen to be suspect because, in general, the combined forecast has a smaller error variance. Second, if σ_1^2 and σ_2^2 are equal, in (3.7) the weights are equal and the combined forecast is the simple average of the components. Third, if the covariance of the forecast errors is positive and greater than one of the variances (for example, if $\sigma_2^2 - \sigma_{12}$ is negative), one of the weights will be negative and the other one greater than one. Notice that a negative weight does not imply that a forecast is, in some absolute sense, a poor one. Fourth, as the error variance of a forecast tends to zero, the weight of that forecast tends to one. Thus the more reliable a forecast is, the higher its weight.

In discussing the properties of optimal combinations of forecasts it is important to remember that it has been assumed that each of the forecasts is unbiased and that the error variances and covariances are constants. In the rest of this chapter we examine ways in which these assumptions can be relaxed.

3.3   The regression method

Granger and Ramanathan (1984) demonstrate that the variance-covariance method of combining forecasts can be interpreted as the estimation of a regression equation. For example, in the case of two unbiased forecasts F_1 and F_2, consider the regression model

$$y_t = \beta_1 F_{1t} + \beta_2 F_{2t} + v_t \tag{3.9}$$

where v is a disturbance with a mean of zero. Since the forecasts are unbiased, $E(F_1)$ and $E(F_2)$ both equal $E(y)$, and taking expectations of (3.9) gives

$$E(y) = \beta_1 E(y) + \beta_2 E(y)$$

or $1 \quad = \beta_1 \quad + \beta_2$

Substituting for β_1 in (3.9) results in the restricted regression model

$$y_t - F_{1t} = \beta_2 (F_{2t} - F_{1t}) + v_t \tag{3.10}$$

Estimating (3.10) by ordinary least squares produces

$$\beta_2 = \frac{\Sigma(y - F_1)(F_2 - F_1)}{\Sigma(F_2 - F_1)^2} \tag{3.11}$$

Substituting from (3.1) and (3.2) results in

$$\beta_2 = \frac{\Sigma u_1(u_1 - u_2)}{\Sigma(u_1 - u_2)^2}$$

$$= \frac{\Sigma u_1^2 - \Sigma u_1 u_2}{\Sigma u_1^2 + \Sigma u_2^2 - 2\Sigma u_1 u_2}$$

Also $\beta_1 = 1 - \beta_2$

$$= \frac{\Sigma u_2^2 - \Sigma u_1 u_2}{\Sigma u_1^2 + \Sigma u_2^2 - 2\Sigma u_1 u_2} \tag{3.12}$$

These are the same as the values of $\hat{\lambda}_1$ and $\hat{\lambda}_2$ given in (3.8). Therefore, a convenient method of implementing the variance-covariance method for unbiased forecasts is to obtain the weights (λ_1 and λ_2) from the regression

(3.10). This method generalises to combinations of more than two forecasts.

There is, of course, no reason to assume that all forecasts are unbiased. Granger and Ramanathan suggest that any biases can be allowed for, in the case of two forecasts, by modifying (3.9) to include an intercept term to give

$$y_t = \beta_0 + \beta_1 F_{1t} + \beta_2 F_{2t} + v_t \tag{3.13}$$

By comparison with (3.10), the regression formula for two unbiased forecasts, it can be seen that the unbiasedness of the individual forecasts allows two restrictions to be imposed on (3.13) – the intercept term β_0 is zero and the sum of β_1 and β_2 is one. It also follows that if (3.10) and (3.13) are each estimated with the same data, then the residuals variance for (3.13) will be at least as small as that for (3.10). That is, the fit of (3.10) will, in general, be worse than that of (3.13) within the estimation period. There is, of course, no guarantee that out of sample forecasts using (3.13) will be any better than forecasts using (3.10) and we will return to this in section 3.6 below.

Before discussing (3.13) in detail we note the similarity between Granger and Ramanathan's approach and a method of evaluating forecasts used in chapter 1 (see (1.39)). For a particular series of forecasts F_t and outcomes y_t, the regression relationship

$$y_t = \alpha + \beta F_t + v_t \tag{3.14}$$

can be estimated. If α is a found to be significantly different from zero and β is significantly different from one then the forecasts are said to be biased and inefficient. If the hypotheses α is zero and β is one are accepted, the forecasts are weakly efficient provided that, for a forecast horizon of k periods, the residual is not serially correlated of order greater than $k-1$ (see Holden, Peel and Thompson 1985, pp. 68–9). However, the estimator of β will be biased away from one if there is any correlation between F and v. That is, even if the forecast is unbiased the estimated value of β can be significantly different from one. To illustrate this point, consider (a) the series of outcomes, y, generated by

$$y_t = m + \varepsilon_t - \rho \varepsilon_{t-1} \tag{3.15}$$

where m is a constant, ε is a white noise error and ρ is a parameter, and (b) the forecast

$$F_t = y_{t-1}$$
$$= m + \varepsilon_{t-1} - \rho \varepsilon_{t-2} \tag{3.16}$$

This forecast is unbiased since $E(F)$ and $E(y_t)$ are equal but the forecast error is

$$v_t = y_t - F_t$$
$$= \varepsilon_t - \rho\varepsilon_{t-1} - \varepsilon_{t-1} + \rho\varepsilon_{t-2} \tag{3.17}$$

which, from (3.16), is correlated with the forecast since

$$E(F_t v_t) = -(1+\rho)E(\varepsilon_{t-1}^2) - \rho^2 E(\varepsilon_{t-2}^2)$$
$$= -(1+\rho+\rho^2)\sigma_\varepsilon^2$$

where σ_ε^2 is the variance of ε.

Another interpretation of (3.14) is in connection with the unconditional mean, μ, of the y series. If y is stationary, we have

$$y_t = \mu + u_t \tag{3.18}$$

where u is an error process with zero mean. In general, as shown in chapter 2, section 3, u has an infinite moving average representation. Now while μ is likely to be a poor forecast of y it is unbiased, and so can be combined with the unbiased forecast F using (3.9) above

$$y_t = \beta_1 \mu + \beta_2 F_t + v_t$$

But we can rewrite (3.14) as

$$y_t = (\alpha/\mu)\mu + \beta F_t + v_t \tag{3.19}$$

so that in (3.14) we are implicitly combining two unbiased forecasts, μ and F with weights (α/μ) and β. Notice that if any other constant replaced μ it would not be unbiased. Now comparing (3.19) with (3.9), the sum of the weights is one or

$$(\alpha/\mu) + \beta = 1 \tag{3.20}$$

since the forecasts are unbiased. This means that in (3.14) the condition for unbiasedness is not that α and β sum to one but (3.20). It turns out that this is a sufficient condition for unbiasedness (see Holden and Peel 1990 for details). Note, however, that the original statement $\alpha = 0$ and $\beta = 1$ is also still a sufficient condition for unbiasedness. The important conclusion from this is that including a constant in the regression has the same effect as including the unconditional mean of the series as an extra forecast.

Now suppose that the forecast F in (3.14) is biased by the constant amount b so that

$$F = F_1 + b \tag{3.21}$$

where F_1 is an unbiased forecast, then substitution into (3.14) gives

$$y_t = (\alpha + \beta b) + \beta F_{1t} + u_t \tag{3.22}$$

and the effect of the bias is to change only the intercept term. Also, note that if the constraint $\beta = 1$ is imposed on (3.22) then the constant in the regression corrects for the bias in F.

Returning now to (3.13), the inclusion of the constant can be seen not only to correct for any bias in the forecasts but also to include implicitly the unconditional mean of the series as an additional forecast. Finally we consider the case where a constant is included but the weights on the forecasts are constrained to sum to one. That is, (3.13) becomes

$$y_t = \beta_0 + (1 - \beta_2)F_{1t} + \beta_2 F_{2t} + v_t \tag{3.23}$$

This can be re-arranged to give

$$y_t - F_{1t} = \beta_0 + \beta_2(F_{2t} - F_{1t}) + v_t \tag{3.24}$$

which, except for the inclusion of β_0, is the same as (3.10), the variance-covariance method of combining two forecasts. The constant term corrects for any bias in the forecasts. It can be shown that, following the argument of (3.21) and (3.22), this is equivalent to correcting each forecast for bias before using (3.10) and so (3.23) does not include the unconditional mean of the series as an extra forecast.

The results of this section readily generalise to a combination of any number of forecasts. The conclusions are that Granger and Ramanathan's suggestion of including a constant term in the combining regression can correct for any bias in the forecasts, but it can also be equivalent to including the unconditional mean of the series as an extra forecast. The way to avoid the latter is to impose the restriction that the sum of the weights on the forecasts (excluding the unconditional mean) is one.

3.4 Serial correlation problems

Granger and Ramanathan (1984, p. 203) comment: 'Even if a pair of forecasts is combined, and each has white noise forecast errors, there is no reason to suppose that the combination will have white noise errors.' Diebold (1988) has examined this point in detail. Returning to the general combining equation for two forecasts, and assuming that the forecasts are biased with

$$y_t = F_{1t} + b_1 + u_{1t} \tag{3.25}$$

$$y_t = F_{2t} + b_2 + u_{2t} \tag{3.26}$$

then from (3.13) we have that the error of the combined forecast is

$$v_t = y_t - \beta_0 - \beta_1 F_{1t} - \beta_2 F_{2t}$$

and substituting from (3.25) and (3.26) for F_1 and F_2 gives

$$v_t = (\beta_1 b_1 + \beta_2 b_2 - \beta_0) + (1 - \beta_1 - \beta_2) y_t + \beta_1 u_{1t} + \beta_2 u_{2t} \qquad (3.27)$$

By construction the mean of v is zero and its other properties can be deduced from this equation. The first term on the right-hand side is assumed to be a constant and so can be ignored as far as serial correlation is concerned. The next term includes y unless the constraint that β_1 and β_2 sum to one is imposed. In general, y will not be white noise and so will be serially correlated, resulting in v also being serially correlated. The final terms include u_1 and u_2 so that v will be serially correlated if either u_1 or u_2 is serially correlated.

This implies that v will be white noise only if (a) y is serially uncorrelated (or the restriction that β_1 and β_2 sum to one is imposed) and (b) both u_1 and u_2 are white noise. Now Diebold points out that a common criterion for selecting forecasts is that they should be free from serial correlation, so in practice (b) is likely to be valid. Serial correlation is therefore more likely to be a problem when the unrestricted equation (3.13) is estimated rather than (3.24).

If serial correlation is present in the errors of the combined forecast then this can be exploited to produce better forecasts. For example if it is found that v satisfies

$$v_t = \rho v_{t-1} + \varepsilon_t \qquad (3.28)$$

where ε is a white noise error then estimating (3.28) allows v_{t+1} to be predicted from v_t. This prediction, $\hat{v}_{t+1}$, can be incorporated into, say, (3.13) to give the improved forecast

$$y_{t+1} = \beta_0 + \beta_1 F_{1t+1} + \beta_2 F_{2t+1} + \hat{v}_{t+1}$$

However, the fact that the individual forecast errors are serially correlated does not necessarily result in the combined forecast error being non-random. For example, consider the two biased and inefficient (serially correlated errors) forecasts F_1 and F_2 where

$$F_1 = \delta_0 \mu + \delta_1 \varepsilon_{t-1} + \delta_2 \varepsilon_{t-2}$$

$$F_2 = \gamma_0 \mu + \gamma_1 \varepsilon_{t-1} + \gamma_2 \varepsilon_{t-2}$$

where the δs and γs are constants and ε_t is a white noise error. If y is a stationary variable generated by

$$y_t = \mu + \varepsilon_t + \pi_1 \varepsilon_{t-1} + \pi_2 \varepsilon_{t-2}$$

then the combined forecast error, from (3.13), is

$$v_t = y_t - \beta_0 - \beta_1 F_{1t} - \beta_2 F_{2t}$$

and substituting for y, F_1 and F_2 gives

$$v_t = \mu(1 - \beta_1\delta_0 - \beta_2\gamma_0) - \beta_0 + \varepsilon_t + \varepsilon_{t-1}(\pi_1 - \beta_1\delta_1 - \beta_2\gamma_1)$$
$$+ \varepsilon_{t-2}(\pi_2 - \beta_1\delta_2 - \beta_2\gamma_2)$$

It can be seen that this reduces to ε_t if

$$0 = \mu(1 - \beta_1\delta_0 - \beta_2\gamma_0) - \beta_0$$

and $\quad 0 = \pi_1 - \beta_1\delta_1 - \beta_2\gamma_1$

and $\quad 0 = \pi_2 - \beta_1\delta_2 - \beta_2\gamma_2$

Therefore, if these three equations are satisfied the combined forecast error here will be white noise, even though F_1 and F_2 have serially correlated errors.

This is a counter example to Diebold's assertion that, in the absence of β_1 and β_2 summing to one, both y and the forecast errors must be white noise for the combined forecast error to be white noise. While the example may seem to be a special case, it is clear that if y is generated by an ARMA$(p, 0)$ process then the p forecasts $y_{t-1}, y_{t-2}, \ldots, y_{t-p}$, each of which have serially correlated errors, can be combined to produce white noise forecast errors. However, if the forecast errors are white noise and the forecasts are unbiased, the combined forecast from the regression method will have white noise errors when the weights sum to unity and serially correlated errors otherwise.

3.5 Other methods of combination

Both the variance-covariance and the regression methods of combining forecasts imply that data on past forecast performance can be used to estimate the variances and covariances of the forecast errors. Using a set of T observations on the forecasts and outcomes (3.8) and (3.11) give the estimated weights. Unfortunately, there are a number of reasons for assuming that, for macroeconomic forecasts, the properties of the forecast errors may vary over time. For example, a shock to the international economy, such as happened with the sudden increase in oil prices in 1973, is likely to result in the errors of economic forecasts having a different pattern (such as non-zero means and larger variances) in the periods immediately following the shock, until the full implications of the shock are realised. Also, as time passes, the macroeconomic models used for forecasting change, because of developments in theory and estimation methods, as do the personnel producing the forecasts and the judgemental adjustments they make. A related point is the Lucas (1976) critique which as we have seen in chapter 1 states that the coefficients in the equations of standard econometric models depend on the existing policy regime, and any change in that regime will alter these coefficients. This point also applies to time-series methods of forecasting such as ARMA and vector autoregression models.

The result of this is that it is unlikely that the variance-covariance matrix of forecast errors is a constant, so that using a fixed weighting scheme may produce poor combined forecasts. Several suggestions have been made to overcome these problems. They assume that the weights might be changing and hope to give extra weight to those forecasts which are improving over time. For simplicity we will limit discussion to the case of combining two forecasts.

One way of allowing the weights to change is to avoid using all the available data (say T observations) to estimate the weights and instead to use only the most recent T^* values. However, the choice of T^* is arbitrary and Diebold and Pauly (1987) have shown that its value can have a big impact on the weights.

Granger and Newbold (1977) have made several suggestions for allowing the weights λ, to vary, such as:

(a) $$\lambda_t = \frac{E_{2t}}{E_{1t} + E_{2t}} \tag{3.29}$$

where $E_{1t} = \Sigma u_{1t}^2$ and $E_{2t} = \Sigma u_{2t}^2$ and u_1 and u_2 are the errors from the forecasts F_{1t} and F_{2t}. The weights are determined by past errors in the forecasts and, in the case of a new forecast, an arbitrary value (say 0.5) might be allocated initially.

(b) $$\lambda_t = \theta \lambda_{t-1} + \frac{(1-\theta)E_{2t}}{E_{1t} + E_{2t}} \tag{3.30}$$

where θ is a constant between 0 and 1. This allows the value of λ to change slowly if θ is near 1. Methods (a) and (b) are suitable if there is little change in the accuracy of the two forecasts as time passes. However, if one forecast improves relative to the other, then this should influence the weights. The next two methods allow this to happen.

(c) $$\lambda_t = \frac{W_{2t}}{W_{1t} + W_{2t}} \tag{3.31}$$

where $W_{1t} = \Sigma w^t u_{1t}^2$ and similarly for W_{2t}, and w, which is greater than one, gives more weight to recent errors. A range of values of w can be tried and the selection based on past errors.

(d) $\qquad \lambda_t = \dfrac{W_{2t} - C_t}{W_{1t} + W_{2t} - 2C_t}$ $\qquad\qquad$ (3.32)

where $C_t = \Sigma w^t u_{1t} u_{2t}$ is the weighted covariance. This is based on (3.7).

For each of these methods there are a number of arbitrary choices to be made so that they are basically *ad hoc*. Also, as Bessler and Brandt (1981) point out, such moving average methods tend to result in weights in the range 0 to $1/N$ when there are N forecasts, which limits the benefits of combining forecasts when one forecast is substantially better than the others. See also Clemen (1986) and Clemen and Winkler (1986).

Diebold and Pauly (1987) outline a number of methods by which time-varying weights can be incorporated into the regression framework. They use the weighted least squares approach, in which rather than minimising Σv^2 in, say, (3.9), the weighted sum $\Sigma w_t v_t^2$ is minimised. Here w_t is the weight attached to the tth observation. If all the weights w_t equal one, this is the same as ordinary least squares. Among the other possibilities are linearly declining weights, where $w_t = t$, so the latest observation has the largest weight, and geometrically declining weights where $w_t = \lambda^t$, with $\lambda > 1$. Another variation they consider makes a direct replacement of the β_1 and β_2 in (3.9) by simple polynomials in time. For example, assuming the β_i vary linearly with time gives

$$\beta_1 = \alpha_1 + \alpha_2 t$$
$$\beta_2 = \gamma_1 + \gamma_2 t$$

and so (3.9) becomes

$$y_t = (\alpha_1 + \alpha_2 t)F_{1t} + (\gamma_1 + \gamma_2 t)F_{2t} + v_t \qquad\qquad (3.33)$$

Diebold and Pauly also propose allowing the weights to vary stochastically with time, using the random coefficient model. They point out that if there are any systematic patterns in the weights then these methods will exploit that pattern and so lead to improved forecasts.

An alternative way of modelling time-varying coefficients, suggested by Engle, Granger and Kraft (1984), is by means of a bivariate autoregressive conditional heteroskedasticity (ARCH) model, in which the covariance matrix of the forecast errors (and hence the weights) adapts over time. For a first-order ARCH model it is assumed that

$$\sigma_{1t}^2 = \alpha_1 + \alpha_2 u_{1t-1}^2$$
$$\sigma_{2t}^2 = \beta_1 + \beta_2 u_{2t-1}^2$$
$$\sigma_{12t} = \gamma_1 + \gamma_2 u_{1t-1} u_{2t-1}$$

so that the forecast errors in period $t-1$ affect the variances and covariances in period t. More generally, extra terms can be added to allow the forecast errors in $t-2, t-3,...$ to have some effect. In their illustration of the technique, Engle, Granger and Kraft include the eight most recent forecast errors. They also outline how to specify and estimate the ARCH model.

Another approach to allowing the weights to vary over time is the Bayesian one, in which a subjective prior distribution of the values of the weights is specified, and the evidence from the data modifies these weights (see Bessler and Brandt 1981 and Gupta and Wilton 1987 for details). Bordley (1982, 1986) has interpreted the variance-covariance and regression methods as Bayesian approaches.

The final method of combining forecasts we examine is the simple average of the forecasts. We saw that in the variance-covariance method the simple average was appropriate when the forecast errors have equal population variances. An alternative rationale is that the optimal weights are likely to be unstable because of changes over time in the variance-covariance matrix of forecast errors. If these changes are not systematic, the weights will change dramatically from period to period and forecasts based on unstable optimal weights will be expected to be poor. In general the simple average will have non-optimal weights but may still give better forecasts than any system of time-varying weights.

3.6   Practical suggestions for combining forecasts

We now turn to the implications of the above discussion for someone faced with a number of different forecasts. The first point that must be made is that the performance of any method of combining forecasts can only be judged by examining its accuracy outside the data used for determining the weights. That is, if we use the record of two forecasters over, say, 1980–8, to determine the weights then the accuracy of the combination can only be determined by the use of data outside this period. Within the data period we would expect more complicated methods, with changing weights, to dominate simpler, fixed-weight combinations since they are more flexible, but the real test is the accuracy outside the estimation period.

Next, we will discuss an issue that is generally neglected in the literature, namely, how many and what type of forecast should be included in the combination. The choice should depend on both statistical and economic factors. From the statistical point of view the forecasts should be 'different' in the sense that they utilise independent information and so do not lead to multicollinearity in the combining equation. The more variation they include, the lower is the variance of the combined forecast error expected to be. This implies that forecasts from different techniques, such as econometric models, time-series models and surveys might be included. Within these groups, only forecasts based on different information should be selected, such as forecasts from a monetarist and Keynesian model, and a naive no-change and an ARIMA model. Once, say, a monetarist forecast is included it is unlikely that a further monetarist forecast will provide a significant addition to the information already included.

From the economic perspective, an agent should devote resources to the forecasting exercise, in both gathering and processing costs, until the expected marginal benefits and the expected marginal costs are equal. This implies that the total number of forecasts to be included is likely to be small. Below we discuss examples in the literature where big gains in accuracy have been obtained with up to six forecasts.

We now examine the evidence from the literature on the usefulness of the different methods of combining. This literature is extensive and includes a special issue of the *Journal of Forecasting* in June 1989. Here we will mention some of the more important original references. Using the 1001 series from the M-competition (see section 3.7 below for details of this), Winkler and Makridakis (1983) examined five weighting procedures (including (3.29)–(3.32) above) for combining forecasts from ten different time-series methods, and found that (3.30) gave the best results (see also Makridakis and Winkler 1983 and Russell and Adam 1987 for similar studies). On the other hand, in a study of weekly forecasts of US money supply, Figlewski and Urich (1983) found that the simple average was preferred to the optimal weighting because of the instability of the estimated weights. Similar results were obtained by Kang (1986). These contrasted with the result of Figlewski (1983) that, for the Livingston inflation expectations survey, the optimal combination of individual responses was better than the simple average. One explanation of these findings is that the respondents to the Livingston survey are a more heterogeneous group than the money supply forecasters who all worked for US goverment security dealer firms. However, in each of these studies the forecasting methods used are rather similar, being from time-series methods or agents with common backgrounds.

A number of researchers have taken forecasts from different techniques as inputs into the combination. Lupoletti and Webb (1986) combine two econometric and a vector autoregression forecast by means of a generalisation of (3.13) and find that the combined forecasts generally outperform the individual forecasts. In contrast, Moriarty and Adams (1984) examine judgemental and ARIMA forecasts of sales and do not get any improvement by combining the forecasts. Holden and Peel (1986) study combinations of three econometric forecasts and three time-series forecasts, and present evidence that the correlations of the forecast errors change over time. In these circumstances the regression based methods are not expected to give good combined forecasts. As well as (3.10) and (3.13), the simple averages were also examined. The best performance was from (3.10) applied to the three econometric forecasts, but the simple average of all six forecasts performed reasonably well. We will discuss this paper further below, after summarising the conclusions from the rest of the literature.

As might be expected, the general picture which emerges from this literature is that the theoretical benefits from combining forecasts do not always occur in practice and no single method of combining forecasts dominates the others in all situations. This follows from the evidence that the properties of forecast errors vary from one sample to another. However, we believe that there is enough agreement in the literature to provide some guidance to agents faced with a number of different forecasts of the same outcome.

First, if there is any choice over which forecasts should be considered then they should be taken from as wide a range of techniques as possible. Then the properties of the forecasts need to be determined. Examine the past accuracy of the forecasts by calculating the mean errors, the root mean square errors and the variance-covariance matrix of the forecast errors. If there are enough observations this should be done both for all the available data and for suitable sub-groups such as the first half and second half of the observations. This will indicate which of the forecasts are unbiased and which are accurate, and also whether the covariances are constant over time. If the covariances do vary over time this implies that the optimal weights will also change and that perhaps a simple average will be a more reliable combination.

Next, it is necessary to decide whether any of the forecasts should be discarded as being inferior ones. Whilst there is no precise way of defining a good or bad forecast, the preferred forecasts are those which are unbiased and have random (rather than predictable) errors. If the errors are predictable they should also be modelled and incorporated into a new forecast series.

Finally a method of combining the selected forecasts needs to be chosen. Probably the best way of selecting a method is by experimenting to find the best fit over the past data. Ideally this would be by saving, say, the last 20 observations to test the accuracy of forecasts based on the earlier data. Once a method is selected it should be re-estimated using the full set of data. If optimal weights are to be obtained, our preference would be to use a regression (like (3.23)) in which a constant term is included (to remove any biases) and in which the sum of the weights is constrained to be one (to avoid inefficiency). However, the varying weights methods should also be considered.

Table 3.1. *Accuracy for 1975(1)–1979(4) (RMSEs)*

Forecast	Growth	Inflation
NI	2.27	4.32
LBS	2.29	4.87
PD	3.05	6.15
ARIMA	3.29	7.28
Naive I	3.75	6.34
Naive II	4.75	7.01

Source: Holden and Peel (1986), table 1.

To illustrate this methodology we will consider the study by Holden and Peel (1986) previously discussed, in which forecasts of growth and inflation in the UK from three economic models and three time-series models are combined. The economic models are those of the National Institute of Economic and Social Research (NI), which is broadly Keynesian, the London Business School (LBS), which has monetarist properties, and the London stockbrokers Phillips and Drew (PD), which has a 'city' rather than academic perspective. The three time-series models are naive I, the simple 'no change' model, naive II, the 'same change' model, and a sequence of ARIMA models. For each of the time-series models the data used were those which were available at the time when the corresponding economic forecasts were produced, so that all the forecasts used the same data base.

Quarterly forecasts for 1975(1)–1984(2) are analysed, with the period 1975(1)–1979(4) being used to form the combinations, and the combinations evaluated for 1980(1)–1984(2). The first step is to check the accuracy for 1975(1)–1979(4). The root mean square errors (RMSEs) are given in table 3.1, where it is seen that the three economic forecasts are more accurate than the three time-series forecasts. In view of this a case can be made for combining only the economic forecasts. However, the results for the individual forecasts and various combinations are given in table 3.2. The combinations considered are the unrestricted regression model, based on (3.13), the restricted regression model, based on (3.10) and the simple average. The regression weights were re-calculated for each quarter as more information became available so that a series of one-step ahead forecasts were produced. The best of the individual forecasts is LBS, for both growth and inflation, followed by the restricted combinations both of the three economic forecasts and all six forecasts. Next come the means of the three economic and all six forecasts. All the unrestricted combinations perform badly, showing the benefit to be gained by imposing the restrictions. From this study the conclusions are that if the best forecast for the period of

Table 3.2. *Forecast performance 1980(1)–1984(2) (RMSEs)*

Forecast	Growth	Inflation
NI	2.33	2.47
LBS	1.16	2.23
PD	3.61	3.68
ARIMA	2.91	4.19
Naive I	3.59	3.78
Naive II	3.94	3.98
Combinations of six:		
Unrestricted	3.26	5.94
Restricted	1.94	2.49
Simple mean	2.18	3.06
Combinations of NI, LBS and PD:		
Unrestricted	3.07	5.06
Restricted	1.90	2.44
Simple mean	1.99	2.61
Combinations of Naive I, Naive II and ARIMA:		
Unrestricted	3.11	6.41
Restricted	2.18	4.15
Simple mean	2.49	3.80

Source: Holden and Peel (1986), tables 1 and 7.

interest can be identified in advance (the LBS forecast here), that one should be used, but otherwise a restricted combined forecast is likely to be an improvement on the simple mean of the best three or all six forecasts. Here the theoretical result, outlined in section 2 of this chapter, that the combined forecast will be at least as accurate as the better of the component forecasts, does not apply. This is because the weights used are based on sample information and are not the population values.

In conclusion, we reiterate our earlier statement that there is much research currently being undertaken on combining forecasts. Until this produces some rules that are widely applicable, the forecaster's judgement will be an important ingredient in deciding how to combine forecasts.

3.7   The Makridakis forecasting competition

Our discussion of the choice of forecasts to be included in a combination raises the question of whether the various time-series extrapolation methods reviewed in chapters 1 and 2 are equally useful for all series. In order to try to provide evidence on this, Makridakis and Hibon (1979) collected together 111 series and examined the accuracy of 22 methods used for forecasting them. For a series of n observations, the first $n-12$ observations were used to fit the forecasting model, and then forecasts for the last 12 observations were made. Finally they analysed the accuracy of these forecasts over horizons of $1, 2, 3, \ldots, 12$ periods. Their general conclusions are that the choice of forecasting method depends on the loss function the investigator intends to minimise, that the methods which minimised the errors in fitting the model did not minimise them in the forecast period and that simpler methods frequently did as well as more complex methods.

Following the comments raised in the discussion of Makridakis and Hibon (1979), Makridakis *et al.* (1982) (reproduced as chapter 4 of Makridakis *et al.* 1984) organised a forecasting 'competition', known in the literature as the M-competition, in which up to 24 methods were used to forecast up to 1001 time series. The same general approach was adopted, with each forecasting model being fitted to the data series and some observations reserved for forecasting. The models were fitted to the data without the forecasters knowing the outcomes for the forecast periods. In fact they were only told the frequency (monthly, quarterly, annual) of the data and had no information about the situation in which each series occurred. They could not use causal variables to help in forecasting since the M-competition was intentionally concerned with a narrow range of extrapolation methods. A basic requirement was that the results should be replicable by other forecasters. That is, anyone using a particular forecasting method should be able to reproduce the forecasts. This meant that the methods used had to be specified in detail, and if a selection criterion was used this also had to be reported.

The series were different from those used in the Makridakis and Hibon (1979) study. Some information about the data is given in table 3.3, where it can be seen that both economic and demographic data are used, the majority being monthly, and most having more than 50 observations. The data also had a variety of different starting/ending dates to avoid possible correlations of errors with external shocks. Newton and Parzen (1984) give the names of some of the series and their graphs.

Since fitting 24 models to 1001 time series was likely to be very time consuming for some of the more complex methods, a systematic random sample of 111 series was selected by taking a random starting point (which was 4), and then taking every ninth series, giving the sample as series numbered $4, 13, 22, \ldots, 994$. These were not the same 111 series as those examined by Makridakis and Hibon (1979) in the study described above.

The methods used for forecasting are explained in appendix 2 of

Table 3.3. *Characteristics of the 1001 series*

Type of data	No. of series	Time unit	No. of series	Length of series	No. of series
Micro data	302	annual	181	0–25	185
Industry data	236	quarterly	203	26–50	276
Macro data	319	monthly	617	51–75	304
Demographic	144			76–100	86
				101–125	102
				126–150	48
Total	1001		1001		1001

Source: Based on Makridakis *et al.* (1982), table 1 and Libert (1984), exhibit 1.

Makridakis *et al.* (1982) and in more detail in the chapters of Makridakis *et al.* (1984). Here we will outline their main features after establishing the notation. Let X_t be the actual value of the series and $\hat{X}_t$ be the forecast for period t made in period $t-1$, then the error, e_t is

$$e_t = X_t - \hat{X}_t, \tag{3.34}$$

and the sum of squares of the errors is

$$\text{SSE} = \Sigma e_t^2 \tag{3.35}$$

If a total of n observations are available, $n-m$ are used in fitting the model, and the remaining m for forecasting, where m is 18 for monthly data, 8 for quarterly data and 6 for annual data. Thus in fitting the model, SSE is obtained by summing for $t=1$ to $n-m$, while for assessing the accuracy of the forecasts, the errors e_t for $t=n-m+1$ to n are used, for the appropriate horizon. Where the values of parameters need to be determined from the data, a grid-search method is used, so that if, for example, α is expected to satisfy $0 \leqslant \alpha \leqslant 1$ then the values $\alpha = 0.00, 0.01, 0.02, \ldots, 1.00$ might be tried, the minimum SSE found, and then a finer grid of values around the minimum could be examined. For example, if the first search yields 0.46 as the minimising value, the second grid could be $0.451, 0.452, \ldots, 0.469$ and the new minimum found. This process can be repeated until no further reduction in SSE occurs.

The forecasting methods are as follows.

1 Naive I: this is the simple 'no-change' or random walk model (1.1) and, for forecasting is given by

$$\hat{X}_{t+1} = X_t \tag{3.36}$$

and this is also used for forecasting, so that all the forecasts are X_{n-m}.

2 Simple moving average: this is a generalisation of (1.9) where the model
   is fitted by

$$\hat{X}_{t+1} = (X_t + X_{t-1} + \cdots + X_{t-N+1})/N \tag{3.37}$$

and N is chosen to minimise SSE over 1 to $n-m$. The same equation is
used for forecasting, with forecast values occurring on the right-hand
side as necessary. If there is a trend in the series the forecasts will always
lag behind the actuals.

3 Single exponential smoothing: this uses (1.26) and has

$$\hat{X}_{t+1} = \alpha X_t + (1-\alpha)\hat{X}_t \tag{3.38}$$

where α is chosen to minimise SSE over 1 to $n-m$, and the same
equation is used for forecasting. It assumes that there is no trend in the
series. We saw in chapter 1 section 3 that an initial forecast is needed to
start off the model and this was obtained by 'back forecasting' or by
taking the last actual value of the series as $\hat{X}_{n-m}$ and using (3.38) to
solve for $\hat{X}_{n-m-1}$, then for $\hat{X}_{n-m-2}$ and so on until $\hat{X}_1$ was given.

4 Adaptive response rate exponential smoothing: this uses (3.38) but
   α varies with t according to

$$\alpha_t = |E_t/M_t| \tag{3.39}$$

where E_t is the smoothed error and M_t is the smoothed absolute error,
so

$$E_t = 0.2e_t + 0.8E_{t-1}$$
and $\quad M_t = 0.2|e_t| + 0.8M_{t-1}.$

For a series of random errors α will be around 0.5, while for a run of
positive errors α will increase. The smoothing parameter, which has
a value of 0.2 for the M-competition, can be varied. As with (3.38), this
method assumes that there is no trend in the series.

5 Holt's two-parameter linear exponential smoothing: this has two
   components, the trend (T) and smoothed series (S), which both follow
   (3.38). These are given by

$$S_t = \alpha X_t + (1-\alpha)(S_{t-1} + T_{t-1}) \tag{3.40}$$

$$T_t = \beta(S_t - S_{t-1}) + (1-\beta)T_{t-1} \tag{3.41}$$

$$\hat{X}_{t+1} = S_t + T_t \tag{3.42}$$

and a grid search of values of α and β is used to minimise SSE. For forecasting k periods ahead

$$\hat{X}_{n-m+k} = S_{n-m} + kT_{n-m} \tag{3.43}$$

This method extrapolates any linear trend in the data.

6 Brown's one-parameter linear exponential smoothing: this applies the smoothing operation (3.38) twice to give a smoothed series S' and a smoothed adjustment S''

$$S'_t = \alpha X_t + (1-\alpha)S'_{t-1} \tag{3.44}$$

$$S''_t = \alpha S'_t + (1-\alpha)S''_{t-1} \tag{3.45}$$

$$\hat{X}_{t+1} = 2S'_t - S''_t + \alpha(1-\alpha)^{-1}(S'_t - S''_t) \tag{3.46}$$

The value of α is selected to minimise SSE. Any linear trend in the data will be smoothed and extrapolated.

7 Brown's one-parameter quadratic exponential smoothing: this extends the previous method to allow for a quadratic trend by applying (3.38) three times, to give (3.44), (3.45) and

$$S'''_t = \alpha S''_t + (1-\alpha)S'''_{t-1} \tag{3.47}$$

$$\hat{X}_{t-1} = a_t + b_t + 0.5c_t \tag{3.48}$$

where

$$a_t = 3S'_t - 3S''_t + S'''_t$$
$$b_t = \alpha\{2(1-\alpha)^2\}^{-1}\{(6-5\alpha)S'_t - (10-8\alpha)S''_t + (4-3\alpha)S'''_t\}$$
$$c_t = \alpha(1-\alpha)^{-2}(S'_t - 2S''_t + S'''_t)$$

Again α is chosen to minimise SSE. Forecasts are given by

$$\hat{X}_{n-m+k} = a_{n-m+k} + kb_{n-m+k} + 0.5k^2 c_{n-m+k} \tag{3.49}$$

8 Linear regression trend fitting: this is the estimate of (1.5) or

$$\hat{X}_t = a + bt \tag{3.50}$$

where a and b are chosen by minimising SSE, and so are the ordinary least squares values. Forecasts are from

$$\hat{X}_{n-m+k} = a + b(n-m+k). \tag{3.51}$$

The average linear trend over the series is extrapolated by this method.

9–16 As 1–8 but the data are first deseasonalised by the simple ratio to (centred) moving average method (see (1.17) and the discussion of the decomposition method) to give the seasonally adjusted series X'_t, and the forecasts $\hat{X}_{n-m+k}$ are re-seasonalised by multiplying them by the seasonal factor.

17 Holt–Winters' linear and seasonal exponential smoothing: for non-seasonal data the method is 5 above otherwise $(1.27)-(1.29)$ are used. The values of the parameters which minimise SSE are found by a grid search method. The result is that the seasonal factors are also smoothed.

18 AEP (automatic) Carbone–Longini: this is a variation of the adaptive estimation procedure of Carbone and Longini (1977) which allows a fixed additive and multiplicative model to have parameters which change over time, and the version used is an autoregressive model with time dependent parameters. Details are given by Carbone (1984).

19 Bayesian forecasting: this can be interpreted as a stochastic version of the Brown, Holt and Winters smoothing model which uses the Kalman filter to produce the forecasts. It requires a number of parameters and probability distributions to be specified *a priori* and these are then updated as the evidence from the data accumulates. Fildes (1984) discusses details of the method.

20 Combining forecasts (A): this takes the simple average of forecasts from methods 11, 12, 13, 14, 17 and 18.

21 Combining forecasts (B): this weights the forecasts used in 20 according to the size of the sample covariance matrix of percentage errors. Winkler (1984) presents details of the method.

22 Box–Jenkins methodology: this follows the cycle of model identification, parameter estimation and diagnostic checking discussed in chapter 2, section 3 above. Andersen and Weiss (1984) explain how the method was applied in the M-competition.

23 Lewandowski's FORSYS system: this is a decomposition method which incorporates exponential smoothing with a varying parameter. Details are outlined in Makridakis *et al.* (1982) and Lewandowski (1984).

24 ARARMA methodology: this starts with a simple non-stationary autoregressive model (the AR model) for which the residuals are determined and the ARMA models are fitted to the residuals. The procedure is interpreted as the AR model transforming the data from being a long-memory series into a short-memory series, which in turn is transformed, through the ARMA model, into white noise. Newton and Parzen (1984) give the details.

The above methods, with the exceptions of Box–Jenkins, Lewandowski and ARARMA, were applied to all 1001 series. The three other methods were limited to the 111 series previously mentioned. In order to be able to make comparisons of accuracy, summary measures are needed. The ones chosen by Makridakis *et al.* (1982) are MSE, MAPE, MdAPE, average ranking (AR) and percentage better (PB). These were discussed in chapter 1, section 5 above. The average rank is obtained by ranking, for each series, the forecasting methods from 1 (most accurate) to 21 or 24 (least accurate), and then finding the average value. The percentage better statistic is obtained comparing the forecast MSEs of each series for each horizon and finding the percentage of time (out of 1001 or 111) that a particular method is better than the other methods. In using these different accuracy methods it is important to bear in mind a point made by Priestley (in the discussion of Makridakis and Hibon 1979): is it valid to use SSE (or equivalently, MSE) to select the model and then use some other measure to assess its accuracy? It would appear to be more sensible to use the same criterion for both purposes.

The results of the competition are presented in 35 tables in Makridakis *et al.* (1982) and are not easy to summarise. However, there are a number of general conclusions arrived at by the authors. These include:

(*a*) Comparisons of the results for the 111 series and 1001 series show that MSE fluctuates more than the other measures of accuracy, while the others are more consistent.

(*b*) The performance of the different forecasting methods depends on the accuracy measure being used, and also on the type of series being forecast. For example, deseasonalised single exponential smoothing performs well for monthly data but not for annual data.

(*c*) With micro data the simple methods are best, while the more complex methods are preferred with macro data.

(*d*) The factors affecting forecast accuracy are trend, seasonality and randomness. Trend is extrapolated too much in the statistically sophisticated methods. Seasonality is best removed by a simple decomposition procedure. The greater the randomness of the series, the less useful are the sophisticated methods.

(*e*) The best methods for horizons 1 or 2 periods ahead are deseasonalised simple, Holt, Brown and Holt–Winters exponential smoothing, for 3–6 periods ahead the deseasonalised Holt, Brown, and Holt–Winters exponential smoothing, and ARARMA do well, while for horizons 7–18, Lewandowski is best.

(*f*) Combining (A) the simple average of six forecasts is better than any of its components and performs very well overall, while the weighted average combining (B) is not as good. Notice that no restricted combinations of the kind discussed earlier in this chapter were tried.

(*g*) The best methods for the 1001 series are deseasonalised single exponential smoothing, Holt, Winters, AEP (automatic) and Bayesian forecasting, and these plus Box–Jenkins, Lewandowski and ARARMA are best for the 111 series.

(*h*) For the data as a whole, when average rankings are examined, no method is significantly better than deseasonalised single exponential smoothing, but this does not apply to sub-groups of series.

(*i*) There is no evidence that forecast accuracy increases with the length of the series.

Since the publication of the M-competition study, a number of researchers have supplemented the results. A general commentary is provided in the *Journal of Forecasting*, volume 2, number 3, 1983 where some experts not involved in the original study present their views, and the authors respond to these. Particular points of criticism concern the presentation of the tables of results, the choice of forecasts to be included in the combinations and the lack of detail in the discussion of the time taken and costs of the various methods. The way the Box–Jenkins models were selected was also questioned. Hill and Fildes (1984), Libert (1984), Lusk and Neves (1984) and Poulos, Kvanli and Pavur (1987) all examine 'automatic' procedures for specifying and estimating Box–Jenkins models and find that, in general, automated systems give forecasts which are about as accurate as those made by experts. Koehler and Murphree (1988) find that an automated procedure for single exponential smoothing and a semi-automatic procedure of the state space method are also as accurate as Box–Jenkins forecasts by experts. On a different aspect of the M-competition, Flores (1986) performs sign tests on the percentage better statistics and shows that many of the apparent differences between the methods are insignificant.

The M-competition revealed the importance of the circumstances of the series – frequency, type, randomness – in determining the best forecasting method. The general approach, of using competing methods on the same series and then examining the accuracy of the forecasts, is one framework for evaluating forecasting methods. Schnaars (1986), for example, has applied it to annual sales forecasts. But one important feature of the M-competition was that the participants had no information about the particular situation of each series and so could not use causal variables to help in forecasting. Thus, the M-competition was intentionally concerned with a narrow range of extrapolation methods. Since the original work for the competition in 1979, important developments (discussed in chapter 2) have occurred concerning tests for stationarity, non-linearities and the differences between deterministic and stochastic trends. It would be interesting to know whether the use of these can help in the choice between the different time-series methods.

PART 2

Applications

CHAPTER 4

Microeconomic forecasting

4.1 Introduction

In this chapter we are concerned with methods of forecasting in the microeconomic environment. That is, at the level of a particular firm or industry rather than with the whole economy (which is the subject of chapter 5). In chapters 2 and 3 we saw various time-series methods which can be applied in any circumstances, given the required data. They are basically non-causal extrapolative methods. Here the approach adopted is to assume that a causal model will help in understanding behaviour and so will produce accurate forecasts. Whether it is worthwhile constructing such a model depends on the costs and benefits of the forecasting process. The costs can generally be estimated but the benefits are more difficult to assess. This is particularly the case when the choice is between a virtually costless naive model, say, a random walk or simple extrapolation model, and a complex causal model which is expected, *ex ante*, to give more accurate forecasts, but requires much judgement by the modeller.

We take as our starting point demand analysis, in which the theory of consumer behaviour is used to model how individuals behave in a perfectly competitive market. By making simplifying assumptions it is possible, in principle, to construct an economic model which attempts to explain demand in terms of observed prices, incomes, advertising and other variables. With further assumptions it is possible to make forecasts of their future values. This follows directly from the basic concepts of micro-economics and in general refers to demand at the level of an industry rather than the individual firm.

An alternative approach, discussed in section 4.3, is taken in the literature on marketing, where the main concerns are sales forecasting and predicting market shares for the products of particular companies. While the factors central to microeconomics (prices, advertising) are still important, there is an emphasis on the role of competing products. Another way of forecasting behaviour is to ask participants what their plans are. Thus firms could be asked about their likely investment over the next few months or consumers asked about future purchases of durable goods. The resulting information, known as anticipations data, can then be used for forecasting. These are examined in section 4.4. Related to this is the possibility that another variable can be found which is a leading indicator of the series of interest. While these are mainly used for business cycle forecasting, other applications are also presented in section 4.4. Scenario analysis, in which alternative pictures of the future are presented qualitatively, is discussed in section 4.5. The chapter ends with a brief review of other techniques.

4.2   Demand forecasting

In chapter 1, section 4 we introduced a simple model of the demand for alcoholic drink as an illustration of the methods of econometric forecasting. It was based on elementary demand theory and took the form

$$q = f(p, Y) \tag{4.1}$$

where q is the quantity of alcohol demanded during a specified period, p is the price of the product relative to the general price level, Y is the level of the consumer's real income, and f denotes a function so that q depends on p and Y. This type of relationship is the starting point for many models of the demand for non-durable consumer products and, since sales are the product of quantity and price, can be used for modelling sales. The variable of interest which is to be explained, q, is a measure of the quantity demanded, using some physical units, of a particular product. The analysis can take place at the level of the individual firm or at the level of the industry. We will not consider complete systems of demand equations which attempt to explain the demand for all products subject to a budget constraint, since the emphasis of research in this area has been on testing demand theory rather than on producing forecasts. See Thomas (1987) for an excellent summary of the literature in this area and De Pelsmacker (1988) for an application to the Belgian car market.

It is obviously important for the retailer or manufacturer of a product to be able to predict its future demand. In elementary consumer theory the product is assumed to be clearly defined (say carrots rather than clothing) and to consist of identical units with a common size (say a hairspray that comes in only one size and perfume) and quality. In these circumstances q could be the number of units sold. This would also be the case with a service such as dry cleaning. More generally, it might be a weight (say grams of coffee) or an index number which takes account of size and quality variations (say an index of the quantity of footwear sold).

Turning next to the price term, p, we notice that it is the relative price rather than the actual price that matters. This is using the property of homogeneity from demand theory which states that demand will be unchanged if all prices in the economy change in proportion. The responsiveness of the quantity demanded to a change in price is measured by the price elasticity of demand, defined by

$$E^p = \frac{\partial q/q}{\partial p/p} \qquad (4.2)$$

where ∂q and ∂p are the changes in quantity and price respectively. This is an important concept in any market. Since E^p is expected to be negative, a large elasticity implies that a small increase in price results in a large reduction in demand. The effects on revenue (or expenditure) can be seen by assuming that q depends only on p so that total revenue is

$$TR = pq$$

and the marginal revenue from a small change in price is found by differentiation with respect to p

$$MR = \frac{\partial TR}{\partial p} = q + p\frac{\partial q}{\partial p}$$

$$= q(1 + E^p). \qquad (4.3)$$

If E^p is -1 then MR is zero and TR is unaffected by a change in price, while if demand is inelastic $(0 > E^p > -1)$ MR is positive so that an increase in price increases total revenue. Whether this increases profits depends on costs. The remaining case is when demand is elastic $(E^p < -1)$ so that MR is negative and an increase in price reduces total revenue. Examples of estimated price elasticities include -0.2 for cigarettes in the USA (see Baltagi and Levin 1986), -0.37 for Canadian beer and -1.27 for imported wine in Canada (see Adrian and Ferguson 1987), -0.08 for cigarettes in Greece (see Stavrinos 1987), and -0.69 for electricity in the Netherlands (see van Helden, Leeflang and Sterken 1987). The effects of a tax on sales of a product can also be examined if the price elasticity is known (see, for example, Townsend 1987 for a discussion of cigarette taxes).

The other variable we included in (4.1) is real income, since this is expected to be a major determinant of a consumer's demand for a product. There are several ways in which real income can be defined. Money income can be taken before or after deductions such as income tax. An alternative which is frequently adopted in studies of consumer demand is to use total expenditure, since this omits savings, and this is justified by arguing that a consumer first allocates income between saving and spending before going on to allocate spending to different products. Additionally, when data are collected by household surveys, it is believed that expenditure figures are more reliable than income figures. Yet another approach is to focus on 'discretionary' income, that is, the income remaining after the consumer has paid for basic living costs. The income elasticity is a similar concept to price elasticity and is defined by

$$E^Y = \frac{\partial q/q}{\partial Y/Y} \tag{4.4}$$

where ∂Y is the change in real income. Again notice that it is not money income but real income that determines demand. From elementary demand theory we know that the income elasticity will be positive for normal goods, since consumers generally want more of the product as income rises. Of particular interest to firms are those products with income elasticities greater than unity (for example foreign holidays), since demand will grow at a faster rate than the general economy. In contrast, negative income elasticities are associated with inferior goods, such as bus travel, where, beyond a particular level, demand declines as incomes rise. Empirical estimates of income elasticities include: for the UK, from Dax (1987), 1.2 for wine 0.7 for beer, 0.5 for coffee and 0.2 for tea; for Canada, from Adrian and Ferguson (1987), 0.23 for Canadian beer, 1.54 for imported beer, 0.7 for Canadian wine and 0.6 for imported wine; for Greece, from Stavrinos (1987), 0.176 for cigarettes, and from van Helden, Leeflang and Sterken (1987), 0.945 for electricity in the Netherlands.

The model consumer demand (4.1) is intended to be a simplification of the real world. There are many other factors which influence demand and we now consider some of them. Note that we are not advocating a modelling procedure in which (4.1) is estimated and then extra variables are added if it is unsatisfactory. We are taking the variables one at a time in order to explain how each is relevant, and it is only when the full equation is specified that the parameters should be estimated.

The first one is the effect of *other products*. In demand theory the consumer is assumed to allocate income to the available goods in such a way as to maximise the utility gained from them. This implies that all goods are competing for the consumer's income and so are potential substitutes. By analogy with the price elasticity of demand we can define the effect of a change in the price of good B on the quantity of good A demanded as the cross elasticity between A and B

$$E^{AB} = \frac{\partial q^A/q^A}{\partial p^B/p^B} \tag{4.5}$$

Thus, E^{AB} measures the response of the quantity of good A demanded when the price of good B changes. If E^{AB} is positive then A and B are substitutes since an increase in the price of B results in an increase in the demand for A. Adrian and Ferguson (1987) found that the cross elasticity between the quantity of Canadian beer demanded and the price of Canadian spirits was

0.34, and for Canadian wine and the price of imported wine, 0.21. If E^{AB} is negative then A and B are complements and an increase in the price of B reduces demand for A. For Canadian spirits, Adrian and Ferguson found the cross elasticities with the prices of Canadian wine and imported wine were -0.26 and -0.13 respectively. The remaining case is where E^{AB} is zero and the products are independent so that a change in the price of one does not affect the demand for the other. Adrian and Ferguson obtained insignificant cross elasticities between both the quantity of Canadian beer and the price of Canadian wine and the quantity of Canadian wine and the price of Canadian beer. While in principle all goods which are not complements are substitutes, so that all their prices should enter every demand function, it is useful in practice to assume that many cross elasticities are effectively zero so that these prices can be dropped from the demand function.

The next variable we consider is *advertising*. The purpose of advertising is to increase the demand for the product at the existing price. That is, the hope of the advertiser is that the demand curve will shift to the right. One approach is to include real expenditure on advertising (A) in (4.1). This implies that advertising has an effect in the current period (this year with annual data) only. An alternative is to assume that advertising is a type of investment which has a long-term effect but that this effect declines as time passes. If the rate of decline is constant, say α per year, this means that, for a value of α of 0.5, an expenditure of 100 units this year will have an effect of 100 this year, 0.5(100) or 50 next year, 0.5(50) or 25 the following year and so on. For an application to the demand for cigarettes in the USA see Baltagi and Levin (1986). To illustrate this method we assume (4.1) is a linear equation and include this year's advertising (A_t), last year's advertising (A_{t-1}), the previous year's advertising (A_{t-2}), and so on. The result is that we can write the equation as

$$q_t = \beta_1 + \beta_2 p_t + \beta_3 Y_t + \beta_4(A_t + \alpha A_{t-1} + \alpha^2 A_{t-2} + \alpha^3 A_{t-3} + \cdots) \quad (4.6)$$

where $\alpha, \beta_1, \beta_2, \beta_3$ and β_4 are unknown parameters which are to be estimated. This is the familiar geometric or Koyck distributed lag model (see, for example, Gujarati 1988 or Johnston 1984) which is very similar to the exponentially weighted moving average model (1.26). The equation can be simplified by writing (4.6) lagged one period

$$q_{t-1} = \beta_1 + \beta_2 p_{t-1} + \beta_3 Y_{t-1} + \beta_4(A_{t-1} + \alpha A_{t-2}$$
$$+ \alpha^2 A_{t-3} + \alpha^3 A_{t-4} + \cdots) \quad (4.7)$$

We can now form (4.6) minus α times (4.7) to give

$$q_t - \alpha q_{t-1} = \beta_1(1-\alpha) + \beta_2 p_t - \alpha \beta_2 p_{t-1}$$
$$+ \beta_3 Y_t - \alpha \beta_3 Y_{t-1} + \beta_4 A_t \quad (4.8)$$

This can be written in the general form

$$q_t = f(q_{t-1}, p_t, p_{t-1}, Y_t, Y_{t-1}, A_t) \tag{4.9}$$

which is easier to estimate than (4.6). However, (4.9) is a dynamic equation in contrast to (4.1) which was based on the static theory of consumer demand. This implies that a better starting point might be some dynamic model of demand which takes account of tastes and habits through the effects of past consumption. This approach is used by Houthakker and Taylor (1970), but we do not follow it here. Another problem with (4.9) is the fact that if a random (white noise) error term is added to (4.6) then the transformation gives a moving average error in (4.9). Ordinary least squares will give biased and inconsistent estimators and so should not be used. A further problem is that (4.9) includes two values of p and Y so that multicollinearity may be present.

As with the other variables, an elasticity for advertising can be defined as

$$E^A = \frac{\partial q/q}{\partial A/A} \tag{4.10}$$

Aaker and Carman (1982) review the literature on advertising and find that the short-run advertising elasticities for products such as soft drinks, coffee, apples and cigarettes are generally small and around 0.1. We will return to a discussion of advertising when we examine methods of forecasting company sales in the next section.

Another assumption of the theory of consumer behaviour is that an appropriate *unit of consumption* has been chosen. For products such as food and clothing it is reasonable to take the individual consumer as the basic unit so that quantity demanded and income are measured per capita. Some allowance for the different requirements of children can be made by the use of 'equivalent scales' (see for example Muellbauer 1977), whereby the demands of children of different ages are measured as a proportion of adult demands. If the total population in the country is not approximately constant then population size should enter the demand function. In his study of the demand for automobiles in the USA, Chow (1960) takes the number of new cars per capita as the quantity variable (see below for further details). Many products, for example cleaning materials, are used by households rather than individuals, so that the corresponding variable is the number of households rather than the total population. If there is a long-term trend in the size of households this will be important. In Great Britain, between 1951 and 1981 the total population increased from 48.8 million to 52.6 million, an increase of 8 per cent, but the number of households rose by 34 per cent with one-person households increasing by 163 per cent. That is, while the total population was more or less constant, the structure changed dramatically and this has important implications for many products. More generally, the demographic and geographical characteristics of households and consumers directly affect consumption. In a study by Ketkar and Ketkar (1987), 19 categories of households in the USA are used, based on their size, region, race, age, employment status etc.

External events or special factors can effect consumer behaviour in some non-quantifiable way. For example the market for cigarettes is thought to have been affected by the various reports warning about the health hazards of smoking. In empirical studies these may be accounted for by 'dummy' variables which take the values zero or one depending on whether the factor is absent or present. Baltagi and Levin (1986), for example, include dummy variables to reflect the 1971 ban on broadcasting cigarette advertisements in the USA. For the market for alcoholic drink in Canada, Adrian and Ferguson (1987) use dummy variables to represent effects that vary between the different provinces.

In the basic model of demand the *quality* of the product is assumed to be fixed. For some agricultural products this may be reasonable, but even with these, the packaging, presentation and freshness may improve over time. With many manufactured goods there are frequent improvements in quality such that a packet of, say, today's soap powder is rather different from one ten years ago. It is difficult to measure quality changes but they should not be ignored. In some cases it may be necessary to represent their effects by dummy variables.

Forecasting the demand for *new products* is particularly difficult, as is evident from failure rates of up to 40 per cent in the USA (see Tyebjee 1987). Many 'new' products are in practice major or minor variations on existing products and their demand can be related to the factors discussed above. But for a genuinely new product, as well as not having information about the relevant elasticities, additional problems are caused by the learning and acceptance period needed by consumers. While advertising can affect the length of this, it is unlikely that a suitable model could be developed and estimated to explain the learning process. However, evidence from a similar stage in the life of other products or the results from test markets might help (see Dodson 1981). In the absence of any data relevant to demand, a completely different method of forecasting is needed. Wind, Mahajan and Cardozo (1981) and Assmus (1984) review the use of diffusion models, behavioural models and managerial models. These rely on experimentation or computer modelling to give information about the potential size of the market, and are unsatisfactory to the extent that the values of many parameters have to be chosen by the modeller.

Another approach is to assume that demand for the new product will follow the typical product life cycle illustrated in figure 4.1. It is the

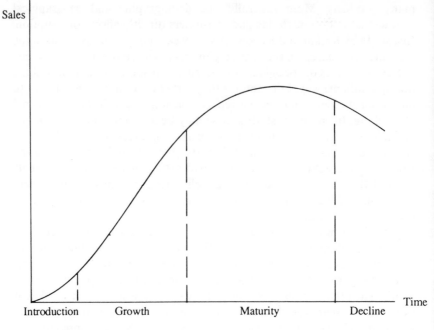

Figure 4.1
A typical product life cycle

introduction and growth stages which are the most important for a new product since these are characterised by a rapid increase in demand. An appropriate way of modelling them might be to fit a non-linear growth curve (see below) using whatever data are to hand. Once the maturity stage is reached a conventional demand function will be appropriate. For a full discussion of the concept of a product life cycle see, for example, Kotler (1988, chapter 12) and for an application to forecasting prices see Dino (1985).

So far we have assumed that the product under consideration is consumed within a single period. For *durable goods*, such as televisions, washing machines and books this is not the case and, when purchased, they are expected to provide services for some time into the future. This means that an important determinant of the demand for durable goods is the stock already held by the consumer. A person who purchases a new car one week is unlikely to purchase another one the following week, even if there is a price reduction.

When a new durable product is introduced the initial demand will be from first-time buyers. However, as time passes, the stock held by consumers will depreciate leading to a demand for replacements. Therefore the quantity sold will depend on these two components of demand. As for non-durable goods, the demand from first-time buyers will depend on the variables already discussed. Replacement demand will depend on the rate of depreciation of the good (the higher the depreciation rate, the higher the demand) and on the level of stocks held by consumers (the higher the stock, the higher the demand). This can be formalised in a stock-adjustment model. From (4.1), suppose that the desired stock (S^*) of a durable good depends only on its relative price (p) and real income (Y), and is given by

$$S_t^* = \alpha + \beta p_t + \gamma Y_t \tag{4.11}$$

but that the actual stock (S) differs from the desired stock. The reasons for this difference will vary with the product but for expensive goods like cars and boats the availability of finance will be important while for others, like new houses and built-in furniture, there may be a delay between ordering and receiving the product. A simple approach to reconciling the difference between S and S^* is to use the partial adjustment model

$$S_t - S_{t-1} = \delta(S_t^* - S_{t-1}) \tag{4.12}$$

where $0 < \delta < 1$. If δ were zero the value of S would never change while if δ were one, S and S^* would always be equal. Thus δ measures the speed of adjustment. If the rate of depreciation (λ) is assumed to be constant for each period there is an identity relating stocks and quantities purchased (q) since the stock at the end of a period is the stock at the beginning less its depreciation plus new purchases

$$S_t = S_{t-1} - \lambda S_{t-1} + q_t \tag{4.13}$$

This can be re-arranged as

$$q_t = S_t - S_{t-1} + \lambda S_{t-1}$$

and substituting (4.12) and (4.11) gives

$$q_t = \alpha\delta + \beta\delta p_t + \gamma\delta Y_t + (\lambda - \delta)S_{t-1} \tag{4.14}$$

The result of this consideration of the properties of durable goods is that (4.14) includes the value of stocks at the end of the previous period. While data on q, p and Y are frequently available, data on S, the depreciated value of stocks, are not. One procedure that has been used by Stone and Rowe (1957) is to take an arbitrary starting value, S_0, say, and, for a particular value of the depreciation rate λ, substitute into (4.13) repeatedly to obtain a series for S. Different values of λ give different series to be used in (4.14). The one giving the best fit (highest R^2) is selected.

Chow (1960) undertook one of the classical studies of the demand for durable goods in his work on automobiles in the USA. He measured stocks in units of 'new car equivalents per head of population' by taking the number of car registrations at the end of each year, weighting them according to the relative prices in 1937 of cars of different ages and dividing by population size. He did not try to allow for quality changes but instead experimented with a trend variable to represent the gradual increase in quality which occurred. An example of his results is, for 1921–53, the linear demand function

$$q_t = 0.08 - 0.020p_t + 0.012Y_t - 0.23S_{t-1} \qquad (4.15)$$
$$(7.6) \qquad (10.9) \quad (4.9)$$

$$R^2 = 0.858 \text{ Durbin-Watson statistic} = 1.43$$

where q_t is the number of new automobiles purchased in year t divided by the population, p is a price index of automobiles divided by the GNP deflator, Y is per capita disposable personal income divided by the GNP deflator, S is the stock variable already mentioned and t-values are in parentheses. The equation has a satisfactory fit; no serious autocorrelation and high t-values on the coefficients. Evaluating the elasticities at the means of the variables, the price elasticity is -0.63 and the income elasticity 1.70. In Chow's formulation the depreciation rate is 0.75 and the adjustment coefficient is 0.48. Chow also checked the effects of replacing Y by permanent income and found values of -0.72 and 1.88 for the elasticities and 0.55 for the adjustment coefficient. He used (4.15) to forecast q for 1954–7 by substituting the actual values of p, Y and S into the equation and obtained small errors except for 1955. These are *ex post* forecasts that could only have been made after the year they refer to. Chow also re-estimated the equation using data to 1957, with minor changes to the estimated coefficients and made an *ex ante* forecast for 1958 in May of that year using his predictions of the values of the independent variables. This forecast is inaccurate because of mistakes in the values of disposable income and the price level. However, the error is not large enough for the estimated model to be rejected.

An alternative method of forecasting the demand for durable goods is to use *growth curves*, which can be considered as extensions of the trend extrapolation methods discussed in chapter 1, section 3. These model the way market penetration (that is the percentage of consumers possessing the product) increases as time passes. The basic assumption is that the growth curve is S-shaped, as in figure 4.2 where a saturation level of 90 per cent is indicated. Penetration is assumed to be a function of time so that causal variables such as prices and advertising have no direct effect. The most

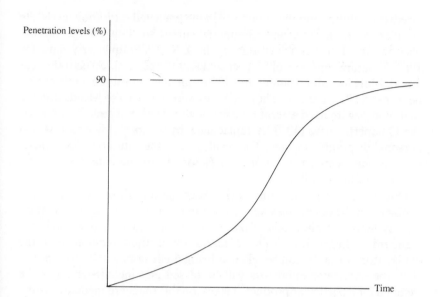

Figure 4.2
A growth curve with a 90 per cent saturation level

commonly fitted growth curves are the logistic and Gompertz curves. The logistic takes the form

$$X_t = \frac{\alpha}{1 + \beta \exp(-\gamma t)} \qquad \alpha, \beta, \gamma > 0 \qquad (4.16)$$

where X is cumulative penetration, exp is exponential and t is time, and α is the saturation level. For estimation purposes, if α is known, (4.16) can be transformed to

$$\log[X_t/(\alpha - X_t)] = -\log \beta + \gamma t$$

The Gompertz growth curve is

$$X_t = \alpha \exp(-\beta(\exp(-\gamma t))) \qquad \alpha, \beta, \gamma > 0 \qquad (4.17)$$

where α is the saturation level. If α is known, (4.17) can be estimated by transforming it to

$$\log[\log(\alpha/X_t)] = \log \beta - \gamma t$$

Given time-series data on X, the remaining parameters, β and γ, can be estimated. Meade (1984) reviews a number of studies using these and other growth curves and finds problems over the choice of model, their forecasting ability, and the variability in the predicted saturation levels. He goes on to fit logistic and Gompertz curves to data on the market penetration of colour televisions in the UK. Using quarterly data for 1968–74 saturation levels of 53.2 per cent and 101 per cent respectively were found, while including data up to 1977 resulted in saturation levels of 62.3 per cent and 72.1 per cent. These changes were worrying so Meade decided that models with fixed saturation levels are unsatisfactory and he modified the Gompertz curve (4.17) by replacing α by $\alpha \exp(\delta Y_t)$ where Y is real personal disposable income. The result is that the saturation level varies with income. This gave a more satisfactory fit to the data but requires forecasts of future values of income.

Once a suitable demand function has been specified there are a number of problems at the *estimation* stage. These can be divided into single equation and systems complications. Taking the single equation ones first, the standard ordinary least squares regression method requires that the explanatory variables can be taken as being predetermined. If this is not so then the parameter estimators will be biased and inconsistent. For the demand for a particular product, it is reasonable to regard income as being exogenous, but prices and advertising are more likely to be jointly determined with demand. This suggests that extra equations are needed to explain each of these variables. These should be based on a suitable theory. Furthermore, we have ignored considerations of supply when theory tells us that it is the interaction of supply and demand that generates the market price and quantity. This raises the question of identification: given data on the variables, is it possible to estimate the structural parameters of each of the equations in the system? Tests for identification are presented in introductory econometrics texts (see, for example, Johnston 1984 and Gujarati 1988). Having obtained a system of identified and/or over-identified equations, the parameters can be estimated by a technique such as two stage least squares, and the results checked to see that they are satisfactory. As we saw in chapter 1, section 4, it may be necessary to adjust the model at this stage.

Finally, predictions of the future values of the exogenous variables are needed before demand can be forecast. For variables outside the control of the forecaster, for example national income, these might be obtained from a time-series model or from an outside source, such as a macroeconomic model. The values of other variables, for example advertising expenditure and relative price, might be chosen by the forecaster. It may be useful to experiment with a range of assumptions in order to see how sensitive the forecasts are to the particular values chosen. These experiments are known as simulations and can be a valuable guide in decision making and determining marketing strategies.

4.3 Sales and market share forecasting for companies

We now turn to forecasting sales of individual brands. There are basically two ways of building causal models: we can apply the methods just described to a particular brand or we can use the identity

$$\text{company sales} = \text{market share} \times \text{total market} \qquad (4.18)$$

and focus on market share. The second of these is more common in the marketing literature. In order to forecast company sales both market share and total market need to be forecast. The methods of the previous section can be used to forecast the total market for the product, leaving the problem of forecasting market share.

We start with modelling the sales of individual brands. Since the real value of sales is simply the number of items sold it is clear that one way of forecasting sales is to construct a model of the demand for the product and use this to forecast sales. Our previous discussion of market demand found that the factors affecting the quantity demanded were relative price, real income, advertising and a list of other factors such as population structure, quality and stocks. The same variables will affect the sales of a particular brand except that the degree of competition in the market is now important. A general sales function can be written

$$SI_t = f(PI_t, PC_t, Y_t, AI_t, AC_t, OI_t, OC_t) \qquad (4.19)$$

where SI = sales of brand I

PI = price of brand I

PC = price of competing brands

Y = income variable

AI = advertising of brand I

AC = advertising of competing brands

OI = other factors affecting brand I

OC = other factors affecting competing brands.

In (4.19) a distinction is made between brand I and competing brands. If there are many competing brands and brand I is relatively unimportant then PC, AC and OC could be index numbers covering the total market for the product, while in a more oligopolistic situation the values of these variables for each of the competitors could be entered. Since (4.19) is a static equation, and following our discussion of the Koyck distributed lag in (4.6), the lagged value of SI could be included to capture dynamic effects.

This type of model was used by Schmalensee (1972) in his study of the six major firms in the US market for cigarettes. He used a variety of specifications for his sales equations. An example of his results, for the Philip Morris brand (see Schmalensee 1972, p. 204) with all the variables in logarithms, is

$$SI_t = 3.6 + 0.26Y_t + 0.31AI_t - 0.20AC_t + 0.73SI_{t-1} - 0.43SC_{t-1}$$

$$(4.20)$$

where SI = number of Philip Morris brand cigarettes sold per person aged 15 and above

Y = real disposable income per capita

AI = real expenditure on advertising Philip Morris brand

AC = real expenditure on advertising other brands

SC = sales of other brands.

In this equation SI is the quantity of cigarettes sold adjusted for population size and there are no price variables included. The lagged value of SC indicates the size of the competitor's market which is the target of the advertising. The higher this is, the more the number of customers who might change over. While the coefficients are plausible, autocorrelation is present so we do not report significance tests. In his exhaustive investigation of the effects of different variables and different functional forms, Schmalensee found that relative price, competitive advertising and real income were never significant and that the lagged dependent variable was 'suspiciously important'. This last point implies the equations are misspecified and dynamic effects are important. However, in his study of advertising, Lambin (1976, p. 105) concludes that advertising has a lower than average effect when there is little quality differentiation between products. This could be the situation with cigarettes and would explain Schmalensee's results.

Lambin (1976) examines the markets for sixteen products in nine European countries, focusing on the effects of advertising. He takes account of such factors as product quality and the number of outlets. An example is the monthly sales of a brand of fruit yoghurt in Belgium

$$SI_t = f(PI_t, AI_t, KI_t, OI_t)$$ $$(4.21)$$

where SI = sales of this brand

PI = price of this brand

AI = advertising of this brand over the last six months

KI = quality measure – the number of packages and flavours being sold

OI = index of seasonal variation.

This equation (see Lambin 1976, p. 151) was found to be more satisfactory than alternatives which included income and the number of outlets. In his conclusions on the relationship between advertising and sales, Lambin states that brand advertising has a significant (but modest) effect on current sales, increases future sales and is less important than product quality.

Leone and Schultz (1980) provide a more general review of the evidence on the effects of company (brand) advertising on sales. They find that there is strong empirical support for the view that brand advertising has a positive effect on sales. The size of the effect is found to be small, with typical elasticities of 0.1. Aaker and Carman (1982) also review the literature on advertising and sales. They examine the question of whether there is too much advertising. One method is to use the model, developed by Dorfman and Steiner (1954), of a monopolist wishing to maximise profits in the short run. The optimal level of advertising is when:

$$\frac{A}{pq} = \frac{E^A}{E^P} \tag{4.22}$$

so that the ratio of the value of advertising to value of sales equals the ratio of the elasticity of advertising (4.10) to the price elasticity (4.2). Of course, most products cannot be regarded as monopolies, and the Dorfman–Steiner model is static. Another method is to examine what happens to sales when advertising is reduced. Taking account of the limited evidence available, Aaker and Carman conclude that over-advertising exists and that the marginal response to some advertising is very low.

Once the equation for sales is specified and estimated, it can be used with forecasts of the exogenous variables to predict future sales.

We now consider the second approach to forecasting company sales, namely that of *forecasting market share* and then using (4.18) to forecast sales. We assume we are dealing with an oligopolistic industry and can define three categories of product: (a) the product whose market we are concerned with, (b) products which are different but are substitutes or complements and (c) the remaining products which are relatively un-important, apart, perhaps, from their influence through aggregate prices. In concentrating on market share we can ignore (b) and (c) since these are taken account of in the forecast of industry sales. Thus we are concerned solely with the market for the product. From our examination of demand forecasting it should be clear that the variables that determine demand – price, advertising, quality and distribution – are likely to determine market share. Also, since market share measures the relative sales of the firm, it will be affected by relative prices, relative advertising and so on. Therefore we can write

$$\text{MSI} = f(p^1, A^1, K^1, D^1) \tag{4.23}$$

where MSI is the market share of firm I, the superscript I denotes firm I relative to the industry, and p is price, A is advertising, K is quality and D is distribution. As with the earlier models, the lagged dependent variable may be included to represent any carry-over effects of the marketing variables. An obvious property of market shares is that when summed over all the firms in the industry they total to one. This can be used in estimation if data are available on all the brands in the market.

A number of different functional forms have been considered for the market share function, the most common being the linear and the multiplicative (that is linear in the logarithms of the variables).

In order to estimate (4.23) data are needed on each of the variables. We will assume that market share and prices are known. For advertising the usual measure is expenditure on advertising but it may be possible to quantify its effectiveness in terms of its potential audience. Product quality is more difficult to measure. For some products there are technical characteristics, such as the horse-power rating of a tractor, which reflect quality. In other cases surveys of consumers may indicate the relative quality of different brands. If no information is available, quality may be represented by a dummy variable, but this will also represent any other variables which differ between brands and which are not explicitly included in the equation. Distribution might be measured by the number of outlets. With all of the variables there may be a lack of variation in the data so that multicollinearity is a problem and unreliable estimates are produced. In the limit, where a variable is constant across brands, such as the demographic structure, this variable should be excluded.

As an illustration of a market share equation we give Lambin's (1976, p. 150) estimate for a brand of electric shavers in Germany. The way quality varies between brands and over time is measured by an index reflecting the characteristics of the leading brands, subjectively rated by the marketing staff of one of the firms. All the variables are in logarithms, making the coefficients elasticities, and the estimation method is two stage least squares.

$$\text{MSI} = -0.512 - 3.726p^1 + 0.147A^1 + 0.583K^1 + 0.344\text{MSI}_{t-1} \tag{4.24}$$

The coefficients have the expected signs. Relative price has a negative effect on the market share of the brand, while relative advertising and quality have positive effects. However, autocorrelation is significant and so we do not report t-values.

Brodie and De Kluyver (1987) review research on market share forecasting and, comparing the types of econometric model we have discussed with naive no-change models, find that no one model dominates all the others. For their own data for three markets in New Zealand the naive models are in fact superior to the econometric ones and they conclude (page 435) that the market share models 'do not capture enough of the important features of the market to be used as "stand alone" forecasting instruments'. This suggests that further research is needed in this area.

4.4   Anticipations data and leading indicators

Many decisions by individuals and firms can only be carried out after a prolonged planning period. A person wishing to buy a house needs to save a deposit and arrange finance before the purchase can occur. Similarly, a firm wishing to build a new factory may have to get planning permission, commission architects, decide on the construction schedule and wait for machinery to be installed before the factory can be opened. In cases like these, where there is a lag between the decision to do something and the event taking place, a survey which asks participants their plans can provide useful information for forecasting. The results are referred to as *anticipations data*. While a case can be made for treating them as a macroeconomic forecasting technique, since they have been used in macroeconomic forecasting, we deal with them in this chapter because it is the views of individuals that matter. The usefulness and reliability of anticipations data depend on the length of the lag and how stable the lag is. Also important is whether the decision to undertake an action always results in that action occurring. There are many types of anticipations data but the most popular cover expectations of inflation, consumer buying intentions, company investment and future production. Examples of consumer intentions surveys include, for the USA, the Survey of Consumer Finances carried out by the Institute for Social Research, University of Michigan which collects data on consumer opinions and buying plans, and for the EEC, the survey reported in *European Economy Supplement C* covering consumer views on inflation and future purchases of durables. Investment and production surveys of firms in the EEC are reported in *European Economy Supplement B* and for the USA in the January issue of *Survey of Current Business*. The literature on these surveys is diverse. Reviews are given by Strigel and Ziegler (1988) and Holden, Peel and Thompson (1985), and illustrations of how the results from particular surveys might be used are given by Laumer and Ziegler (1982) and Oppenlander and Poser (1984).

A question mark remains over the usefulness of anticipations data for forecasting because of the conflicting evidence on the accuracy of survey data. The most researched area concerns expectations of inflation. For example, Batchelor (1982) examines results from the EEC survey of firms in which the questions concern changes in the firm's own prices over the next 'three or four months'. The answers are qualitative – whether prices will be the same, lower or higher – but are transformed by Batchelor into inflation rates. These are found to be biased forecasts of inflation. Batchelor also compared the accuracy of a naive no-change model of inflation, where the forecast is simply the latest observed value of inflation, and an ARIMA model fitted to past values. The ranking of the accuracy, from best to worst, is ARIMA, survey data and naive model. That is, the ARIMA model gives better forecasts than the survey data.

Other researchers who find that surveys give biased forecasts of inflation include De Leeuw and McKelvey (1981) for the US Bureau of Economic Analysis survey of businessmen, Saunders (1983) for the Australian Department of Industry and Commerce Survey of Manufacturing Activity (SOMA), and Figlewski and Wachtel (1981) for the Livingston survey of economists in the USA. What is noteworthy about this last study is that the analysis was at the level of individual respondents. An alternative analysis by Brown and Maital (1981) of these survey results averaged across respondents found that, while the forecasts were unbiased, they could be improved by taking account of lagged values of changes in money supply and wholesale prices. Also, while Saunders' (1983) study of the SOMA data found biasedness at the level of total manufacturing industry and twelve sub-categories, this was not the case in Saunders (1980) where the analysis was at the aggregate level.

A comparison of anticipations data and econometric forecasts of US business investment has been provided by Landefeld and Seskin (1986). They consider three anticipations surveys – the Bureau of Economic Analysis (BEA) in the US Department of Commerce, McGraw-Hill Publications Co., and Merrill Lynch Economics – and two econometric models – Data Resources Incorporated (DRI) and Wharton Economic Forecasting Associates. The BEA survey is the largest, covering a stratified sample of 13000 firms, while the other two focus on up to 1000 large firms. For annual data for 1970–80 Landefeld and Seskin find that the BEA survey is the most accurate of the surveys, with a root mean square error (RMSE) of 2.25, while that of the Merrill Lynch series is 4.03 and for the McGraw–Hill series, 4.11. The differences are explained by the inclusion of small firms in the BEA sample. When the econometric forecasts are added to the comparison, for 1974–80, the ranking (with RMSEs in brackets) is BEA (2.56), DRI (3.37), Merrill Lynch (4.86), McGraw-Hill (4.91) and Wharton (5.33). Thus the BEA anticipations survey is found to be superior to the econometric forecasts for this period.

This agrees with the results of an earlier study by Jorgenson, Hunter and Nadiri (1970) in which the US Office of Business Economics and the Securities and Exchange Commission (OBE-SEC) survey of business investment results are examined for 15 industry groups. The quarterly forecasts of investment for 1949(1)–1964(4) from the OBE-SEC survey are compared with forecasts from four econometric models, and also with a simple time-series model, a fourth order autoregressive scheme. While the autoregressive model has a superior explanatory power over the estimation period to the econometric models in 35 out of 60 comparisons, the anticipations data are superior in 57 out of 60 cases and are always preferred to the autoregressive model. See also Liebling *et al.* (1976).

The conclusion from this consideration of anticipations data is that there is a limited amount of evidence that forecasts based on surveys can turn out to be better than forecasts from an econometric model. Whether this result extends to current econometric models of the USA, or other countries and time periods is a matter for further research. However, care must be taken in interpreting the results and, rather than regarding surveys and econometric models as competitors, perhaps a more fruitful approach is to look at ways in which the information they each use can be combined together, and linked with that from other methods of forecasting. An illustration of how this might be done informally is provided by Keating (1985). We discussed other ways of combining in chapter 3 above.

A related topic to anticipations data concerns *leading indicators*. These are series which are used to predict turning points (peaks and troughs) in economic activity. It should be clear that many of the quantitative forecasting methods described in chapters 1 and 2 attempt to model the trend in a series and will not predict turning points since they imply that past trends will continue in the future. A different type of information is needed, and one approach, as we have just seen, is to find anticipations data from surveys. The assumption is that agents' behaviour will change as a turning point is approaching and this will be reflected in the survey results. Another approach, which we now consider, is to find series, known as leading indicators, which have turning points which precede the turning points of the variables of interest – thus leading indicator series forecast turning points.

Much of the work on leading indicators has been concerned with aggregate economic activity, that is, the business cycle, but the same principles apply to microeconomic series, such as company sales and investment at a disaggregated industry level. The first attempts at identifying leading indicators were by Harvard University Committee on Economic Research at the end of the first World War (see Gordon 1961, p. 514). Three curves, the speculation curve (based on stock prices), the business curve (based on bank debits) and the money curve (based on short-term interest rates) were found to be apparently related in the period before 1914. The business curve rose following an upturn in the speculation curve and a fall in the money curve. This pattern did not continue in the 1920s and the method fell into disuse. More recently, work on indicators has been conducted at the US National Bureau of Economic Research (NBER). Three types of indicator are covered: leading, coincident and lagging. Here we limit consideration to the leading ones since these are of interest for forecasting.

The first problem in leading indicator analysis is in deciding what series to consider. For microeconomic applications the choice is usually obvious, but even here there may be different patterns for production and sales because of variations in stocks. At the aggregate level, Burns and Mitchell (1946, p. 3) define the business cycle as consisting of 'expansions occurring at about the same time in many economic activities, followed by similarly general recessions, contractions and revivals which merge into the expansion phase of the next cycle'. Thus the 'economic activities' are not specified as, say, nominal gross national product, but are kept vague. The reason for this is that no single measure of economic activity is believed to be reliable enough (because of data errors) or available for a long enough historical period. Also, any particular variable may move differently from others. Moore (1983) points out that at the start of a recession, nominal GNP might rise because of inflation when real GNP is falling and unemployment is rising. The result is that the NBER identifies peaks (*ex post*) by making comparisons with historical records of previous peaks in order to determine when a period of expansion ends and the contraction starts. The duration of the contraction from the peak, the relative depth of the decline and how widespread the contraction is between sectors and regions are all considered. The variables considered include nominal and real GNP, total sales, the index of industrial production, unemployment and employment. An extra factor taken into account is 'diffusion' which measures the percentage of non-farm sector industries which have declining employment. The higher this is, the more severe is the contraction. For example, in April 1980 the diffusion percentage was 77, while in January 1975 it was 88 (see Moore 1983, p. 456), indicating that the 1975 recession was deeper.

Examination of these variables allows the NBER to date business cycles and so identify which series act as leading indicators. The twelve selected include (see Klein and Moore 1983) the average work week in manufacturing, initial claims for unemployment insurance, new orders for consumer goods and materials, the change in business inventories, the stock price index, and the change in consumer instalment debt. They are selected through a combination of prompt availability, economic theory and empirical observation. Economic theory is relevant because a causal relationship is likely to be stable. The empirical behaviour is important because data problems may result in a theoretically correct variable having an unsatisfactory performance. Rather than use individual series, an index of leading indicators is constructed, using subjectively chosen weights based on the properties of the series. Klein and Moore present evidence showing that for 1948–75 the leading indicator index predicted cyclical peaks with a mean lead of five months and troughs with a mean lead of seven months. However, the standard deviations were five months and eight months respectively, showing there was considerable variation in the lead times.

Klein and Moore also checked the performance of the 12 US indicators in nine other economies and found that, in general, they were satisfactory. The main exception was industrial materials prices, which lead peaks and troughs by one month for the USA but lag for the UK (five months), West Germany (eleven months), France (three months), the Netherlands (seven months) and Sweden (one month). These variations are not surprising given the differences in the economies considered. What is more remarkable is the agreement for the other 11 indicators. More detailed information about leading indicators for seven countries is given in Moore and Moore (1985), which includes monthly values of the indices up to the end of 1982, as well as sources and compilation details. Strigel and Ziegler (1988) give a brief summary of 160 business cycle and consumer sentiment surveys in 42 countries.

For the UK, cyclical indicators are published each month in *Economic Trends*. There are two leading indicators, a longer one with a mean lead of 12 months, and a shorter one with a mean lead of five months. The components of the longer one are a three month interest rate, the financial surplus/deficit of industrial and commercial companies deflated by the GDP deflator, the number of dwellings started, the Financial Times Actuaries 500 share index and the change in optimism in the Confederation of British Industry quarterly survey of firms. Details of the behaviour of the components of the composite indicators are given in the mid-month of each quarter issue of *Economic Trends*.

Klein (1986) has applied the leading indicator approach to forecasting inflation in seven countries. He points out that fluctuations in inflation rates are closely tied to the growth cycle, but six of the countries had experienced a growth recession during which inflation continued to rise. The leading indicators examined are the percentage of the working age population employed, the annual rate of change of basic industrial market prices, and the annual rate of change in total credit outstanding in the economy. These all have economic justifications for their role: as the labour market tightens, labour costs rise and higher wages and employment increase demand, basic industrial prices tend to change before other prices, and domestic credit expansion feeds directly into inflation. A composite index based on these three indicators is also calculated. These leading indicators had all performed satisfactorily for the USA previously and now did so for the six other countries, with median leads of two to eight months at the peaks and troughs of inflation. Klein then relates changes in the leading indicators to changes in the inflation rate in order to forecast the inflation rate and finds correlations (R^2) varying from 0.09 for Italy up to 0.90 for the UK. There is therefore some support for the technique but further evidence of its forecasting ability is needed.

Leading indicators are used by Holmes (1986) to forecast industrial employment in British Columbia. Twenty-one series, covering the stock market, building permits, financial variables, economic variables for British Columbia and leading indicators for Canada, Japan and the USA, are combined into a six month and a twelve month leading indicator. The series are processed first, by smoothing, deseasonalising, inverting (if the series varies counter-cyclically) and standardising for variation, and then combined into a composite index. Rather than choosing the weights subjectively (as in the NBER studies), Holmes determines them by regressing the cyclical variation of the series being forecast on the cyclical variation of each component series, with leads of six or twelve months as appropriate. The relationship between the composite index and industrial employment is then determined by fitting a transfer function model. For the twelve month leading indicator (I) the result is

$$(1 - L^{12})IE_t = 0.75\, I_{t-12} + \{(1 - 0.89\, L^{12})/(1 - 0.74\, L)\}e_t \quad (4.25)$$
$$\phantom{(1 - L^{12})IE_t = } (8.4) \qquad\qquad (31.2) \qquad\quad (12.0)$$

where IE is industrial employment, L is the lag operator and t-values are given in brackets. This equation is used for out-of-sample forecasting for 1981–5 and the accuracy is compared with forecasts from Holt's two parameter linear exponential smoothing model (see (3.40)–(3.42) above). The leading indicator models are more accurate, having smaller mean absolute percentage errors (MAPE) for forecasts 1–12 months ahead. For example, for one-month forecasts the MAPEs are 1.84 for the leading indicator model and 2.80 for Holt's method, and for 12-month forecasts the values are 5.08 and 7.77 respectively. This study illustrates that leading indicators can be used successfully in forecasting.

Leading indicators have also been used by Layton, Defris and Zehnwirth (1986) in forecasting outgoing telephone traffic in Australia. Since there is only one firm in the telephone industry, the research can be interpreted as an industry study or a firm study. They report evidence for 1971–83 which shows that telecommunications traffic is cyclical and correlated with Australia's coincident indicator, so that leading indicators can help in forecasting. Using the techniques of cross-spectral analysis (see for example Chatfield 1980), an average lead time of six months is found to occur between the Australian leading indicator series and telephone traffic. This provides the motivation for building a statistical model of the relationship. The modelling approach used follows Haugh and Box (1977) in which first, separate ARIMA models are fitted to the series to give random (pre-whitened) residuals, the residuals are computed, and then the two series of residuals are related. The estimated ARIMA models for the telephone traffic and leading indicator series are

$$(1 - 0.461L^{12})X_t = (1 - 0.722L)v_t + 0.011 \qquad (4.26)$$
$$\quad (5.62) \qquad\qquad\qquad (12.2) \qquad (5.5)$$

$$(1 - 0.479L)Y_t = u_t. \qquad\qquad\qquad\qquad (4.27)$$
$$\quad (6.39)$$

where L is the lag operator, X is the first difference of the natural logarithm of telephone traffic, Y is the first difference of the natural logarithm of the leading indicator, and v and u are residuals. The numbers in parentheses are t-values. The two series of residuals are found to satisfy

$$v_t = \rho u_{t-5} + w_t \qquad\qquad\qquad\qquad (4.28)$$

where ρ is a constant and w a white-noise residual. By substituting the form of the ARIMA models (4.26) and (4.27) into (4.28) a model relating X and Y is obtained, which is estimated by non-linear least squares to give

$$X_t = 0.010 + 0.490X_{t-12} + 0.742Y_{t-5} - 1.063Y_{t-6}$$
$$\quad (5.00) \quad (5.90) \qquad\quad (1.97) \qquad\quad (1.91)$$

$$+ 0.741Y_{t-7} + (1 - 0.794L)a_t \qquad\qquad (4.29)$$
$$\quad (2.22) \qquad\qquad (13.23)$$

where a is the residual. The forecasting performance of (4.29) was compared with that of (4.27), the ARIMA model, using 36 post-sample observations and was found to give a smaller root mean square error. That is, by using the leading indicator better forecasts are obtained.

The final method of cycle analysis which we consider is the 'average recession and recovery' method suggested by McLaughlin (1982) and used by him for a number of years. This can be applied to any cyclical series and relies on finding the average behaviour of each variable after the peak. For the USA, this is done by starting from the peaks as defined by the NBER and setting the value of the series at each cyclical peak to 100. For each of the six post-war peaks, data for the months following the peak are found and averaged to give a typical pattern for the recovery. This can be plotted on a time-series graph, the standard deviation for each month calculated and an interval of one standard deviation either side of the mean added to the graph to indicate typical uncertainty around the average. Finally the data on the present situation are added to the graph and, by comparison with the average, an idea of the future path of the variable can be found. McLaughlin points out that all the data should be seasonally adjusted. This method is potentially useful in the early months of a recession but, because of the variations in the length of cycles, will be less reliable for predicting the recovery and the next peak.

Research on leading indicators was initially concerned only with the business cycle. The extension of the technique to other areas of activity is still in its infancy, but the evidence we have reviewed suggests that it is likely to be fruitful.

4.5   Scenario analysis

The quantitative forecasting methods with which this book is mainly concerned rely on fitting a model to past data and using the model to extrapolate into the future. This obviously assumes that past trends are a guide to the future and that the model can incorporate changing circumstances. Qualitative, subjective views about developments are generally ignored. Also, there is a tendency, with quantitative forecasts, to produce a single value as the prediction and ignore possible variation around that value. A different approach is to use what are known as 'scenarios' or 'alternative futures'. These are attempts to get away from the possibly misleading precise forecasts given by quantitative methods and instead to adopt a more flexible approach in which extra information can be utilised. While scenarios can be used for both short-term and long-term forecasting, they are probably more useful for the latter.

A scenario may be defined as a 'narrative description of alternative futures' (see Ashley and Hall 1985, p. 66) or 'an account or story about a projected course of action in a possible environment' (see Armstrong 1985, p. 510). It is set up as a case history of the future, in which, for example, details of the environment, competitors' strategies, new discoveries and government actions are all specified. The scenario is presented as a realistic possibility, frequently using persuasive language and colourful imagery. The method of scenario analysis consists of examining a number of different scenarios which are plausible paths to the future. The intention is to persuade decision makers to cope with uncertainty by designing strategies which are adaptable to whatever circumstances arise. It is claimed that by considering a range of possibilities, the chance of an unexpected outcome occurring should be reduced. Also, decision makers will be made aware of the inherent uncertainty in forecasting, so that they will place less confidence in the possibility of any one outcome.

Fildes and Chrissanthaki (1988, p. 15) suggest that this can be achieved by setting up, say, two scenarios for the environment and determining the appropriate company policies for each of them. Then the results of implementing the first policy under scenario two are examined and similarly for the second policy under scenario one. This gives some idea of how sensitive the outcomes are to the policy and the scenario.

The use of scenarios in long-term forecasting is illustrated by Coates (1985) who considers how telecommunication and computer developments might affect the financial services industry in the USA in 1995. Two types of scenario are developed for 1995: one for the state of US society (the macro scenario) and the other for the impact of information technology (the financial services scenario). There are four macro scenarios, chosen to illustrate plausible rather than probable future states of US society in 1995. They are

i continuity and change: business as usual,

ii booming prosperity,

iii regional America and,

iv America goes global.

The first of these extrapolates present trends with no radical changes: a slow growth of real incomes, a small decline in unemployment, larger increases in the percentages of workers in information industries, of homes with cable television and with home computers. The second allows the economy to boom, with real incomes rising by 4.2 per cent per annum, unemployment falling, a smaller increase in workers in information industries (because of the use of robots), and more home computers. The third emphasises a general move away from the national markets towards regional ones, as a result of high transport costs and the growth of smaller-scale manufacturing plants. The final scenario assumes that there is a big growth in US international trade following reductions in trade barriers so that different economies are closely interlinked. Each of these scenarios is specified by a narrative and a table of data. Coates also presents six financial services scenarios, covering institutional diversification, nationwide services, slower growth, regionalisation, global links and international financial chaos. The different types of scenario are examined in combination, but not all combinations are considered likely.

An example used by Schnaars and Topol (1987) to examine the effectiveness of scenarios in sales forecasting involved taking sales data for five years, which showed an upward trend with some lessening of the rate of increase in the last year. Forecasts were required for the next two years. Three scenarios were considered: optimistic, middle ground and pessimistic. The optimistic scenario stated that last year's slowing in growth could be an aberration and that it was likely that sales over the next two years would resume their upward growth. The middle ground scenario suggested that the product was maturing and that sales over the next two years would be steady. The pessimistic scenario assumed that sales had reached a peak and would decline.

In their experiments, Schnaars and Topol compared the accuracy of forecasts both with and without the scenarios. Without the scenarios simple extrapolative models were used. Their conclusion was that there was no evidence that the scenarios improved the accuracy of the forecasts. Also, the use of scenarios caused the forecasters to become more confident about their forecasts, instead of being more aware of other possibilities as is expected by the proponents of the scenario method.

Other applications of scenarios are in strategic planning (see Brauers and Weber 1988) and long-term forecasting (see Leontief 1986, chapter 16). In conclusion, it is clear that scenario analysis has the potential of being a worthwhile alternative (or supplement) to quantitative forecasting. However, there are many problems in its implementation. Little evidence is available on how many scenarios should be used, how they are best constructed, and whether they result in better forecasts. There is a need for research into these matters.

4.6   Other techniques

Various methods have been suggested for generating forecasts using judgement. One of the simplest is *PERT* (Program Evaluation and Review Technique), which arose in the operational research literature in the solution of network problems. Strictly, this is not a method of forecasting: it is a way of processing information about forecasts in order to make them more reliable. An expert is asked to make three forecasts of, say, sales next year. These are (i) pessimistic or low (L), (ii) most likely or middle (M) and (iii) optimistic or high (H). If it is assumed that the distribution of the variable is approximately normal then an estimate of the mean forecast is

$$\text{Mean} = \frac{L + 4M + H}{6} \tag{4.30}$$

and an estimate of the standard deviation of the forecast is

$$\text{Standard Deviation} = \frac{H-L}{6} \qquad (4.31)$$

For example, forecasts $L = 50$, $M = 130$ and $H = 150$, give an estimated mean of 120 with standard deviation 16.7. Thus an approximate 95 per cent confidence interval, covering two standard deviations either side of the estimated mean, is 86.6 to 153.4.

The advantages of the PERT method are its simplicity, since it can be used by managers with few quantitative skills, and the fact that confidence intervals, which give an idea of the uncertainty in the estimated mean, can be calculated. It assumes that reliable values of L, M and H can be found, and that the normal distribution applies.

The uncertainty in forecasts can also be allowed for by the *expected-value method*. This starts by assuming that a probability can be attached to each of the different outcomes of the variable being forecast. The expected value is simply the mean of the probability distribution. In general, these probabilities are decided subjectively, but they must satisfy the laws of probability in that they have a minimum value of zero (the outcome never happens), a maximum value of one (the outcome always happens), and they sum to one. For example, sales of a product next year (S) may be forecast to be 50, with a probability of 0.1, 80 with a probability of 0.3, 130 with a probability of 0.4, and 150 with a probability of 0.2. These can be combined by forming the expected value of sales, defined by

$$E(S) = \Sigma P(S_i)S_i \qquad (4.32)$$

where i denotes a particular forecast and the summation is for all values of i. For the example,

$$E(S) = 0.1(50) + 0.3(80) + 0.4(130) + 0.2(150) = 111$$

That is, the expected value of sales is 111. Notice that this is not one of the values which was given a positive probability, and so this can be regarded as a weakness of the expected-value method. A variation is to allocate probabilities to ranges of outcomes rather than single values. As with the PERT method, interval estimates can be obtained by calculating the variance using the formula variance $= \Sigma P(S_i)(S_i - E(S_i))^2$.

The concept of expected value can be extended to apply to conditional events, leading to the use of *Bayesian decision theory*. For example, sales of a product may be affected by the general state of the economy, and suppose that there are three situations which are considered likely to occur: a general expansion, no change and a depression, which have probabilities of 0.2, 0.5 and 0.3, respectively. More formally, if E_1 is the event that there is a general expansion of the economy, E_2 is the event that there is no change in the economy and E_3 is the event that there is a depression, then

$$P(E_1) = 0.2, P(E_2) = 0.5, P(E_3) = 0.3 \qquad (4.33)$$

Each of these will result in a different value of S, the level of sales next year, and, using (4.32), the expected value of sales in the three cases might be 150, 130 and 90. That is, using the standard notation for conditional events,

$$E(S/E_1) = 150, E(S/E_2) = 130, E(S/E_3) = 90 \qquad (4.34)$$

These are alternatives which depend on the appropriate conditions being satisfied. The final stage is therefore to use the rules of conditional probability to combine the probabilities of these alternatives and the expected values of sales to give the expected value of the combined events of the state of the economy and the levels of sales. The result is

$$E(S) = \Sigma P(E_i)E(S/E_i) \qquad (4.35)$$
$$= 0.2(150) + 0.5(130) + 0.3(90) = 122$$

This is the expected value of sales next year, taking account of the three possible states of the economy and the effects these have on the level of sales. The approach can be generalised to include further factors (see, for example, Targett 1983, chapter 8 or Gross and Peterson 1976, chapter 2). A good introduction to Bayesian statistics is given by Hey (1983) and to the wider use of Bayesian methods in forecasting by Fildes (1984).

This consideration of uncertainty leads to our final technique which is concerned with forecasting probabilities. An example of this arises in predicting whether a particular firm will go bankrupt during the coming year. If the probability of bankruptcy can be estimated then this can be used for forecasting. Peel, Peel and Pope (1986) relate the probability of bankruptcy to accounting measures such as the ratio of working capital to total assets, sales divided by total liabilities and the flow of funds divided by total liabilities. Other examples relate the probability of buying a product to the level of income, age and housing status (see Fisher 1962), and the probability of voting for a particular candidate to the age and education level of the voter (see Pindyck and Rubinfeld 1981, p. 283).

Two general approaches are available for forecasting probabilities. The first, known as the *linear probability model* uses a zero-one dummy variable, representing the absence or presence of the appropriate characteristic, as the dependent variable which is related to a number of explanatory variables. For example, suppose that the variable Y_i takes the value one if person i owns a car, and the value zero otherwise, and that car ownership varies with the level of income (X_i). The linear probability model is

$$Y_i = \alpha + \beta X_i + u_i \qquad (4.36)$$

where u_i is a disturbance term. If P_i is the probability that person i owns a car (so that Y_i is 1) then $(1 - P_i)$ is the probability that Y_i is 0. It follows that the mean value of Y is

$$E(Y_i) = (1 - P_i).0 + (P_i).1$$
$$= P_i$$
$$= \alpha + \beta X_i$$

so that P_i is the conditional probability of Y_i, given the value of X_i. Thus, estimating (4.36) is a way of forecasting P_i. However, as explained in standard econometric texts (see Gujarati 1988, Maddala 1988), there are a number of statistical problems with the linear probability model. The major ones are that the error term is not normally distributed and is heteroskedastic, and that the predicted probability is not limited to the range zero to one.

The second approach is to observe groups of individuals, say firms in a certain industry or households in particular income ranges and composition categories, and get a direct measure of the value of P_i. This is then explained by the other variables. Care is needed in the way the groups are defined. In the *logit model* the basic equation is

$$\log_e(P_i/(1 - P_i)) = \alpha + \beta X_i + u_i \tag{4.37}$$

Extra explanatory variables can be added in the usual way. In the *probit model* the observed probability is converted to a utility index by assuming that a cumulative normal distribution applies, and this index is related to the explanatory variables. With both the logit and probit models heteroskedasticity remains a problem but the functional forms ensure that the predicted probabilities lie in the range zero to one. Further details are given in the references mentioned above.

CHAPTER 5

Forecasting with macroeconomic models

5.1 Introduction

In this chapter we consider the role of macroeconomic models in the forecasting process. The use of macroeconomic models has developed extensively since the 1960s. In the US private institutions have been able to obtain forecasts of the US economy based on the Wharton model since 1963 and for the UK the London Business School has been modelling the economy since 1966. Since that date the number of forecasts based on macroeconomic models has been the subject of considerable expansion and Fildes and Chrissanthaki (1988) suggest that over 100 agencies are involved in making macroeconomic forecasts for the UK. Many of these agencies utilise macroeconomic models for this purpose but, for commercial reasons, details of their forecasting methods are not published. In section 5.2 we examine the general nature of macroeconomic models, followed by the presentation of a simple illustrative model in section 5.3. In section 5.4 we demonstrate how forecasts are prepared using this simple model as an example and in section 5.5 consider the role of judgemental adjustments. Forecasts of the 1980–82 recession are examined in section 5.6 and the decomposition of forecast errors in section 5.7. In section 5.8 we discuss the accuracy of macroeconomic forecasts and our conclusions are presented in 5.9.

5.2 Nature of macroeconomic models

Essentially a macroeconomic model is an attempt to describe an economy. This description may be presented in verbal form, diagrammatic form or in the form of mathematical equations. Standard macroeconomic texts are firmly based in the first two approaches with some use of mathematics. In contrast a macroeconomic model is expressed entirely in the form of equations which are based on the relevant economic theory. It is also empirical in as much as it is estimated from data obtained from the real world. These equations can be divided into three categories. First behavioural equations which describe the activities of economic agents, such as, for example, the consumption function. Second there are the relationships based on technology rather than economic behaviour. An example of a technical relationship is the production function. Finally there are relationships which are true by definition. These are termed identities and the familiar national income identity shown below is just one example

$$Y = C + I + G + X - Im \tag{5.1}$$

where $Y = $ GNP, $C = $ consumption expenditure, $I = $ investment expenditure, $G = $ government current expenditure on goods and services, $X = $ purchases of exports by non-residents and $Im = $ purchases of imports by residents. The general form of a behavioural equation is

$$Y_{1t} = \beta_0 + \beta_1 Y_{2t} + \beta_2 Y_{3t} + \cdots + \gamma_1 X_1 + \gamma_2 X_2 + \cdots + \varepsilon_t \tag{5.2}$$

Within this relationship the βs and the γs are parameters, the Ys are endogenous variables (those variables determined within the model) and the Xs the exogenous variables (those variables determined outside the model). Exogenous variables may be either variables external to the economy concerned, for example general world economic conditions, or goverment policy variables. The error or residual term, ε, is usually assumed to have a mean of zero and represents the impact of unusual events, the effect of items not covered in the model and/or errors in the data. Note in contrast to the endogenous and exogenous variables, values of ε cannot be measured directly since they represent the residual element after the inclusion of other variables. Which variables are endogenous and which are exogenous depends critically on the purpose for which the model is being constructed. Thus, for example, a model intended to forecast foreign trade flows may include imports and exports from a number of countries as separate endogenous variables, while one intended to forecast domestic employment may treat 'world trade' as exogenous. Since an equation or identity is required for each endogenous variable, there is a trade-off between simplicity, which points in the general direction of a small-scale model, and greater detail, indicating a larger-scale model which, it would be hoped, would provide greater accuracy. This trade-off helps to explain the observed wide variation in the size of existing macroeconomic models. For example, for the UK model sizes range from some eight behavioural equations and 24 identities for the Liverpool model (see Minford, Marwaha, Matthews and Sprague 1984) to over 500 equations and identities for recent versions of the Treasury model (see HM Treasury 1987).

Equation (5.2) does not allow for the time necessary for changes in the exogenous variables to have an impact on the endogenous ones. This implies that adjustment takes place immediately so that the economy is always in equilibrium. Clearly this is unrealistic. To allow for lags in the adjustment of the endogenous variables a dynamic specification may be achieved in a number of ways. One method is to include lagged values of the variables $Y_2, Y_3, \ldots, X_1, X_2, \ldots$, which already appear on the right-hand side of the equation. The problem with this simple approach is two fold. First the choice of the lags can be quite arbitrary. Second the number of parameters to be estimated can rise dramatically unless restrictions are placed on the number of lags. A more general approach is to include the dependent variable lagged one period as an explanatory variable on the right-hand side of the equation. This follows from either assuming that a partial adjustment to the desired position occurs in any one period (see (4.12)) or assuming a Koyck distributed lag (see (1.24)). A simple example is

$$Y_t = \beta_0 + \beta_1 X_t + \beta_2 Y_{t-1} \tag{5.3}$$

where stability of the equation requires that the coefficient on the lagged dependent variable (β_2) is less than one. A third approach is the 'error correction' method which has already been discussed in relation to cointegration (see (2.130)). This method has the advantage of distinguishing between long-run influences and short-run adjustment to the desired position. A simple example of the use of the error correction principle is

$$\Delta Y_t = \beta_0 + \beta_1 (Y_{t-1}/X_{t-1}) + \beta_2 \Delta X_t + \varepsilon_t \tag{5.4}$$

The long-run relationship between Y and X is obtained by setting ΔY and ΔX equal to 0 and solving (5.4) to obtain

$$Y = -(\beta_0/\beta_1)X \tag{5.5}$$

which gives the steady state relationship between Y and X. Note this relationship could also be expressed in terms of growth rates rather than levels. A similar steady state relationship can be derived from (5.3) by assuming that $Y_t = Y_{t-1}$ so that

$$Y = (\beta_0 + \beta_1 X)/(1 - \beta_2) \tag{5.6}$$

A further problem pertinent to all, not just macroeconomic, models arises with regard to expectations of future values of variables. In many economic relationships the relevant value of a variable is the expected future value of that variable rather than its current value. For example, investment theory is concerned with the net return expected from a project over a number of years. In fact, expectations are relevant to all decisions taken by economic units and the problem posed is how to model them. One approach is to use survey data. For example Joseph Livingston, a US financial journalist has conducted a twice yearly survey of professional economists in a variety of posts (business, government and academic) to seek their views as to the future course of inflation. See Holden, Peel and Thompson (1985) for a discussion of this. The problem with this approach is that it is not clear that survey data represent the view of all agents. There is a difference between voicing an opinion on the future course of inflation and actually taking economic decisions based on this view. Furthermore the time period of the survey data may not coincide with that required for the model. A second method is to use the adaptive expectations approach in which expectations are determined by past values of the variable. This is achieved by including the lagged value of the dependent variable. A third approach is to derive an expected series through use of a technique such as instrumental variables (see, for example, McCallum 1976). The series derived would then be checked against the actual series using standard diagnostic statistical tests. A fourth method is to assume that the rational expectations hypothesis holds. In this case the model predictions of future values of the relevant endogenous variables are used as the expectations series. For this reason this approach is sometimes termed 'model consistent' expectations in as much as the expectations are those predictions generated by the model.

To sum up therefore construction of a macroeconomic model requires the following steps:

1 Select the appropriate body of economic theory relevant to the model, including the method of expectations formation and dynamic adjustment.

2 Write the theory in a system of equations in a form in which they may be estimated.

3 Obtain the data necessary to estimate the parameters of the model.

4 Use appropriate statistical techniques to estimate the equations.

5 Test the performance of the model. The model has to be acceptable both statistically and economically. Statistical tests concern the properties of the residuals (which should be random), the stability of the parameters and the within-sample forecasting ability. Economic tests include simulating the properties of the model. Two types of simulation are possible. The first uses actual variables for all predetermined variables and is termed 'static' simulation. The second method uses model predictions of the relevant variables for the previous periods for predetermined variables. This method is termed 'dynamic' simulation. These give insights into the way the model responds to shocks.

We will assume that points 1 to 5 have been completed.

5.3   A simple macroeconomic model

In this section we present a simple small-scale macroeconomic model and examine how such a model may be used for forecasting the future course of an economy. At the outset, it should be emphasised that the model is used purely for illustrative purposes and has no relationship to any real economy. We adopt this approach in order to illustrate the general principles of using a model for forecasting without becoming bogged down in the details of any real economy. The model listed below in equations (5.7) to (5.14) is based on that contained in appendix A.2 of Holden, Peel and Thompson (1982). The parameters are therefore imposed rather than estimated.

$$Y = C + I + G + X - IM \tag{5.7}$$

$$C = 0.4*(Y - T/P) + 0.001*(FA/P) + 0.5*C_{t-1} + \varepsilon_1 \tag{5.8}$$

$$T = 0.3*P*Y + \varepsilon_2 \tag{5.9}$$

$$IM = 0.2*Y + \varepsilon_3 \tag{5.10}$$

$$\Delta FA = P*G - T + P*(X - IM) \tag{5.11}$$

$$FA = FA_{t-1} + \Delta FA \tag{5.12}$$

$$\Delta P = 0.00018*(Y - Y_c) + E_t \Delta P_{t+1} + \varepsilon_4 \tag{5.13}$$

$$P = P_{t-1}(1 + \Delta P) \tag{5.14}$$

All variables are timed at current period t unless otherwise stated.

Endogenous variables (8)

C = consumption expenditure (real)

FA = stock of financial assets (nominal)

ΔFA = the change in financial assets (nominal)

IM = volume of imports (real)

P = the price level (index)

ΔP = the rate of inflation

T = tax receipts (nominal)

Y = gross domestic product (real)

Exogenous variables (4)

G = government expenditure (real)

I = investment expenditure (real)

X = volume of exports (real)

Y_c = capacity output (real)

Lagged dependent variables (3)

Consumption (real)

Stock of financial assets (nominal)

Price level (index)

Expectational variable (1)
Rate of inflation

The ε_i refer to the error terms of the behavioural equations. For convenience the period t can be assumed to be one year so that the rate of inflation (ΔP) is measured per annum.

At this stage a brief description of the model is appropriate. The first equation is the national income identity while (5.8), (5.9), (5.10) and (5.13) are the behavioural equations. Equation (5.8) is a simple consumption function in which consumption in real terms depends on real disposable income, the real value of the stock of financial assets and consumption lagged one period representing partial adjustment to desired consumption. Equations (5.9) and (5.10) describe tax receipts and imports as functions of gross domestic product. We assume in (5.9) that the tax rate is set by the government as a policy variable. A Phillips curve is depicted by (5.13) in which the rate of inflation depends on the extent of capacity utilisation and expected inflation. For this latter variable the coefficient is equal to 1, implying a vertical long-run Phillips curve. The identity (5.11) links the growth of financial assets to the budget deficit and the current account of the balance of payments. In (5.12) and (5.14) changes in financial assets and the price level are defined. Again at this stage we would like to reiterate that this model is not put forward as a serious explanation of any economy but rather as a means to explain the use of models in forecasting. For example, obvious defects in the model include the absence of any explanation (or for that matter incorporation of) interest or exchange rates.

5.4   Preparing the forecast

We now move on to consider how the model may be used for forecasting future values of the endogenous variables, for example for the next four years. At this stage we shall assume that expectations are formed according to the adaptive expectations model discussed earlier with the coefficient on lagged inflation $= 1$ (i.e. $E_{t+1}\Delta P_{t+i+1} = \Delta P_{t+i-1}$). This means that (5.13) is respecified as

$$\Delta P = 0.00018*(Y - Y_c) + \Delta P_{t-1} \tag{5.15}$$

In addition all the error terms (ε_i) are assumed to be zero. We will return to these assumptions later. At the outset of the process, the forecaster is faced with a number of problems. These involve (i) the data set available, (ii) the assumptions made about the future course of government policy and (iii) the predicted values of the exogenous variables during the forecast period.

Dealing with the information set, we first of all assume that, with the exception of the tax rate, all the model parameters are known to the forecaster in that they have been estimated previously. This does not mean that all the coefficients are accurate estimates of the unknown coefficients but rather that they are the best estimates available. As we have noted earlier the tax rate is a policy variable set by the government. Consequently it may be altered during the forecast period. Turning now to the data set, we note that in the real world information becomes available at different times and that frequently data for the current period will not be available when forecasts for future periods are made. Thus, for example, national income data are only available after quite a long lag whereas interest and exchange rates are immediately available. Consequently, it is often necessary to forecast the current values of endogenous variables before forecasting future values. For expositional purposes at this stage we ignore the complication that information becomes available at different times and assume that, at time t, the forecaster has knowledge of all variables up to but no later than time $t-1$. Assumptions have to be made about the whole range of policy variables such as, for example, the various tax rates, monetary policy instruments and government expenditure. Because of the difficulties of predicting government expenditure over a long period, alternative forecasts are often produced with each forecast based on a specific assumption regarding future policy. Finally predictions of the future values of the exogenous variables must be made. One method which can be adopted is to use the time-series forecasting methods discussed in chapter 2. Alternatively survey data on, say, investment intentions may be used. A third approach is to take forecasts from highly aggregated models of the world economy. This procedure is followed by the London Business School (see Keating 1985). Alternatively forecasts from international organisations such as the OECD could be used.

The assumptions relevant for preparing forecasts for our simple model are:

1 Data for $Y_{t-1}, C_{t-1}, T_{t-1}, FA_{t-1}, \Delta FA_{t-1}, IM_{t-1}, P_{t-1}$ and ΔP_{t-1} are available but no data for period t are available.

2 Fiscal policy will be unchanged so that the tax rate and the level of government expenditure remain constant at 0.3 and £3500m respectively.

3 The assumed values of the exogenous variables are: exports (X) remain constant throughout the period, investment (I) increases by £100m per period and capacity output (Y_c) increases by £200m per time period.

Because of 1 five forecasts are required from time t to $t+4$ inclusive. It is also worth noting that the model forecasts are conditional upon the forecasts of the exogenous variables and of the tax rates so that inaccurate forecasts may be attributable to either model deficiencies or inaccurate predictions of exogenous variables or of government policy. We return to this point later.

We now turn to how the forecasts or the solution of the model are obtained. If the equations within a model can be ordered in such a way that each equation can be solved sequentially then the model is said to be recursive. Consider the following equation set

$$Y_{1,t} = \beta_{1,1} Y_{2,t-1} + \beta_{1,2} Y_{3,t-1} + \gamma_{1,1} X_{1,t} + \gamma_{1,2} X_{2,t} \tag{5.16}$$

$$Y_{2,t} = \beta_{2,1} Y_{1,t} + \beta_{2,2} Y_{3,t-1} + \gamma_{2,1} X_{1,t} + \gamma_{2,2} X_{2,t} \tag{5.17}$$

$$Y_{3,t} = \beta_{3,1} Y_{1,t} + \beta_{3,2} Y_{2,t} + \gamma_{3,1} X_{1,t} + \gamma_{3,2} X_{2,t} \tag{5.18}$$

Here it is possible to solve (5.16) for Y_{1t} and use the solved value in (5.17) to obtain a solution for Y_{2t} and then obtain a solution for Y_3 from (5.18).

In practice, exact mathematical solutions to macroeconomic models are virtually impossible to obtain due both to the number of equations involved and also the inclusion of non-linear relationships. Consequently an approximate solution is often obtained by an iterative process such as the Gauss–Seidel method. This involves specifying an accuracy or tolerance level and a solution is reached when the change in every endogenous variable is less than the tolerance level prescribed by the user. We illustrate this method using the following two equations, though, of course, it is perfectly general and can be used for any number of equations

$$Y_{1,t} = \beta_{1,1} Y_{2,t} + \cdots + \beta_{1,j} X_{1,t} + \cdots \tag{5.19}$$

$$Y_{2,t} = \beta_{2,1} Y_{1,t} + \cdots + \beta_{2,j} X_{1,t} + \cdots \tag{5.20}$$

where Y_1 and Y_2 are the endogenous variables. The first equation (5.19) is solved for Y_1 using the observed value for $Y_{2,t}$ and the exogenous variables. Subsequently the solved value for $Y_{1,t}$ (say Y_1^*) is then substituted for Y_1 in the second equation (5.20) and a solution obtained for Y_2 (say Y_2^*). The round of iterations is repeated obtaining values for $Y_{1,t}(Y_1^{**})$ using Y_2^* and the exogenous variables. A similar solution is then obtained for $Y_{2,t}(Y_2^{**})$ using Y_1^{**} and exogenous variables. The change in values between Y_1^{**} and Y_1^* and also for Y_2^{**} and Y_2^* are then compared with the tolerance level. If either of the values exceeds the tolerance level specified (say 0.001 for example) then the whole process is repeated until all the changes in the values of the endogenous variables fall within the tolerance level. This procedure is repeated for each time period. Appendix A2 of Holden, Peel and Thompson (1982) contains an example of a computer programme written in 'Basic' to solve a simple macroeconomic model by the Gauss–Seidel method.

As noted earlier the values of the ε_is are set to zero and the starting values for the exogenous variables (in £ millions) are:

Government expenditure $(G)=£3500$ Exports $(X)=£2000$
Investment (I) $=£2500$

Predetermined variables are given the following initial values

Consumption (C) $=£6000$ Financial assets $(FA)=£10000$
Price Level (P) $=1$ Δp $= 0.1$

The model listed in (5.7) to (5.14) is then solved for period t using the Gauss–Seidel method. The forecast for period t would then be used as an input for period $t+1$; for example in period $t+1$ the lagged value of consumption expenditure would be that forecast for period t. Assuming a four period forecasting horizon, this process would be continued until the forecast for period $t+4$ had been prepared. The results are shown in table 5.1.

Notice that the values for the expected inflation variable conflict with the model predictions. Thus, for example, in period $t+4$ the model predicts an inflation rate (ΔP_{t+4}) of -6.39 per cent whereas the expectation of inflation incorporated within the model $(E_{t+3}\Delta P_{t+4})$ is $+3.19$ per cent. Hence we can say that expectations are not model consistent. This follows from our assumption that expectations of inflation within the model are formed adaptively according to the past behaviour of inflation whereas the predictions of the model refer to the future. One way of resolving this problem is to incorporate model predictions of future values as current expectations, that is, adopt the rational expectations hypothesis.

The rational expectations approach ensures that expectations are consistent with the predictions generated by the model solution. There are, however, a number of other problems. For sake of ease of exposition we shall assume, as in (5.13) above, that expectations are formed in period t and relate to period $t+1$ $(E_t\Delta P_{t+1})$. The following discussion is however perfectly general and nothing of significance hinges on this assumption with similar results being obtained with differing timing of expectations formation. Given this assumption and that of rational expectations, inflation in the current period is affected by inflation in period $t+1$. Consequently we could assume any value for $E_t P_{t+1}$ and work back to a solution for ΔP_t. In other words, usually there is no need for there to be a unique solution to equations such as (5.13) in the absence of other restrictions. One such restriction might be the imposition of a terminal condition for the period after the last period of the simulation. Con-

Table 5.1. *Model predictions* (*assuming adaptive expectations*)

Period	Y	C	IM	T	ΔP	FA
	£m	£m	£m	£m	% p.a.	£m
t	12100	6500	2400	3900	7.35	9400
$t+1$	12400	6800	2500	4200	5.54	8600
$t+2$	12700	7000	2500	4400	3.19	7700
$t+3$	12900	7200	2600	4500	−0.62	6600
$t+4$	13100	7300	2600	4300	−6.39	5400

sequently $E_{t+n}\Delta P_{t+n+1}$ is set equal to the imposed terminal condition where n is the forecasting horizon. Generally the imposed terminal condition is related to an equilibrium value, for example the long-run model solution where this is readily available, or perhaps for the exchange rate, the value asserted by purchasing power parity, or for interest rates, interest rate parity, etc. Sensitivity analysis reported in Minford and Peel (1983) suggests that simulation results are not particularly sensitive to changes in the terminal values provided they are set sufficiently far beyond the forecasting horizon which is of interest. Our discussion has followed an intuitive approach and the reader who prefers a more analytical approach is referred to Minford and Peel (1983).

The solution of a rational expectations model requires a substantial amendment to the Gauss–Seidel procedure discussed earlier. The solution reached earlier would be just the first stage of the iteration process and the solutions for the rate of inflation for period $t+1$ and the terminal value would then be substituted into the model to form the expected values for period t. The cycle of iterations would then be repeated until a further set of solutions is obtained for periods t to $t+1$. The values for the expectation series for this second cycle of iterations would then be compared with those obtained from the first cycle. If the differences exceeded a pre-set tolerance level then the whole process would be repeated until the differences fell within the tolerance level. To sum up, therefore, there are two tolerance levels set by the user which serve as criteria for the iteration process. First, given the expectations, there is a tolerance level prescribed for changes in the endogenous variables. Second, once solutions have been obtained for the endogenous variables, a tolerance level is prescribed for changes in the expectations series between cycles of iterations. Both must be satisfied before a solution for the model has been obtained.

Following this procedure, our model was then solved with an imposed terminal condition of the rate of inflation = 0 for period $t+5$. The results of this simulation are shown in table 5.2. Note in this simulation expected

Table 5.2. *Model predictions (assuming rational expectations)*

Period	Y	C	IM	T	ΔP	FA
	£m	£m	£m	£m	% p.a.	£m
t	12600	6660	2500	5200	37.67	9600
$t+1$	13000	7000	2600	7000	30.90	8700
$t+2$	13300	7200	2700	8800	22.21	7300
$t+3$	13500	7400	2700	10100	13.48	5400
$t+4$	13700	7600	2700	10900	5.84	3100

inflation is model consistent since the predicted inflation for period $t+1$ becomes the expected inflation in period t. It is also interesting to note the differing predictions obtained for this simulation, as compared with those shown in table 5.1, thus illustrating the importance of the correct specification of a model.

5.5   Judgemental adjustments and forecast errors

Howrey, Klein and McCarthy (1974) have stressed the need for 'tender loving care' in using models. In other words models should not be used mechanistically but modified to allow for changing circumstances. One method of doing this is to adjust the residuals (the ε_is) from their expected value of zero in (5.7) to (5.14) to make allowance for other factors. This process is termed constant adjustments, residual adjustments, add factors or sometimes simply 'adjustments'. A number of reasons may be advanced for adjusting the residuals. First additional information may have become available and a quick method of introducing the new information into the model is by adjusting the residual. Keating (1985) terms the use of outside information together with the formal use of the model as 'conjectural analysis'. A second justification concerns the past performance of a specific equation within a model. For example it may be known that a specific equation has performed badly in the past in as much as it generally under or over predicts so that the residual between the actual and forecast error is consistently different from zero. One way to resolve the problem is to make allowance for this bias in the equation by incorporating an offsetting adjustment in the constant term. Of course it may be argued that the correct procedure is to re-estimate the offending equation and this is obviously the preferred long-run solution. On the other hand, constant adjustments provide a quick method of introducing a correction. The third reason for adjusting the residuals arises where the model prediction differs from the modeller's *a priori* beliefs. This is a case of pure judgement and the modeller may wish to adjust the prediction in line with his beliefs. The criticism often levelled against this approach is that the user of the forecast is unaware of how the model has been modified to produce the forecast. An empirical assessment of the effects of adjustments is presented in section 5.7, after we examine some forecasts for the United Kingdom.

5.6 Forecasting the 1980–1982 recession

As an illustration of the analysis of forecasts made at a particular time we will examine an interesting study in which Barker (1985) compares various forecasts made in the United Kingdom during 1979 and 1980. Other examples of this approach are provided by Wallis (1989), for the 1974–5 recession and Artis (1982), for forecasts published late in 1981. We select the 1980–2 recession because in May 1979 there was a general election at which the Conservative party won power. In the June budget following the election new economic policies were introduced which have become known as the 'Monetarist Experiment' and 'Thatcherism'. These are discussed in various places including Buiter and Miller (1981) and Barker (1980), and the details are set out in the *National Institute Economic Review*, August 1979, p. 57. The major changes were:

1 an increase in value added tax from 8 per cent to 15 per cent,

2 a reduction in the standard rate of income tax from 33 per cent to 30 per cent,

3 a refusal to consider short-term demand management policies,

4 a statement of the intention to cut public spending,

5 a proposal to control inflation by tight monetary policy,

6 a commitment to a floating exchange rate.

The introduction of these policies coincided with a steep rise in oil prices in mid 1979 and an appreciation of sterling. In late 1979 a severe recession started, described by Barker (1985, p. 133) as 'comparable to the great depression 1929–1933'. Between 1979 and 1981 output fell by 5 per cent, and unemployment increased from 1.3 million to 3 million. Retail price inflation rose from 10.3 per cent in May 1979 to a peak of 21.9 per cent in May 1980 before declining to 5.4 per cent by the end of 1982.

Since a correctly specified economic model should have been able to forecast the outcome of these policies, Barker examines the accuracy of forecasts made around this time. Forecasts from five organisations are

Table 5.3. *Forecasts of the growth of GDP in 1975 prices (% change per annum)*

Forecaster	Date of forecast	Measure used	1979	1980	1981	1982
CE	March 1979	(a)	0.8	1.8	2.3	1.9
	June 1979	(a)	−0.7	−0.5	−0.3	0.2
LBS	Feb 1979	(a)	2.4	3.0	2.0	2.3
	July 1979	(a)	1.6	−0.4	1.7	3.4
NI	May 1979	(b)	1.6	2.1	−	−
	Aug 1979	(b)	0.5	0.5	−	−
CEPG	April 1979	(c)	3.0	1.6	0.2	0.9
	April 1980	(c)	1.1	−6.1	−3.6	−1.3
LPOOL	March 1980	(b)	−	0.0	1.6	2.9
Outcome		(a)	2.5	−2.8	−2.3	1.0

Note: − no forecast published.

GDP measure: (a) output at factor cost,
(b) average at factor cost,
(c) average at market price.

Source: Compiled from tables 1 and 2 of Barker (1985).
The outcome series is from *Economic Trends* 1983.

reviewed: Cambridge Econometrics (CE), the London Business School (LBS), the National Institute of Economic and Social Research (NI), the Cambridge Economic Policy Group (CEPG) and the Liverpool Research Group in Macroeconomics (LPOOL).

Barker considers *ex ante* forecasts of percentage changes of GDP, unemployment and inflation for each year from 1979 to 1982. The GDP forecasts made before and after the June 1979 budget are presented in table 5.3. The first point to notice is that three different definitions of GDP are used which makes comparisons of outcomes awkward. In fact, the different measures moved closely together over this period so this turns out to be unimportant. Before the June 1979 budget the LBS forecast for 1979 was the most accurate, with CE and NI being rather pessimistic and CEPG being too optimistic. Also, only CEPG expected 1980 to have lower growth than 1979. After the June 1979 budget, the forecasts for 1979 were all revised downwards by at least 0.8 per cent, with CE being the only one forecasting a decline in GDP. While NI now expected growth in 1980 to be the same as in 1979, CE and LBS expected a further decline and CEPG forecast a big fall in the growth rate. Over the four years, CE and CEPG were expecting an overall decline in GDP, whereas LPOOL (which first published forecasts in March 1980) was much more optimistic. Both LBS and CEPG expected 1980 to be the year with the lowest growth, with increases in the growth rate to 1982. The outcomes show the true picture was relatively high growth in 1979, a sharp fall in 1980, a further fall in 1981 and then an increase in 1982. Thus it can be seen that prior to the June 1979 budget the LBS forecast for 1979 was reasonably accurate, but the revisions made by LBS and the other groups after the budget over-estimated the speed of impact of the measures taken. The new forecasts for 1980, 1981 and 1982 were too optimistic (except for CEPG, which was too pessimistic) and the depth of the recession was incorrectly forecast. However, when the total change in GDP between 1978 and 1982 is considered, the June 1979 CE forecast of an average growth rate of -0.3 per cent per annum is remarkably close to the outcome of -0.4. The other groups were less successful, with LBS forecasting 1.6 in June 1979 and CEPG -2.5 in April 1980. Barker also examines forecasts of unemployment, which turn out to be similar to GDP, and inflation, where LPOOL forecast lower rates than the outcomes and the other groups higher rates. Also, the forecasts based on quarterly models (LBS and NI) were, on the whole, better for the current year while the annual models gave better long-term forecasts.

Our general conclusion from this study is that the various organisations did not successfully predict the timing or depth of the recession. There are a number of possible explanations for this. First, the change in the growth rate from 2.5 per cent in 1979 to -2.8 per cent in 1980, a drop of 5.3 per cent, was large by recent standards and was therefore not predicted accurately. Models fitted to less turbulent data did not give the correct response to the large changes which occurred in 1979 and 1980. Second, in the early months and years of the Thatcher government there was much speculation in the press and on television about the likelihood of a 'U-turn', with an abandonment of monetarism and a return to conventional demand management policies, so the forecasters may have taken account of this in their forecasts. That is, the models might have predicted a severe recession but the proprietors could have assumed that the goverment would act to prevent this occurring and so made judgemental adjustments to the forecasts to make the recession less serious. Third, there was an apparent change of behaviour by manufacturing industry in 1980–81 in that the financial squeeze on the company sector resulted in a large reduction in the levels of stocks which was not predicted on the basis of previous behaviour. This allowed consumption to remain high while output fell.

5.7 Decomposition of macroeconomic forecasts

The total forecast error may be attributable to three components; model error, incorrect projection of exogenous variables and residual adjustments discussed above. As an indication of the impact of incorrect projection of

Table 5.4. *Model predictions (increased government expenditure of +£500m)*

Period	Y £m	C £m	IM £m	T £m	ΔP % p.a.	FA £m
t	12600	6600	2500	4400	17.03	9700
$t+1$	13000	7000	2600	5800	26.01	8900
$t+2$	13300	7300	2700	8000	35.17	7600
$t+3$	13500	7400	2700	11600	43.00	5400
$t+4$	13700	7600	2700	17500	48.82	1800

the exogenous variables in our simple model, suppose the prediction of future government expenditure was inaccurate and it actually increased by £500m in period t to £4000m and remained constant thereafter. The revised forecast incorporating this assumption in the model (the non-rational expectations version) is shown in table 5.4. In comparison with the details shown in table 5.1 the most dramatic effect is on ΔP. However, too much should not be made of the precise figures which reflect the imposed structure of the simple stylised model and the size of the error. The model is quite sensitive to changes in GNP via the inflation equation (5.13) and the size of the forecast error is relatively large (£500m error against a forecast of £3500m). The main point is to note that the model predictions have changed due to a change in the underlying assumption concerning government macroeconomic policy. As far as the purchaser of a forecast is concerned, the relative importance of the individual errors components is not particularly important. What matters is the accuracy of the forecast however arrived at. For example if the forecaster's model always provided bad predictions but these were corrected by judgemental adjustments, then the end user of the forecast would be perfectly satisfied. Obviously, if the model itself is being appraised, then this is no longer true and the important error component would be model error.

In this connection we now consider a study by Artis (1982) of the forecasts produced late in 1981 by CEPG, LBS, LPOOL, NI and the Economist Intelligence Unit (EIU) for 1980 to 1983. In this case outcomes were not known and so the emphasis is on explaining the differences between the forecasts.

Three types of forecast were examined from each organisation. The first are those published in the usual manner in October/November 1981, the 'main forecasts', being the organisation's views about the future state of the economy. As explained earlier, these rely on the estimated model, assumptions about the future path of exogenous variables, and judgemental adjustments to the forecasts produced by the models.

The next ones are a set of forecasts using 'common assumptions' that had earlier been commissioned by the House of Commons Select Committee on the Treasury and Civil Service. These assumptions concerned the percentage change from the second quarter of 1981 to the fourth quarter of 1982 of a number of exogenous variables including North Sea oil output, the world oil price, the $/£ exchange rate, world and domestic interest rates, world trade, government expenditure and tax rates. For details see the companion paper by the Bank of England included with Artis (1982). It was assumed that these forecasts were also subjected to judgemental adjustment so that differences between these and the first ones are attributable to differences in assumptions about exogenous variable behaviour.

The third set of forecasts, with 'constant residuals', arose from trying to remove the effects of judgemental adjustments on the forecasts. In practice, these adjustments are a mixture of mechanical rules (such as adding a constant equal to the negative of the average error over the last three periods to an equation in order to set the model back on track), and the more subjective incorporation of extraneous information (for example from the CBI survey of employers' expectations about future trends in output and exports). For the present study it was thought important to make some adjustments to the model projections. Rules were specified so that the same adjustments would be made to each forecast. For equations in first-difference form, the errors were set to zero while, for equations in levels, a constant was added to make the average error over the previous four quarters zero.

The effects of these adjustments are illustrated in table 5.5 for quarterly forecasts of GDP growth from NI, LBS and EIU. The EIU forecasts are from using the Treasury model. Artis notes that the 'common assumptions' forecasts are close to the main forecasts suggesting that differences in assumptions about the values of exogenous variables are not important, but this is not the case when constant residuals are imposed. The differences between the main forecast and the constant residuals forecast are due to intervention by the forecaster, and so reflect judgement. This is therefore an important influence on the forecasts.

A similar decomposition of forecasts for the UK has been carried out by Wallis *et al.* (1984), for LBS, NI, CUBS and LPOOL forecasts of growth, inflation and unemployment for 1984 and 1985. The use of common assumptions about the exogenous variables does not affect the divergence of the forecasts, unlike in Artis (1982), but reduces average GDP growth from 5.5 per cent to 4.75 per cent. When constant residuals are imposed along with common assumptions, there is no further effect on the average GDP growth forecast but individual forecasts change. Wallis *et al.* also examine the effect of setting residuals to zero, which is large in the initial

Table 5.5. *Autumn 1981 forecasts of GDP growth* (%)

| | Percentage growth | | |
	1980/81	1981/2	Cumulative
NI			
Main forecast	−3.08	0.58	−2.52
Common assumptions	−2.94	0.61	−2.35
Constant residuals	−3.19	1.44	−1.80
LBS			
Main forecast	−2.87	1.68	−1.24
Common assumptions	−2.96	1.93	−1.09
Constant residuals	−1.29	1.30	0.00
EIU			
Main forecast	−1.34	0.57	−0.78
Common assumptions	−1.39	0.60	−0.80
Constant residuals	−1.56	−2.43	−3.95

Source: Based on table 6 of Artis (1982). GDP is measured at 1980 prices.

period but this lessens as the forecast horizon increases. The conclusions from this are that judgemental adjustments by forecasters are important and also that, once the assumptions and residuals are standardised, there still remain sizeable differences due to the influence of the models.

These studies by Artis (1982) and Wallis *et al.* (1984) did not have the outcomes series available so that they could not consider the accuracy of the forecasts. However, Wallis *et al.* (1986) examine the forecasts for 1984 and 1985 just discussed to see the effects of errors in the assumptions about the exogenous variables. A selection of their results is given in table 5.6. They consider the published forecast, a forecast using the actual values of the exogenous variables (AE) and one using both the actual values of the exogenous variables and zero residuals (ZR). The last of these is essentially the 'hands-off' or *ex post* mechanical forecast, before any adjustments are made. These forecasts can be seen to be inaccurate, suggesting that the models are likely to be misspecified. A comparison of the forecast with AE and the forecast with both AE and ZR gives the effects of residual adjustments, and, as previously, these are seen to be important. Finally, the use of the actual values of the exogenous variables instead of the assumed values generally worsens the forecasts. Of course, if these values had been known when the forecasts were made, the judgemental adjustments to the forecasts would have differed, resulting in different forecasts being pub-

Table 5.6. *Autumn 1984 forecasts of real GDP growth* (%)

	1984	1985
LBS		
Published forecast	2.4	2.4
Forecast with AE	3.8	1.2
Forecast with AE and ZR	6.4	2.0
Actual	3.1	3.4
NI		
Published forecast	2.0	1.0
Forecast with AE	3.1	−0.2
Forecast with AE and ZR	6.1	1.9
Actual	3.1	3.4
CUBS		
Published forecast	4.9	3.3
Forecast with AE	7.1	4.5
Forecast with AE and ZR	4.5	6.3
Actual	3.1	3.4
LPOOL		
Published forecast	3.4	3.0
Forecast with AE	3.7	6.3
Forecast with AE and ZR	5.6	7.9
Actual	1.7	3.3

Note:
AE = actual values of exogenous variables.
ZR = zero residuals.
GDP is at 1980 prices and is the output measure except for LPOOL which is expenditure measure.

Source: based on Wallis *et al.* (1986), table 4.7.

lished. In their conclusions, Wallis *et al.* (1986) comment that residual adjustments tend to compensate for errors in the models and/or errors in the exogenous variables, indicating that the forecasters' judgement is correct. However, this also implies that the models are not particularly good forecasting tools. Wallis (1989) arrives at similar conclusions concerning the decomposition of forecast errors.

Wallis *et al.* (1986) go on to look at the effects of data revisions on forecasts. The basic problem is that macroeconomic data are imperfect measures of the true values of the variables and, for many series, as time passes more information becomes available. This results in the previously published figures being revised to be, hopefully, more accurate estimates of the true values. There are a number of effects these revisions might have on forecasts. They might change

1 the forecasters' understanding of how the economy works,

2 the estimated coefficients of the macroeconomic model,

3 the projected pattern of future values of the exogenous variables,

4 lagged values of variables in the forecast equations,

5 recent residuals and therefore the residual adjustments made to any forecasts.

Wallis *et al.* limit consideration to the way revisions affect data for the previous six quarters so that only 4 and 5 are relevant. After re-computing the residuals and forecasts, the conclusion is that the changes are small and unimportant for this particular data set.

5.8   Accuracy of macroeconomic forecasts

Next we turn to the analysis of time series of macroeconomic forecasts. In this a straightforward comparison of forecasts and outcomes is made in order to see which forecasts are the most accurate. Comparisons are made of forecasts made at the same time over particular horizons. This method is easy to carry out but it is important to realise its limitations. First, there is an assumption that aggregating forecasts over time is sensible. However, it is well known that economic circumstances change so that in some periods (for example when a war breaks out or immediately after a stock market collapse) forecasting can be particularly difficult. Also, a few bad forecasts over a restricted period can result in a poor overall performance. Related to this is the fact that comparisons are made for particular historical periods and changing the period may change the result. Second, models develop as time passes so that a series of forecasts is from a sequence of slightly different models, sometimes with changing staff. Because of the judgemental input into forecasts, any comparison reveals the ability of the forecasting organisation rather than the truth or otherwise of the model. Third, we have seen that there are a number of alternative criteria for measuring forecast accuracy – mean square error, mean absolute error, mean square percentage error, etc. – which can give different rankings so that there is no guarantee that a method that performs well under one criterion is satisfactory under the others. The result is that any conclusions from a given data set should be regarded only as indicators of forecasting ability and not as proof of the correctness or otherwise of the underlying model.

A number of studies of macroeconomic forecasting accuracy have been carried out, including Cooper (1972), Zarnowitz (1979), Holden and Peel (1983), Fildes (1985) and Wallis *et al.* (1987). We consider two of the more comprehensive recent ones. The first is by McNees (1986) for quarterly forecasts for the USA. He is particularly interested in the performance of Bayesian vector autoregression (BVAR) modelling technique (see, for example, Litterman, 1986b) compared to forecasts from conventional econometric models. As mentioned in chapter 2, section 5 above, in vector autoregression (VAR) models every variable is regarded as endogenous and depends on lagged values of itself and every other variable in the system. This means that VAR models have a large number of variables included in each equation, and so usually suffer from multicollinearity, with the coefficients being imprecisely determined. As mentioned in chapter 2, in BVAR models the prior assumption is that initially each variable follows a random walk, with the data determining whether other variables have an impact. Therefore estimated BVAR models have fewer parameters than VAR models. For forecasting, the main difference between these and conventional econometric models is that VAR and BVAR models, being autoregressive, do not require explicit assumptions about the future course of the economy. That is, they generate unconditional forecasts.

The variables we will consider are quarterly forecasts of the growth (measured at annual rates) of real GNP and the implicit GNP price deflator for the period 1980(2)–1985(1), giving 20 observations. In order to keep the information available to the different forecasters as similar as possible, McNees distinguishes between the release times of the quarterly forecasts. He defines 'early' as those released immediately after the publication of the preliminary estimate of the actual value for the previous quarter, 'mid' as those released after the first revision of the previous quarter's actual, and 'late' as those issued in the third month of the quarter after the second revision. We will consider forecast horizons of one, four and eight quarters ahead, using the root mean square error (RMSE) as the accuracy measure. The list of forecasters is given in table 5.7 and the results are in table 5.8.

The first point about table 5.8 is that the RMSEs generally decline moving down the table, so that the extra information on the previous quarter's actual value improves the forecasts. For real GNP, the accuracy improves as the forecast horizon increases, while this is not so for the GNP deflator. Considering the individual forecasters, it is clear that, while no one forecaster is best over each horizon for both variables, the BVAR forecasts are the best for real GNP over horizons four and eight, and generally the worst for the GNP deflator over all horizons. McNees also examines the performance of forecasts of nominal GNP, money stock, real non-residential fixed investment, 90-day Treasury bill rates and unemployment,

Table 5.7. *Forecasting organisations*

ASA	American Statistical Association and National Bureau of Economic Research Survey
BEA	Bureau of Economic Analysis, US Department of Commerce
BVAR	Litterman's Bayesian Vector Autoregression
Chase	Chase Econometrics
DRI	Data Resources Inc.
GSU	Economic Forecasting Project, Georgia State University
KEDI	Kent Econometric and Development Institute
MHT	Manufacturers Hanover Trust
RSQE	Research Seminar in Quantitative Economics, University of Michigan
TG	Townsend-Greenspan & Co., Inc.
UCLA	University of California Los Angeles, School of Business
WEFA	Wharton Econometric Forecasting Associates, Inc.

Table 5.8. *RMSEs for US real GNP and GNP deflator quarterly forecasts*

	Real GNP			GNP deflator		
Forecaster Horizon	1	4	8	1	4	8
Early quarter						
BEA	3.7	3.4	–	1.4	1.1	–
BVAR	4.2	2.2	1.7	2.1	3.3	4.1
Chase	4.4	3.0	2.0	1.4	1.7	2.4
DRI	4.0	2.8	2.0	1.6	1.6	2.5
GSU	3.7	2.6	2.1	1.9	1.8	2.3
RSQE	3.3	2.6	–	1.6	1.4	–
WEFA	4.2	2.7	2.0	1.7	1.9	2.4
Mid-quarter						
ASA	3.6	2.8	–	1.5	1.4	–
BVAR	3.6	2.1	1.4	2.0	3.3	4.1
KEDI	3.9	2.8	2.6	2.2	1.5	2.3
MHT	4.1	2.8	–	2.0	1.7	–
TG	3.2	2.6	–	1.7	1.8	–
UCLA	3.1	2.5	–	1.4	1.2	–
WEFA	3.1	2.4	1.7	1.9	1.7	2.4
Late quarter						
BVAR	2.8	1.9	1.3	2.5	3.3	4.1
Chase	2.4	2.7	2.0	1.4	1.4	2.2
DRI	2.0	2.5	2.0	1.4	1.4	2.2

Number of observations: 20 for 1 quarter horizon, 17 for 4 quarter horizon and 13 for 8 quarter horizon.

Note: – no forecast published.

See table 5.7 for the names of the forecasting organisations.
Source: based on McNees (1986), tables 1 and 5.

over all horizons from 1 to 8. He finds that the BVAR forecasts of real GNP, unemployment and real non-residential fixed investment are generally among the most accurate forecasts of these variables, while for the GNP deflator and the 90-day Treasury bill rate the BVAR forecasts are among the least accurate.

McNees discusses the relative merits of conventional econometric models and VAR/BVAR models. While unconditional forecasting might seem to be an advantage, it does ignore any non-model information (such as announced policy changes, strikes and other external events) which economists expect to influence the future. He concludes that rather than regarding them as rivals, they should be used as complementary tools, providing different kinds of information to forecasters. Similar conclusions are reached by Lupoletti and Webb (1986) in a study which includes a discussion of alternative VAR models.

The second study of forecasting accuracy we consider is Holden and Peel (1986), in which the emphasis is on combining forecasts from different sources. Quarterly forecasts of the rate of inflation (based on the consumers' expenditure deflator) and the rate of growth of real output (based on the average estimate of GDP) in the UK are examined for 1975(1)–1984(2). The horizon adopted is four quarters, from the current quarter, t, to quarter $t+4$. Since the latest known observation is for $t-6$ to $t-2$ because of publication lags, six-period ahead forecasts are required. Forecasts from three organisations using economic models, London Business School (LBS), the National Institute (NI) and the London stockbrokers Phillips and Drew (PD), are compared with three extrapolation methods. The latter methods are:

1 naive I, a naive 'no change' model, with the forecast being the most recent observed value of the variable (i.e. for $t-6$ to $t-2$);

2 naive II, a 'same change' model, with the forecast being the most recently observed value to which is added the last observed change, so that if the observed value for $t-6$ to $t-2$ is 2 per cent, and for $t-7$ to $t-3$ is 3 per cent, the forecast is 1 per cent;

3 an ARIMA forecast (see chapter 2) from a sequence of models estimated using data available at the time the forecast is required.

The results are presented in table 5.9 where it can be seen that the smallest RMSEs in the first period are for NI and for the second period are LBS. These two forecasters are clearly more accurate than the others, with the NI being slightly better on inflation for the combined data, and LBS better on growth. This reinforces the evidence from McNees (1986) discussed above showing that no single organisation dominates on every variable for every period. Naive II is always inferior to naive I, and while the ARIMA

Table 5.9. *RMSEs for UK quarterly growth and inflation forecasts*

	Period			
	1975(1)–1979(4)		1980(1)–1984(2)	
	Growth	Inflation	Growth	Inflation
LBS	2.29	4.87	1.16	2.23
NI	2.27	4.32	2.33	2.47
PD	3.05	6.15	3.61	3.68
Naive I	3.75	6.34	3.59	3.78
Naive II	4.75	7.01	3.94	3.98
ARIMA	3.29	7.28	2.91	4.19

Source: Holden and Peel (1986), table 1.

forecasts for growth are better than these, the inflation ones are the worst of all. These poor results for the extrapolation models are partly because the forecasts are for the four-quarter rate of change of the variable starting six periods beyond the data. Since extrapolation models are intended for short-term forecasting it could be argued that they are inappropriate in these circumstances.

5.9   Conclusions

Use of a macroeconomic model imposes consistency over the forecasts of a number of series. Thus to take a trivial example, forecasts of the individual components of GNP must be consistent with the forecast of total GNP because of the imposition of the national income identity. This is just one example of the series of relationships underlying a model of the whole economy. Furthermore any model can easily be adapted to include additional relationships required by the user. For example, demand for a specific industry of interest to the user of the model could easily be the subject of additional equation(s). In this case consistency could be ensured between forecasts for the economy and the specific industry. In a similar way, government requirements for policy design can be accommodated through the inclusion of detailed tax and government expenditure functions. On the other hand the use of macroeconomic models is not without its critics. We mentioned earlier that an assumption is made that the estimated coefficients are constant. The important question is whether they are really invariant to changes in the economic environment, including changes in government policy regimes. Would the behaviour of economic agents really remain the same if the UK adopted a fixed exchange rate by joining the EMS? This caveat is known as the Lucas critique (Lucas (1976)) – see chapter 1, section 1. In principle a change in behaviour can show itself in two ways. First, the expectations held by agents may change. Second, their actual behaviour pattern may change so that parameter values are different. The adoption of the rational expectations hypothesis takes care of the first change but this still leaves open the case of change in behaviour. One way round this is to make 'residual' adjustments as discussed earlier.

The construction of a macroeconomic model requires considerable resources and expertise though, in practice, forecasts (or even access to a model) may be purchased. The advantage to the end user of forecasts based on macroeconomic models relative to other forecasting methods is essentially an empirical question. Are such forecasts better? This aspect is considered in chapter 7.

CHAPTER 6

Forecasting asset market prices

6.1 Introduction

In this chapter we examine whether it is possible or, for that matter, necessary to forecast asset prices. In this connection a useful distinction has been made by Hicks (1974) between a fix price market (where prices are relatively sticky) and a flex price market (where prices are free to move). In this latter type of market prices fluctuate according to conditions of demand and supply. A wide range of types of contracts exist including contracts for both immediate delivery (spot deals) and also for delivery in the future (futures). Arbitrage between traders for both spot deals and futures should produce a set of market prices which provide forecasts of future prices, thus eliminating the need to forecast asset prices through the use of formal forecasting methods. In other words, is forecasting futile when market forces already provide forecasts of future prices within the market price structure? In section 6.2 we consider the efficient markets hypothesis (EMH) which states that a market is efficient if market prices reflect all the available information. We examine the evidence for and the implications of this hypothesis from the foreign exchange market, stock market and commodities markets in sections 6.3, 6.4 and 6.5 respectively. These topics have been the subject of a considerable volume of literature so our discussion has, of necessity, to be selective. We therefore concentrate on work which indicates current thinking, giving more space to the foreign exchange market because it has been the subject of much recent discussion. We shall also restrict the analysis to the forecasting of spot rates rather than futures. Our conclusions are presented in section 6.6.

6.2 The efficient markets hypothesis

The term efficiency when applied to markets can take a number of forms. The first meaning of efficiency is concerned with whether markets operate at a low level of cost. This facet is termed operational efficiency. A second meaning concerns the role of market prices in the allocation of resources. This is termed allocative efficiency. The third aspect is informational efficiency which relates to whether market prices reflect all the available information. It is this last form of efficiency to which the efficient markets hypothesis is applicable. More precisely, a market is said to be efficient if the prices of assets traded in the market always reflect all the information in a defined information set. Fama (1970) has categorised informational efficiency as:

i Weak efficiency: In this case prices reflect all the information contained in the past prices of that asset.

ii Semi-strong efficiency: In this case prices reflect all the information that is publicly available.

iii Strong efficiency: In this case prices reflect all information, both private and public, relevant to the market.

These categories are interdependent since strong efficiency implies semi-strong and weak efficiency and similarly semi-strong efficiency implies weak efficiency. Nevertheless the term efficiency must be hedged to some extent since it is unlikely that any market could be so completely efficient that all prices adjust instantaneously to new information. If this were so there would be a serious question over the incentive to seek out new information since, by definition, it would always be discounted within the market price. This point has been discussed in the relevant literature (see for example Grossman and Stiglitz 1976 and Hellwig 1982). A further factor is that agents other than market traders tend to observe prices at discrete intervals. Thus, for example, the prices quoted in the financial press normally refer to end-of-day trading prices so that consequently the assumption is often made that arbitrage has taken place during the trading period to eliminate abnormal profit/loss situations.

Organised markets such as financial and commodity markets are 'flex price' markets and have special features which suggest that they may be approximately efficient. First, the assets traded are durable assets in the sense that the return includes both a running yield and a capital gain. This is more appropriate to financial markets than commodity markets where the return refers to changes in price relative to the general rate of inflation. The second feature of these markets is that there is continuous trading. Many of these markets are truly international so that there is trading for virtually 24 hours each day. This has been assisted by the revolution in information technology which ensures that prices are determined according to world trading conditions. Moreover, the trading costs are particularly low for large lots. This point is true not only for financial markets but also for commodity markets where title to the goods is easily traded. The effect of these points is that the prices are free to move immediately in response to changes in conditions of demand and supply so that actual market prices should approximate the equilibrium price. In addition many of these markets contain a wide range of types of transactions. First all the markets deal in spot transactions where the asset is traded for immediate delivery. A second type of transaction concerns 'futures' in which a price is agreed now but actual delivery of the commodity/asset takes place at a specified future date thus implying a forecast of the future price of the asset. The actual title of the asset may well be traded more than once before delivery takes place. Finally there are options whereby the trader buys or sells the right (but not the obligation) to purchase or sell an asset. One of the determinants of the prices of futures and options is an expectation of how the price of the underlying asset will move between the time of the agreement and the date of delivery. Hence, given an efficient market, prices would be expected to reflect both current and expected market conditions.

In much of the literature, the assumption has been made that, in an efficient market, prices will follow (approximately) a random walk. Now whilst it is true that a random walk is a sufficient but not a necessary condition for market efficiency, it is worthwhile describing briefly the random walk process. As noted in chapter 2 (2.126), a random walk may be described by

$$Y_t = Y_{t-1} + \varepsilon_t \tag{6.1}$$

where ε is the white noise error term with $E(\varepsilon_t) = 0$, $E(\varepsilon_t \varepsilon_s) = 0$ for $s \neq t$ and $E(\varepsilon^2) = \sigma^2$ for all t. Allowance for a trend (or drift) can be made by including a constant (d)

$$Y_t = Y_{t-1} + d + \varepsilon_t \tag{6.2}$$

Assuming no time trend (i.e. $d = 0$) a forecast can be made for period $t + 1$

$$
\begin{aligned}
E_t(Y_{t+1}) &= E(Y_t, \ldots) \\
&= Y_t + E(\varepsilon_t) \tag{6.3} \\
&= Y_t \tag{6.4}
\end{aligned}
$$

Similarly the forecast two periods ahead

$$
\begin{aligned}
E_t(Y_{t+2}) &= E(Y_{t+1}, \ldots) \tag{6.5} \\
&= E_t(Y_{t+1} + \varepsilon_{t+2}) \\
&= E_t(Y_t + \varepsilon_{t+2} + \varepsilon_{t+1}) \\
&= Y_t \tag{6.6}
\end{aligned}
$$

Consequently if prices do follow a random walk then today's price provides a forecast of future prices since the price will only change in response to the receipt by the market of new information which is, by definition, not forecastable. A slight modification is necessary if a time trend exists so that $d \neq 0$, then $E_t(Y_{t+1}) = Y_t + d$ and $E_t(Y_{t+2}) = Y_t + 2d$, etc.

As noted earlier no market can be perfectly efficient in this respect so that market efficiency is essentially a practical matter for the would-be forecaster. The crucial question is whether imperfections are large enough for market operators to exploit and earn an above-normal profit through forecasting future price movements. It is for this reason we are examining in the following sections evidence of the degree of efficiency within the three markets mentioned earlier.

6.3 Foreign exchange markets

The market for foreign currency is truly international with the three major centres being London, New York and Tokyo. Because of overlapping time zones, trading is virtually 24 hours per day. The services offered by the markets include *spot deals* (the purchase of currency for delivery within two days) and *forward sales* (prices are agreed now for delivery at a specified time in the future). In addition there are related markets in options and financial futures. The distinction between forward and futures contracts is that a forward contract is not transferrable and will be carried out by both parties. A futures contract on the other hand is a financial instrument which may be terminated before maturity by an agreed payment normally made through the market authorities. Note also that most futures contracts require payments of margins which are adjusted in the light of price movements of the underlying asset. This involves extra cost to the transactors as compared with forward purchases of currency. During the first ten days of March 1986, the Bank of England (Bank of England Quarterly Bulletin (1986), undertook a survey into the type of business carried out in the London foreign exchange market. The daily average trading was found to be $90 billion per day, with the major currencies traded being the £ and the $ (30 per cent), the DM and the $ (28 per cent) and the $ and the Yen (14 per cent). Eighty-nine percent of the business was between banks. From this it is apparent that the business is wholesale, being carried out by specialist dealers, so it might be expected that prices would reflect the operator's views on the future movements of exchange rates. To pursue this matter further we look at the forecasting performance of spot and forward rates.

There is quite a volume of evidence which suggests that exchange rates approximately follow a random walk, at least for weekly and monthly changes – see for example Frattiani, Hur and Kang (1987) – so that the current spot price would provide a good prediction of the future spot price. On the other hand if persistence can be found in the movement of exchange rates, then, assuming no risk premium, profitable trading rules (such as the use of filter rules discussed in chapter 1, section 2) could exist to beat the market through the use of information readily available. In this connection the hypothesis being tested is weak efficiency. Two important studies of filter rules are Dooley and Shafer (1976) and Logue and Sweeney (1977). Both of these cover a number of currencies and suggest that profits above a 'buy and hold' strategy were obtainable but that losses were incurred in some sub-periods. Similar profit opportunities were identified by Taylor (1986) for the £/$ exchange rate (with daily observations) for the period 1974–82 through the estimation of price trends, though in fact the improvement of the forecasts over market prices was quite small. This raises the question whether the profit is compensation for the risk involved.

Similarly it can be argued that the forward rate should provide predictions about future movements in the spot rate. In the discussion we shall assume initially that speculators are *risk neutral* so that they are indifferent towards risk and are solely motivated by profit. If the current forward rate is above the spot rate expected to exist in the market at the maturity of the forward contract, risk-neutral speculators will sell the currency forward, hoping to buy the currency spot at the maturity of the contract at the lower price. For example assume today's three month forward rate for sterling is 1.75$ per £ and speculators expect the spot rate to be 1.74$ per £ in three months time. If the expectation is realised they would make a profit of 0.01$ per £ for every £ sold forward by purchasing the necessary £s spot on the day of the maturity of the contract. Clearly they would make a loss if the exchange rate moves in the opposite direction and this illustrates the inherent nature of risk neutrality, i.e. that the possibility of such a loss does not deter the speculators from their attempt to take advantage of potential profits. Since the converse also applies, speculative arbitrage should drive the forward rate to be equal to the expected spot rate. This is probably an over-statement since the forward rate reflects the totality of demand for and supply of forward currency, including interest rate arbitrage, not just the speculative demand we are considering. Abstracting from this last caveat the analysis suggests that, given the critical assumption of risk-neutral speculators and the existence of an efficient market,

$$F_{t-1} = E_{t-1}S_t \qquad (6.7)$$

where F_{t-1} is the forward rate in period $t-1$ for delivery of currency in period t and S_t is the spot rate in period t. We follow the convention in the literature of defining the variables as logarithms of the original variables so that (6.7) becomes

$$f_{t-1} = E_{t-1}s_t \qquad (6.8)$$

where the variables are defined as in (6.7) but the lower case letters refer to logarithms. Throughout the remainder of this chapter lower case letters will always denote logarithms. There are a number advantages from doing this. First, a change in the scale of the measurement of a variable (say from units of pounds to units of pence) changes the logarithm by a constant. Second, changes in logarithms are (approximately) percentage changes and so are elasticities. Third, the disturbances in behavioural equations have more desirable properties when logarithms are used. But one of the alleged advantages is that using logarithms avoids the problem of deciding whether to measure exchange rates in units of domestic currency or in units of foreign currency (see Hansen and Hodrick 1980, page 831). The original problem is that if S is the exchange rate measured in units of domestic currency and S' is the exchange rate measured in units of foreign currency then

$$S' = 1/S \tag{6.9}$$

but by Jensen's inequality (see Hall 1988)

$$E(f(Z)) > f(E(Z)) \tag{6.10}$$

Here $f(Z) = 1/S$ so that

$$E(S') > 1/E(S) \tag{6.11}$$

Therefore the following two statements cannot both be true

$$E(S_t) = F_{t-1} \tag{6.12}$$

$$E(S'_t) = F'_{t-1} = 1/F_{t-1} \tag{6.13}$$

where F and F' are the appropriate forward rates. Thus even with efficient markets (6.7) may not be satisfied suggesting that potential profits exist for purely statistical reasons which appear to have no economic rationale. If we now switch to logarithms of the variables where, as before the lower case letters refer to logarithms, then

$$s' = \log(1/S) = -s \tag{6.14}$$

Taking expectations,

$$E(s') = -E(s) \tag{6.15}$$

so that it is now possible for both of the following statements to be true:

$$E(s) = f_{t-1} \tag{6.16}$$

$$E(s') = f_{t-1} \tag{6.17}$$

However a problem still remains. If $E(S) = F_{t-1}$ then, as before by Jensen's inequality,

$$E(\log(S)) > \log E(S)$$

so that

$$E(\log(S)) > \log(F_{t-1}) \text{ (or in our notation } E(s) \neq f_{t-1})$$

This is called Siegel's paradox. However this seems to be a theoretical rather than a practical problem. McCulloch (1975 p. 172) shows that the distortion due to the paradox is 'empirically virtually imperceptible'.

To illustrate the predictive performance of the spot and forward rates we will examine the monthly changes in the \$/£ exchange rate for the period November 1982 to March 1988, giving 65 observations. A number of forward rates are quoted in the financial press and we concentrate on the one month forward rate. Since the data are also monthly, we avoid all the problems of overlapping time horizons. These occur when the data availability and the forecast horizons do not coincide, for example if the data are produced monthly and the forecasting horizon is three months. In the case of overlapping forecasts, the forecast errors are serially correlated up to an order of $m-1$ where m is the forecast horizon defined in terms of the frequency of data observations. In the example quoted above, the data are monthly and the forecasting horizon is three months so $m-1=2$. The data are presented in the table 6.1.

The first stylised fact is that the *forward premium* defined as $f_{t-1} - s_{t-1}$, is less variable than changes in the spot rate. This is substantiated by the data quoted above where the variance (in percentages) of the forward premium and changes in the spot rate are 1.03 and 10.02 respectively. This leads us to doubt the use of the forward rate as a forecast of the future spot rate. In fact a number of studies have shown that the current spot rate is a better predictor of the future spot rate than the appropriate forward rate. For our data table 6.2 gives some simple statistics describing the performance of the two predictors. As would be expected the mean error for both predictors is quite small because positive and negative errors cancel each other out. The other measures point to the current spot rate being a better predictor of the spot rate in one month's time than the one month forward rate. We examine below the role of a risk premium in this context.

Reverting back to (6.2) and assuming a constant trend the spot rate is given by

$$S_t = S_{t-1} + d + \varepsilon_t$$

and a forecast of its change is

$$E_{t-1}(S_t - S_{t-1}) = E_{t-1}(S_t - S_{t-1})/I_{t-1}) \tag{6.18}$$

Table 6.1. *Log sterling/dollar exchange rate October 1982 to March 1988 (end-of-month values)*

	Spot rate	Forward rate		Spot rate	Forward rate
Nov. 1982	0.4811	0.4660	Aug. 1985	0.3576	0.3334
Dec. 1982	0.4316	0.4800	Sept. 1985	0.3590	0.3547
Jan. 1983	0.4234	0.4296	Oct. 1985	0.3845	0.3560
Feb. 1983	0.3818	0.4214	Nov. 1985	0.3585	0.3816
Mar. 1983	0.4479	0.3806	Dec. 1985	0.3390	0.3557
Apr. 1983	0.4614	0.4469	Jan. 1986	0.3913	0.3352
May 1983	0.4290	0.4605	Feb. 1986	0.3898	0.3876
June 1983	0.4217	0.4291	Mar. 1986	0.4229	0.3860
July 1983	0.4165	0.4220	Apr. 1986	0.4020	0.4196
Aug. 1983	0.4043	0.4168	May 1986	0.4120	0.3994
Sept. 1983	0.4038 .	0.4043	June 1986	0.3999	0.4095
Oct. 1983	0.3825	0.4042	July 1986	0.3935	0.3969
Nov. 1983	0.3673	0.3831	Aug. 1986	0.3694	0.3900
Dec. 1983	0.3382	0.3670	Sept. 1986	0.3423	0.3661
Jan. 1984	0.3778	0.3386	Oct. 1986	0.3544	0.3383
Feb. 1984	0.3714	0.3784	Nov. 1986	0.3721	0.3502
Mar. 1984	0.3411	0.3729	Dec. 1986	0.4281	0.3694
Apr. 1984	0.3269	0.3430	Jan. 1987	0.4314	0.4243
May 1984	0.3012	0.3287	Feb. 1987	0.4768	0.4276
June 1984	0.2795	0.3039	Mar. 1987	0.4896	0.4739
July 1984	0.2694	0.2789	Apr. 1987	0.4875	0.4871
Aug. 1984	0.2174	0.2703	May 1987	0.4766	0.4861
Sept. 1984	0.1920	0.2180	June 1987	0.4687	0.4750
Oct. 1984	0.1841	0.1915	July 1987	0.4846	0.4669
Nov. 1984	0.1572	0.1834	Aug. 1987	0.4950	0.4820
Dec. 1984	0.1139	0.1563	Sept. 1987	0.5339	0.4930
Jan. 1985	0.0857	0.1103	Oct. 1987	0.5862	0.5321
Feb. 1985	0.1882	0.0815	Nov. 1987	0.6028	0.5846
Mar. 1985	0.2149	0.1839	Dec. 1987	0.5735	0.6024
Apr. 1985	0.2350	0.2111	Jan. 1988	0.5688	0.5722
May 1985	0.2549	0.2310	Feb. 1988	0.6066	0.5670
June 1985	0.3402	0.2507	Mar. 1988	0.6304	0.6050
July 1985	0.3368	0.3363			

Source: Chase: Econometrics

Table 6.2. *Relative forecasting performance for a one month horizon. The current spot rate and the one month forward rate for the $/£ exchange rate October 1982 to March 1988*

Predictor	Mean error %	Mean absolute error %	Root mean square error %
Spot rate	0.253	2.44	3.13
One month forward rate	0.427	2.51	3.23

where I_{t-1} defines the information set

$$= E_{t-1}(S_t/I_{t-1}) - S_{t-1}$$
$$= (S_{t-1} + d) - S_{t-1}$$
$$= d$$

An estimate of d can be obtained from the lagged change in the spot rate. However, this forecast will always miss turning points in the series of spot exchange rates since they will involve a change in the sign of d. As noted above, an alternative predictor of the future spot rate is the forward rate. Subtracting s_{t-1} from both sides of (6.8) gives

$$f_{t-1} - s_{t-1} = E_{t-1}s_t - s_{t-1} \qquad (6.19)$$

The left-hand side of (6.19) is the forward premium and, in principle, should capture turning points in the original series, again given the critical assumption that speculators are risk neutral. In fact, further analysis of the data set out in table 6.1 shows that the forward premium correctly predicts the direction of future changes in the spot rate only 26 times out of the 65 observations.

The conclusion to be drawn so far is that the forward rate is a poor predictor of the future spot rate. Negative correlation between the forward premium and the future change in the spot rate has been documented in a number of currencies against the dollar (for example Fama 1984, Meese and Rogoff 1983) and this is also present in our data set. The two possible reasons that have been suggested to explain this are that the forward market is not efficient and that a risk premium exists. It is to the concept of a risk premium we now turn.

If speculators are risk averse, that is they require some compensation for incurring additional risk, then the equality between the forward rate and the expected spot rate would not be achieved by market arbitrage because of the risk involved. Hence (6.8) would be replaced by

$$f_{t-1} = \rho + E_{t-1}s_t \qquad (6.20)$$

where ρ is a risk premium. Thus the forward premium can be split into two components: the expected change in the spot rate and the risk premium. This is because the forward premium can be written as

$$f_{t-1} - s_{t-1} = (f_{t-1} - E_{t-1}s_t) + (E_{t-1}s_t - s_{t-1}) \qquad (6.21)$$

The first term on the right-hand side of (6.21) is the risk premium and the second term the expected change in the spot rate. Fama (1984) carried out regressions of the following form based on (6.21) advanced one period

$$f_t - s_{t+1} = \alpha_1 + \beta_1 fp_t + \varepsilon_{1,t} \tag{6.22}$$

$$s_{t+1} - s_t = \alpha_2 + \beta_2 fp_t + \varepsilon_{2,t} \tag{6.23}$$

where fp is the forward premium ($f_t - s_t$) and the dependent variable in (6.22) is the *ex post* risk premium (ρ), and that in (6.23) the change in the spot rate. Since $f_t - s_{t-1}$ is equal to the risk premium plus the forecasting error (random in the case of rational or efficient forecasts), evidence that β_1 is significantly different from zero implies that the risk premium has a variation which shows up reliably in $f_t - s_{t+1}$. Similarly if the estimate of β_2 is significantly different from zero, this implies that the forward premium has power to predict the future change in the spot rate. The least squares estimators of the coefficients are

$$\beta_1 = \text{cov}(f_t - s_{t+1}, \, fp_t)/\text{var}(fp_t) \tag{6.24}$$

$$\beta_2 = \text{cov}(s_{t+1} - s_t, \, fp_t)\text{var}(fp_t) \tag{6.25}$$

Further insight into the relationship between β_1 and β_2 can be gained by assuming that the expected future spot rate component is rational and efficient and using the definition

$$fp = f_t - s_t = [(f_t - E(s_{t+1})) + (E(s_{t+1}) - s_t)]$$

where the first term in the square brackets is the risk premium (ρ) and the second term the forecast error. Substituting into (6.24) and (6.25) produces:

$$\beta_1 = [\text{var}(\rho_t) + \text{cov}(\rho_t, \, E(s_{t+1} - s_t))]/A \tag{6.26}$$

$$\beta_2 = [\text{var } E(s_{t+1} - s_t) + \text{cov}(\rho_t, \, E(s_{t+1} - s_t))]/A \tag{6.27}$$

where $A = [\text{var}(\rho_t) + \text{var}(E(s_{t+1} - s_t)) + 2\text{cov}(\rho_t, \, E(s_{t+1} - s_t))]$.

Note that when ρ is constant over time (not necessarily zero) the values of the two coefficients are 0 and 1 respectively. The difference between the two coefficients is given by:

$$\beta_1 - \beta_2 = [\text{var}(\rho_t) - \text{var}(E(s_{t+1} - s_t))]/A \tag{6.28}$$

where the first term of the numerator is the variance of the risk premium and the second term the variance of the forecasting error. Consequently the sign and magnitude of the gap between β_1 and β_2 provides evidence on the importance of the two sources of variation in the forward premium. If this gap is positive, it implies that the variance of the risk premium is greater than that of the forecasting error so that a greater proportion of the variation in the forward premium is attributable to the existence of a time varying risk premium. Fama (1984) and most other studies of this type show a positive figure for $\beta_1 - \beta_2$ – see for example Koedijk and Ott (1987) and Hodrick and Srivastava (1984). Similar regressions for the data on the sterling exchange rate quoted above produced the following results for estimation by ordinary least squares

$$f_t - s_{t+1} = 0.013 + 9.158 fp_t \qquad (6.28)$$
$$(2.56) \quad (4.62)$$

$$R^2 = 0.2408. \qquad DW = 2.116$$

where the figures in parentheses are t-values.

$$s_{t+1} - s_t = -0.013 - 8.158 fp_t \qquad (6.29)$$
$$(2.56) \quad (4.11)$$
$$R^2 = 0.1990 \qquad DW = 2.116$$

The gap between β_1 and β_2 is positive (t-value 4.36) and significant, indicating the greater variance of the risk premium as compared with that of the forecasting error. Also, the negative sign of the coefficient β_2 indicates the negative correlation between changes in the spot rate and the forward premium referred to earlier. Reference to (6.20) shows that the forward rate is the sum of a risk premium plus the expected spot rate. Therefore the existence of a time varying risk premium with a relatively large variance suggests that the forward rate would be a poor predictor of the future spot rate. Consequently, the evidence indicated above supports the view that the poor forecasting performance of the forward rate is due to the risk premium. However, Frankel and Froot (1986) using survey data to derive the expectational series argue that, although a time varying risk premium exists, its size was too small to account for other than a small proportion in the variation of the forward premium.

If there is a risk premium, the question arises as to whether any information can be derived about it so as to improve the predictive behaviour of the forward rate. While estimation of functions explaining the risk premium have not been overly successful, Wolff (1987) provides evidence of the practicability of using time-series methods to purge the forward premium of the risk premium content. Advancing (6.20) one period and subtracting s_{t+1} from both sides provides

$$f_t - s_{t+1} = \rho + (E_t s_{t+1} - s_{t+1}) \qquad (6.30)$$

Given the efficient markets hypothesis, that prices reflect all available information, the second term on the right-hand side of (6.30) is a forecast error and therefore pure white noise. Consequently the problem of obtaining information about the risk premium is equivalent to obtaining a signal from a series consisting of a systematic signal and white noise. Wolff adopts a filtering technique known as the Kalman filter to obtain information about the risk premium (for a more precise discussion of this methodology see Kmenta 1986, p. 423). A forecast series is then obtained by modifying the forward premium for the existence of the risk premium and comparing the predictive power of the forward rate with that of the spot rate. The conclusion reached is that the spot rate (i.e. the random walk model) still possesses superior forecasting power to the models developed by Wolff though the margin in its favour is reduced as compared with the unadjusted forward rate.

So far we have examined the predictive power of the spot rate against the forward rate. It is pertinent to consider whether economic models of exchange rate determination (as distinct from the macroeconomic models discussed in chapter 5) can perform better than the spot rate. One of the problems associated with this approach is the absence of a single model of exchange rate determination which commands a wide measure of acceptance. One model put forward is the simple monetary model associated with Bilson (1978) and Frenkel (1976). The basis of this model is that the exchange rate is the relative price of different moneys. In a two country model, assuming equilibrium in the money market so that the demand for money equals the supply of money, then the exchange rate will reflect the relative demands for money. Assuming a money demand equation of the general form

$$M/P = kY^{\alpha}e^{-\beta R} \tag{6.31}$$

where α, β are the income elasticity and the semi-interest elasticity of the demand for money respectively and P is the price level. Hence

$$P = M/(kY^{\alpha}e^{-\beta R}) \tag{6.32}$$

Similarly using * to indicate foreign variables the foreign price level is given by

$$P^* = M^*/(k^*Y^{*\alpha}e^{-\beta R*}) \tag{6.33}$$

Assuming that purchasing power parity holds so that $S = P/P^*$, dividing (6.33) into (6.32) and taking logarithms gives

$$s = (m - m^*) + \alpha(y^* - y) + (k^* - k) + \beta(R - R^*) \tag{6.34}$$

where lower case letters represent logarithmic values of the upper case variables. A variation of this simple monetary model is the Dornbusch model (see for example Dornbusch 1976) which suggests that the price levels are sticky and purchasing power parity does not hold in the short run. In this case relative price levels would also act as a determinant of the exchange rate. An extension of the second model is provided by Hooper and

Morton (1982) to allow for changes in the long-run real exchange rate. These changes are assumed to be correlated with unanticipated shocks to the trade balance.

Meese and Rogoff (1983) examine the forecasting performance of a number of structural exchange rate models for three major currencies (£, DM and the Yen; all against the dollar) and also a trade weighted index of the dollar exchange rate. The approach is to set up a quasi reduced form equation to represent the three exchange rate models noted above

$$s = \alpha_0 + \beta_1(m - m^*) + \beta_2(y^* - y) + \beta_3(R - R^*)$$
$$+ \beta_4(E\pi - E\pi^*) + \beta_5(tb - tb^*) \tag{6.35}$$

where m, y, R, $E\pi$ and tb represent money, income, the rate of interest, the expected rate of inflation and the trade balance respectively while $*$ indicates a foreign variable. Applying appropriate restrictions to the parameters, this general model gives the following special cases:

 a Simple monetary model; with the assumption of purchasing power parity so that $\beta_4 = \beta_5 = 0$

 b Sticky price monetary model; with $\beta_5 = 0$

 c Hooper–Morton model; no parameter constraints

The model was first estimated over the period January 1975 to November 1978 and a series of out of sample forecasts prepared using actual values of the exogenous variables. The use of actual exogenous variables was justified to remove the forecasting errors for the exogenous variables required for the model. The first series of forecasts for a variety of time horizons was then prepared. A rolling regression technique was adopted so that the parameters of the model were re-estimated before a subsequent forecast was prepared. The conclusion drawn from this study is that the random walk model provided superior forecasts to the alternative models. Somanath (1986) re-examined the performance of structural models for the DM/$ exchange rate for period November 1978 to December 1983. Slight modifications were made to the estimating equation (financial wealth was included) and a number of alternative models considered but the main difference between this study and that of Meese and Rogoff was the inclusion of the lagged dependent variable to capture the possibility of lagged adjustment (see chapter 5, section 2 for a discussion of this). It was found that the inclusion of this variable improved the performance of the structural exchange models and, in fact, they provided better predictive power than the simple random walk model. Somanath then considered whether the existence of a lagged adjustment was consistent with the efficient markets hypothesis which postulates immediate adjustment of asset prices in response to new information. He decided that this evidence was consistent with the efficient markets hypothesis provided there was either a perception of uncertainty about the new information received or that there was a dispersion of information among the operators.

We now turn to the question of whether the foreign exchange market provides better forecasts than those provided by professional forecasting agencies. A limited number of such studies have been carried out, for example Goodman (1979), Levich (1979), Bilson (1983) and Blake, Beenstock and Brasse (1986). Goodman analysed data for the period June 1976 to June 1978. A distinction was made between economic orientated services and technical orientated services. The former produce forecasts based on models whereas the latter use technical rules based on past behaviour of the exchange rate. Criteria included (i) accuracy in predicting the direction of the change, (ii) the accuracy of point estimates and (iii) the speculative return on capital at risk. It was only possible to evaluate technical orientated services on the basis of criterion (iii). Goodman found that the predictive ability of the forecasts based on economic models was relatively poor. They predicted accurately the direction of the trend 50 per cent of the time for three month forecasts and 61 per cent of the time for six month forecasts. They faired poorly under test (ii). In fact under both these criteria their performance is no better and generally worse than the forward rate. As far as speculative return on capital at risk, the figure is a derisory 0.92 per cent per annum. The technical orientated services had a stronger performance averaging 8.38 per cent return on capital at risk. Levich found that the forward rate gave quantitatively better results but in the case of some agencies inferior qualitative (i.e. directional) results. This no doubt reflects the negative correlation between the forward premium and the future change in the exchange rate already noted in this chapter. Blake, Beenstock and Brasse (1986) built on earlier work by Brasse (1983) who found that the forward rate generally gave more accurate forecasts for a number of currencies in terms of the Theil coefficient (see chapter 1 (1.48)) than the six forecasting agencies considered in the study. Blake *et al.* carried out a quantitative test on the accuracy of three of these forecasting agencies and found that it was possible to reject the hypothesis of unbiasedness for the forecasts of the agencies and, for that matter, the forward rate. Moreover this defect continued even if the forecasts were combined according to the regression method outlined in chapter 3 (3.13) with the weights not constrained to equal 1.

Finally, in this section, we turn to a more detailed study carried out by Bilson (1983). Initially he examined the performance of the spot rate and the forecasts provided by a forecasting agency against performance of the forward rate for the Canadian dollar, French Franc, DM, Yen and the pound sterling. The criterion was a 'right side of the market' approach. If the forward price of sterling is 1.75\$ per £ and the forecast for the spot rate was 1.73\$ per £, then the speculator could expect to profit by selling £s forward and buying £s spot on maturity of the contract. Consequently, provided the outcome was less than 1.75\$ per £, the speculator would make a profit whereas, if the outcome was above 1.75\$ per £, the speculator would lose. The right side of the market approach recognises this by allocating a score of $+100$ if the forecast proves to be on the right side of the market and -100 if the forecast is on the wrong side. Note the proximity of the forecasts to the right outcome does not necessarily enhance the score. For example, an outcome of 1.65 against the forecast of 1.73 would score $+100$ whereas the closer outcome of 1.76 would score -100. Using this criterion there were only marginal differences between the spot rate and the forecasts provided by the agency. Bilson then considered the gain from combining forecasts and adopting a 'portfolio' approach involving more than just a single currency. Bilson concludes that the analysis of such an approach indicates potential profits which should justify the substantial initial investment in forecasting services, equipment and staff.

6.4   Stock market prices

Share valuation depends on the expected dividend and the price expected at the end of the period. Thus the current price of an individual security may be written as

$$P_t = (E_t \mathrm{DIV}_t + P_{t+1})/(1 + r_d) \tag{6.36}$$

where $\mathrm{DIV} = $ dividend, $P = $ market price of the share, $r_d = $ required discount rate. Since the price at the beginning of period $t+1$ can be expressed in terms of the dividends expected during period $t+1$ and the price at the end of the period $t+1$, forward substitution in (6.36) produces

$$P_t = \Sigma(\mathrm{DIV}_{t+1})/(1 + r_d)^{t+i} \tag{6.37}$$

Equations such as (6.37) are framed in terms of 'price fundamentals'. Prediction of stock/share prices requires prediction of future dividends or alternatively the rate at which dividends will grow together with an assessment of the required rate of discount over time. An alternative approach would be to use the past history of the security price to predict future movements. Such an approach embraces 'chartism' and filter rules as discussed in chapter 1, section 2. In this section we discuss the applicability of using filter rules to predict share prices (i.e. weak efficiency) and then move on to consider evidence of the accuracy of predictions by market experts (i.e. strong efficiency).

One of the most notable early studies of filter rules was that carried out by Alexander (1964) which purported to find that filter rules could generate profits above a 'buy and hold strategy'. These conclusions were subsequently modified in the light of biases in the original study. Later Fama and Blume (1966) carried out an exhaustive study based on daily price observations for the 30 individual securities contained in the Dow-Jones industrial average share index and a wide range of possible filters. The observation period varied per security but generally covered the time period end of 1957 to September 1962. There were, therefore, 1200 to 1700 observations for the 30 series. Fama and Blume conclude that, after taking commissions into account, the largest profits accrue to the brokers who earned the commissions on the transactions indicated by the filter rules. In contrast, the average returns per security are less than a 'buy and hold' strategy. Even if commissions are ignored filter rules provided a more profitable strategy than 'buy and hold' only in the case of four securities out of the total of 50. Taylor (1986) examines the possibility of forecasting financial series through the use of time-series models. In the case of stock market prices he examines the behaviour of the daily prices of 15 individual US shares over the period 1966 to 1976 so that the number of observations in each series was 2750. He finds that the daily prices follow a first order moving average process and that whilst this may be an input into a trading rule, transaction costs are likely to eliminate any profits so derived. The impact of these studies is therefore to suggest that, so far, it has not been possible to detect profitable forecasting methods for stock market prices based purely upon the past history of share prices. Of course, the possibility exists that a method has been detected and is being reserved for private use.

We now turn to consider the accuracy of predictions carried out by market analysts. Two important studies representing this aspect of market efficiency were carried out by Dimson and Marsh (1984) for UK data and Bjerring, Lakonishok and Vermaelen (1983) for Canadian and US data. Both of these studies concentrate on forecasts provided for customers rather than those circulated to the public at large. It is also important to remember that we do not know how the analysts' forecasts were prepared so that this section does not support a particular forecasting method. Dimson and Marsh describe an empirical study covering 3364 specific share forecasts made by 35 brokers for a large UK investment institution during the calendar years 1981/2. Briefly, in advance of the empirical work, brokers were requested to provide, where possible, one year ahead forecasts of excess returns for specific shares assuming an excess return on the market of zero. Over 95 per cent of the forecasts were for the one year horizon. In addition the fund's own internal analysts also provided 823 forecasts. The method of analysis was to compute the excess return on the security so as to ascertain whether the forecasts were successful. The excess return was calculated using the capital asset market pricing model whereby the price of a security is related to the market return on the 'risk free' asset (see, for example, Sharpe 1964). Thus

$$R_{jt} = (1 - \beta)R_{ft} + \beta R_{mt} + \varepsilon_{jt} \qquad (6.38)$$

where R_{jt} is the return on the jth security, R_{mt} is the market return, R_{ft} is the return on the risk free asset, β is the systematic risk of the jth stock and ε_{jt} is the error term or specific return on security j. Inverting (6.38) produces an estimate of ε_{jt} where β is estimated using data for the previous five years. The calculated excess return can then be related to the forecast by the regression equation with δ providing an indication of the forecasting efficiency of the forecaster

$$\varepsilon_{jkt} = \alpha_0 + \delta_{jk} F_{jkt} + u_{jkt} \qquad (6.39)$$

where F_{jkt} is the forecast for the jth security provided by the kth broker in time t. Estimation of (6.39) by ordinary least squares (and weighted least squares to allow for potential heteroskedascity – see e.g. Kmenta 1986, p. 269) showed a small but significant forecasting ability of both brokers and internal analysts. In order to verify whether these forecasts were profitable in practice, a record was kept of all transactions carried out by the fund. Near-neutral forecasts generated no transactions, other forecasts led to trading in the stock on the day of the forecast and subsequent days to avoid market disturbance. In all, 2950 transactions were recorded and the profits of these transactions calculated according to the inversion of (6.38). The weighted average of these transactions produced a positive return of 2.2 per cent which was believed to be more than adequate to cover transaction costs including the internal costs of evaluating the forecasts. Checks were also made to verify if the forecasts were independent of each other and the simple correlation coefficients between the forecasts ranged from -0.15 to $+0.30$ with an average of only 0.08. The stability of the forecasting performances of the various brokers were also examined and the conclusion reached that all brokers possessed the same degree of forecasting ability. Finally, a combination of the forecasts with equal weights allocated to each forecast further improved the predictive ability.

A similar study was carried out by Bjerring, Lakonishok and Vermaelen (1983) in respect of the recommendations of a Canadian brokerage house for forecasts involving both US and Canadian stocks. The forecasts were published weekly and the stocks categorised as 'recommended', or 'speculative' and monthly as 'representative'. Bjerring *et al.* examined the performance of these stocks against the normal return predicted by the 'market' model (a variant of the capital asset pricing model (6.38) discussed earlier) where the excess return depends on the market return only, i.e.

$$\varepsilon_t = R_{jt} - (\alpha + \beta_j R_{mt}) \tag{6.40}$$

The coefficients α and β were estimated from the data by ordinary least squares, where necessary making allowance for thin trading. The Canadian and US stocks on the recommended list provided a mean abnormal return which was significantly different from zero, whereas the return for those stocks on the representative list was insignificantly different from zero. The return on those stocks on the speculative list provided a negative return which verged on statistical significance. After allowing for transaction costs Bjerring *et al.* calculate that the investor who followed the recommended list would make 9.3 per cent more than those who bought and held the market.

The conclusion that may be drawn from these studies is that reliance solely on the past behaviour of a security is unlikely to produce forecasts which beat the market. On the other hand there is evidence that forecasts produced by market analysts do provide positive returns but we do not know whether these are sufficient to outweigh any risk premium which may exist given that security speculation is a risky activity.

6.5   Commodity prices

In this section we consider the evidence concerning asset prices on commodity markets. The question remains the same: how far do market prices provide forecasts of future prices? Bird (1985) analysed the behaviour of the daily prices of tin, copper, lead and zinc on the London Metal Exchange over the period 1972 to 1982. Searching for profitable filter rules, Bird found strong evidence for profitability in the case of copper, weaker but positive evidence for lead and zinc but no such evidence for tin. Interestingly, sub-division of the period into two sub-periods up to and from the middle of 1977 suggested that the performance of the filters was substantially better in the first sub-period. Bird suggests that this could be due to the 1972/5 commodity price boom. The evidence of price dependence leading to profitable filter rules is confirmed by Taylor (1986, p. 195) who suggests that price trend forecasts can provide 'very small reductions in the means square forecast error'. MacDonald and Taylor (1988) also examined the efficiency of the London Metal Exchange with respect to the same four metals as Bird over the period January 1976 to March 1987 (but to October

1985 for tin) using monthly data. Their methodology was to use an nth order bivariate regression of the general form

$$\Delta s_t = \alpha_1 \Delta s_{t-1} + \cdots + \alpha_n \Delta s_{t-n} + \beta_1 (f-s)_{t-1} + \cdots + \beta_n (f-s)_{t-n} + \varepsilon t \qquad (6.41)$$

$$(f-s)_t = \gamma_1 \Delta s_{t-1} + \cdots + \gamma_n \Delta s_{t-n} + \delta_1 (f-s)_{t-1} + \cdots + \delta_n (f-s)_{t-n} + \eta_t \qquad (6.42)$$

where Δs is the change in the spot rate and $(f-s)$ is the forward premium for the metal concerned (lower case figures representing logarithms of variables). MacDonald and Taylor then test for the restrictions implied by the joint hypothesis of rational expectations and risk neutral speculators. They were able to reject this hypothesis in respect to zinc and tin only. In a subsequent paper MacDonald and Taylor (1989) use the Fama (1984) approach described earlier with respect to the exchange rate equations (i.e. (6.22) and (6.23)) and conclude that time varying risk premia exist for tin and zinc but there is only weak evidence for their existence in the case of other metals. Fama and French (1987) also investigated the possible existence of time varying risk premia for a number of agricultural products, metals, wood and animal products. The methodology was again that developed by Fama (1984) and this supported the existence of risk premia for a number of commodities including copper, coffee, cotton, soya oil, lumber, orange juice and plywood. On the other hand no evidence was found in the case of broilers, eggs and hogs.

6.6   Conclusions

We have examined the evidence from a number of auction (price flex) markets to ascertain whether the forecasting of prices would be a futile exercise because observed prices in the markets contain all available information. The evidence is mixed and suggests that current prices do contain predictive power but that it may be possible to prepare forecasts which lead to an increase, albeit a small one, in the predictive power of market prices. Whether this increase in predictive power leads to abnormal profits is a moot question. Speculation is a risky form of business and the increased average return may be compensation for the additional risk incurred, i.e. a normal profit.

CHAPTER 7

Conclusions

7.1   The choice between different techniques

This book has been concerned with the methods used in economic forecasting. For this final chapter we first consider the problem of choosing an appropriate technique. The remainder of the chapter examines current developments in forecasting methods (section 7.2), and the interaction between forecasting and government policy (section 7.3).

From our review of the benefits of combining forecasts in chapter 3 it is clear that in many circumstances no particular technique dominates all others. It should also be apparent that many of the studies which compare different methods of forecasting are not comprehensive in their coverage of these methods. Initially we will examine the general approaches to forecasting, with a view to seeing what sort of information is needed before they can be used, then we will review some evidence on what techniques are employed in practice and taught in universities and other institutions of higher education.

In chapter 1 we saw that there are various ways of classifying forecasting methods such as subjective versus model-based or causal versus non-causal. Here we will limit consideration to quantitative forecasts with particular reference to judgement, surveys, extrapolation procedures and econometric models. Starting with judgement and surveys, these require very little extra information since the respondents use their own methods of producing forecasts. In particular there is no need to have a past history of the event being forecast. Therefore they may be the only methods that can be used when a completely new situation arises, for example when a new consumer product is to be marketed or following some major upheaval, which means that past experience will be a poor guide to the future. A macroeconomic example of the latter would be when the major developed economies switched from fixed to floating exchange rate regimes in the early seventies.

The more simple extrapolation procedures, such as naive 'no change' models can be used when there are very little past data on the variable of interest. However, if the appropriate model is to be selected on the evidence of its past forecast performance, it is beneficial to have more data available. This point also applies to smoothing and decomposition methods, where the reliable estimation of seasonal patterns in particular needs several years data. The more complex extrapolation methods, such as Box–Jenkins models, require a substantial number of observations (say more than 40) in order to have any faith in the procedures of identification, estimation and validation. Of course it has to be recognised that having more data is only helpful in giving better estimates of the parameters when these parameters are constant over the observations. If the data exhibit a changing structure it may be appropriate to discard some observations. For example, data on the consumption of basic foods may be available for the last eighty years, but changes in shopping habits and access to refrigerators mean that perhaps only the most recent 20 year's data should be used. When an econometric model is to be estimated, there is an implicit assumption that the parameters are constants, and data are needed on not only the past values of the variables of interest but also on the explanatory variables. If this information is not available an alternative forecasting technique has to be adopted. Also, forecasting with an econometric model requires forecasts of the future values of the exogenous variables. Ashley (1983) points out that if the forecasts of the latter are poor, more accurate forecasts of the variables of interest might be obtained from univariate models. See also Ashley (1988).

To summarise, when there are no data on past values, only judgement and survey methods can be used. With a few observations, simple extrapolative methods are possible, while much more data are required with Box–Jenkins and econometric methods.

Turning now to which techniques are used in practice, a number of surveys have been conducted to answer this question. Mentzer and Cox (1984) and Dalrymple (1987) report the results of surveys of the sales forecasting methods used by US business firms. The most popular methods are found to be sales force surveys and the Delphi (or jury of executive opinion) method, both of which are subjective rather than model-based techniques. Various extrapolation methods, including naive models, moving averages and leading indicators are the next most popular methods; with regression and econometric models, and exponential smoothing being less popular and Box–Jenkins models being rarely used. Dalrymple also asked respondents which methods had been abandoned and he found that the methods mentioned most frequently here are the Box–Jenkins, econometric and regression approaches. Possible explanations for these results are the data requirements of the methods and the heavy demands on forecaster time and skills. Sparkes and McHugh (1984) carried out a similar survey of British manufacturing industry and likewise found a bias towards the simpler techniques.

Fildes and Chrissanthaki (1988, chapter 1) examined the question of how forecasts are used. In a survey of business economists in the UK they found that macroeconomic forecasts are useful for sales forecasting and long-term profit/cash flow planning, but not for investment appraisal. The particularly valuable forecasts are for economic growth, consumers' expenditure, interest rates and exchange rates. Most respondents utilise both their own internal forecasts and ones purchased from external agencies (mainly academic research units, private forecasting services and banks). The factors determining the choice of agency were found to be whether the variables of interest were forecast with the required time-horizon, the accuracy of the track record of the agency and the policy discussion and interpretation service provided. One criticism was on the lack of sector and regional detail which would have satisfied company needs. The users believed that the state of the economy had an important effect on their organisation and that, while macroeconomic shocks were a source of risk, macroeconomic forecasts were more accurate now than in the past. One interesting comment was that the coherence of the forecasts was recognised to be important.

An alternative assessment of the value of different forecasting methods is provided by Makridakis (1986) who, in reviewing the literature, concentrates on studies where direct comparisons of methods are made. We will also include comments which refer back to earlier chapters. He summarises the empirical evidence as:

1 Contradictory results come from different data sets so no single method dominates all others. To some extent this is due to the range of material covered by Makridakis, which varies between monthly, quarterly and annual data, between micro and macro data, and covering engineering, economic and medical series. However, tables 5.8 and 5.9 provide evidence from macroeconomic data.

2 Judgemental methods are generally not more accurate than quantitative methods. Makridakis also comments that they are usually more expensive. This is clearly true where simple extrapolation methods are concerned, but might be arguable with Box–Jenkins or econometric models. There is surprisingly little evidence as to what the costs of different methods are in practical situations.

3 Econometric methods are not always more accurate than time-series models. For example, in the study by McNees (1986) discussed in chapter 5, section 8, Bayesian vector autoregression (BVAR) forecasts come out well compared with econometric forecasts. However, this should not lead us to abandon econometric models since they help in

understanding the causal relationships between variables and can provide evidence on the validity of economic theory.

4 Simple methods frequently give better forecasts than complex and sophisticated methods. In table 5.9 we saw that naive models were sometimes more accurate than ARIMA models, even though the naive models were special cases of the ARIMA models.

5 Adaptive methods, such as those discussed in chapter 3, section 7, are not generally better than fixed-parameter models. This is a special case of the previous point.

6 Discounted least squares, in which more weight is given to recent data, is more accurate than ordinary least squares. This result is expected when the patterns in the data are changing, so that recent observations provide the most useful information.

In his discussion of this evidence, Makridakis points out that many of the M-competition series (see chapter 3, section 7) show a change in behaviour between the fitting and the forecast periods. This might explain the two main results above – that empirical studies produce contradictory evidence about accuracy and theoretical improvements in accuracy do not always arise in practice – since any method of forecasting assumes that the existing pattern (or data generating process) will persist in the future. If patterns change then the wrong model might be selected, resulting in poor forecasts.

The next aspect of forecasting we consider is which methods are taught in business schools, since presumably the academics involved will have an up-to-date knowledge of the subject from both the theoretical and practical points of view and the techniques learnt will be used by managers in the future. Hanke (1984) conducted a survey of US business schools at the under-graduate and post-graduate levels to find how important forecasting is. Forecasting courses were taught in 58 per cent of the respondents' institutions but only in 26 per cent of the positive responses was a forecasting course compulsory. The subject areas in which forecasting was generally taught were economics (28 per cent), management science (22 per cent), business economics (16 per cent), or decision science (10 per cent). Where particular techniques are concerned, over 90 per cent regard a knowledge of regression as important or very important, followed closely by simple time-series methods, exponential smoothing and Box-Jenkins methods. The only techniques which were regarded as not important are adaptive filtering and the Census II method, but it is not clear from Hanke's paper whether judgemental methods were included in the list. Most forecasting courses involve practical exercises, using a wide variety of computer packages, as an integral part of the course.

7.2   Current developments

In 1988 the *International Journal of Forecasting* had a special issue on 'The Future of Forecasting' in which a number of experts reviewed the way in which they think forecasting will develop in the future. Gardner and Makridakis (1988) acknowledge the many conflicts, discussed in the previous section, between the theory of forecasting and the empirical evidence. The aim of the special issue is to identify the major problems and to propose a research agenda to solve them.

Fischhoff (1988) points out that all forecasting methods require the use of judgement, if only in deciding what method to select and whether to accept the results. He suggests four conditions which will lead to better judgement and hence improved forecasts:

1 Repeated practice in similar situations. This allows the forecaster to get experience in exercising judgement.

2 Evaluation of past forecasts. Forecast errors occur for a variety of reasons and can provide useful information for improving judgement.

3 Task specific reinforcement. Forecasters should be rewarded for accurate forecasts.

4 Recognition of a need for learning. Forecasters should accept that they can always improve the accuracy of their forecasts.

For the future of macroeconomic forecasting, McNees (1988) offers what he admits to be assertions or unsupported forecasts based on his recent experiences in the USA. First, he argues that the distinction between 'structural' models, based on economic theory, and time-series models, based on data, will gradually disappear. Economic models will incorporate the time-series properties of data and economic theory will influence the development of time-series models. Second, he believes that selection between alternative models will be increasingly based on post-sample forecasting performance. That is, it will become accepted practice that model selection and model evaluation should be done using different data. Third, he expects formal modelling to increase and hunch and intuition to play a diminishing role in forecasting. An example of where this has occurred is in the 'ragged edge' problem (see Wallis 1986) where with, say, a quarterly model, up-to-date monthly data may be available for some series. This partial information can be incorporated into the model. Fourth, he hopes that in the future more attention will be paid to the quality of the evidence where evaluation of models and techniques are concerned. He mentions that simple comparisons of judgement, time-series and econometric forecasts can be misleading since forecasts from bad econometric models (or inappropriate Box–Jenkins models) are likely to be worse than those from naive extrapolation. McNees's final prediction is that more attention will be paid to how forecasts are to be used, since the object of forecasting is to help in decision making.

From a rather different perspective, Ord (1988) also emphasises the purpose for which the forecast is needed, how important the forecast is, and the role of background information. He argues that future developments in forecasting will come from a synthesis of current knowledge. He comments that there is a need for understandable models, with estimates of parameters being regularly updated and some possibility of structural change to occur, and he suggests that the Kalman filter approach (see chapter 2, section 5), rather than the conventional fixed sample size procedures, is the way forward. He also mentions that, while linear models can be reasonable approximations in many situations, non-linearities become important as the forecasting horizon extends.

Chatfield (1988) comments that the recent increase in interest in multivariate (as opposed to univariate) methods is partly due to improvements in computing software. He expects this interest to continue because of the large number of packages now available. While many of the univariate techniques can be implemented automatically, multivariate methods generally require some subjective input from the forecaster, for example, in the choice of variables. Chatfield hopes that future research will make multivariate methods more useful.

In an important article, Harvey (1984) has attempted to provide a unified view of statistical forecasting methods by using the state-space formulation. Once a model is in this form the Kalman filter can be used to estimate the unknown parameters and to give optimal predictions. This contrasts with the situation where, as in chapter 3, section 7, *ad hoc* models are used with arbitrary parameter values and for which the statistical properties of the resulting model are not always known. Harvey shows how the exponentially weighted moving average method, the classical decomposition method, Bayesian methods, ARIMA models, explanatory variables and structural change can all be expressed in the state space framework. However, Ledolter (1984) points out that some of the flexibility of the general ARIMA model is lost, and that Harvey exaggerates the difficulties of selecting these models.

Long-term trends in forecasting methods are discussed by Armstrong (1985), who points out the general moves from subjective to objective methods and from naive methods to causal ones. This is reflected in economic modelling, where the simple models of the sixties have been replaced by the much larger macroeconomic models of the eighties. With the increasing availability of computer packages, it is becoming easier to use more complex methods for the estimation and evaluation of these models. However, we saw in chapter 2 that there has been a convergence of the time-series approach (with univariate models and an emphasis on the statistical properties of the data) and the econometric approach (with multivariate models based on economic theory) to give simpler multivariate models (such as vector autoregression models) based on economic theory. These models are still in their infancy, but developments in the theory of cointegration are promising and point the way for a fruitful amalgamation of approaches.

In chapter 3 we saw that there is evidence of improved accuracy for combining forecasts, and that the biggest benefits are likely to occur when different types of forecast are combined. Whether this will prove to be an enduring result is an open question. If forecasts from, say, a univariate model and an econometric model can be combined to give an improved forecast, this suggests that each of these models is inadequate and can be improved. A better model might arise from a union of the two models. In other words, using a correctly specified combined model may dominate combining forecasts from simpler models.

7.3   Economic forecasting and government policy

The design of government macroeconomic policy involves consideration of the question what will happen if a policy variable is changed. This requires explicit or implicit evaluation of both forecasts of the future course of the economy given that the policy variables remain unchanged, and prediction of the changes induced in key endogenous variables if some policy variables are altered. Clearly the latter can only be obtained through the use of a causal model. Time-series analysis is inappropriate in this context because of the underlying assumption that past history will repeat itself. On the other hand macroeconomic models are ideal since the impact of the policy change can be examined by comparing two simulations; one with an unchanged policy (the base or the control run) and the other incorporating the projected policy change. In a similar manner analysis of the past behaviour of an economy can be carried out through what is called 'counterfactual exercises' – see for example Saville and Gardiner (1986) or Mackie, Miles and Taylor (1989). Basically the idea is to simulate the economy with each exogenous variable (including policy variables) held to a trend or a neutral value. This provides a path for the endogenous variable(s) of interest conditional on the assumption made for the exogenous variables. This path is called the counterfactual path. The gap between this path and the actual path of the variable(s) concerned is then analysed so as to identify the individual impact of the exogenous variables.

Nevertheless this type of exercise is not as simple as appears at first sight. Neutral or unchanged policy is not always an unambiguous concept. For example does an unchanged monetary policy refer to a constant quantity of money, or a constant level of interest rates or yet a constant monetary feedback rule? Moreover the margins of error in such exercises have caused some economists to raise questions over their real value. Forecast errors as we have seen in chapter 5, section 7 can arise from three sources: model errors, errors in predictions of exogenous variables and errors in judgemental adjustments. It is really the first category which concerns the use of macroeconomic models for policy appraisal. The rationale for a macroeconomic model varies between models, so that predictions of the individual models will themselves differ, particularly in medium or long-term policy simulations. This problem is enhanced by the way models develop over time and it is often true that changes in one or two key equations can have important effects on simulations of policy changes.

Finally, in this context, there is the problem of the Lucas critique discussed in chapter 5, section 9. This is partly met since most models now include 'model consistent' expectations which permit expectations to change in response to policy changes. Nevertheless this critique still applies to the extent the equation parameters themselves vary in response to changes in the policy regime. Naturally any changes in expectations and equation parameters depend on the credibility of the policy change. If we assume that the choice of policy is optimal, and so maximises the government objective function, it is possible that the policy may be 'time inconsistent' which means that in future periods the adopted policy may become suboptimal. In this case there is an incentive for the government to change its policy which, in turn, affects the credibility of the policy. Odling-Smee (1989) argues that, over the last decade, governments have paid less attention to the short-term effects of policy and more attention to the medium-term impact and its sustainability. If this is so, then two facets may be important. First the problem of time inconsistency is less relevant and second the use of cointegration techniques discussed in chapter 2, section 6 may become useful to derive long-term equilibrium conditions of the model equations.

Despite all these caveats we would argue that forecasting is important for policy design and that use of macroeconomic models will remain one of the methods used to assess the impact of policy proposals.

References

Aaker, D. A. and Carman, J. M. (1982), 'Are you overadvertising?', *Journal of Advertising Research*, vol. 22, no. 4, pp. 57–70.

Adrian, M. and Ferguson, B. S. (1987), 'Demand for domestic and imported alcohol in Canada', *Applied Economics*, vol. 19, pp. 531–40.

Akaike, H. (1970), 'Statistical predictor identification', *Annals of the Institute of Statistical Mathematics*, vol. 22, pp. 203–17.

— (1973), 'Information theory and an extension of the maximum likelihood principle' in B. N. Petrov and F. Csaki (editors), *Second International Symposium on Information Theory*, Budapest: Akademini Kiado.

Alexander, S. S. (1964), 'Price movements in speculative markets: trends or random walks', *Industrial Management Review*, vol. 5, pp. 25–46.

Andersen, A. and Weiss, A. (1984), 'Forecasting: the Box–Jenkins approach', pp. 167–200 in Makridakis *et al.* (1984).

Armstrong, J. S. (1985), *Long-Range Forecasting*, second editon, New York: Wiley.

Artis, M. J. (1982), *Why do Forecasts Differ?* Papers presented to the Panel of Academic Consultants, No. 17, London: Bank of England.

Ashley, R. (1983), 'On the usefulness of macroeconomic forecasts as inputs to forecasting models', *Journal of Forecasting*, vol. 2, pp. 211–23.

— (1988), 'On the relative worth of recent macro-economic forecasts', *International Journal of Forecasting*, vol. 4, pp. 363–76.

Ashley, R., Granger, C. W. J. and Schmalensee, R. (1980), 'Advertising and aggregate consumption: an analysis of causality', *Econometrica*, vol. 48, pp. 1149–68.

Ashley, W. C. and Hall, L. (1985), 'Nonextrapolative strategy', pp. 61–75 in Mendell (1985).

Assmus, G. (1984), 'New product forecasting', *Journal of Forecasting*, vol. 3, pp. 121–38.

Baillie, R. T., Lippens, R. E. and McMahon, P. C. (1983), 'Testing rational expectations and efficiency in the foreign exchange market', *Econometrica*, vol. 51, pp. 553–74.

Baltagi, B. H. and Levin, D. (1986), 'Estimating dynamic demand for cigarettes using panel data: the effects of bootlegging, taxation and advertising reconsidered', *Review of Economics and Statistics*, vol. 68, pp. 148–55.

Bank of England Quarterly Bulletin (1986), vol. 26, pp. 379–82.

Barker, T. (1980), 'The economic consequences of monetarism: a Keynesian view of the British economy 1980–90', *Cambridge Journal of Economics*, vol. 4, pp. 319–31.

— (1985), 'Forecasting the economic recession in the UK 1979–1982: a comparison of model-based *ex ante* forecasts', *Journal of Forecasting*, vol. 4, pp. 133–51.

Batchelor, R. A. (1982), 'Expectations, output and inflation', *European Economic Review*, vol. 17, pp. 1–25.

Bates, J. M. and Granger, C. W. J. (1969), 'The combination of forecasts', *Operational Research Quarterly*, vol. 20, pp. 451–68.

Bessler, D. A. and Brandt, J. A. (1981), 'Forecasting livestock prices with individual and composite methods', *Applied Economics*, vol. 13, pp. 513–22.

Bilson, J. F. O. (1978), 'The monetary approach to the exchange rate', *International Monetary Fund Staff Papers*, vol. 25, pp. 48–75.

— (1983), 'The evaluation and use of foreign exchange rate forecasting services' in R. Herring (editor), *Managing Foreign Exchange Rate Risk*, Cambridge University Press.

Bird, P. J. W. N. (1985), 'The weak form efficiency of the London Metal Exchange', *Applied Economics*, vol. 17, pp. 571–87.

Bjerring, J. H., Lakonishok, J. and Vermaelen, T. (1983), 'Stock prices and financial analysts recommendations', *Journal of Finance*, vol. 38, pp. 187–204.

Blake, D., Beenstock, M. and Brasse, V. (1986), 'The performance of UK exchange rate forecasters', *The Economic Journal*, vol. 96, pp. 986–99.

Bordley, R. F. (1982), 'The combination of forecasts: a Bayesian approach', *Journal of the Operational Research Society*, vol. 33, pp. 171–4.

— (1986), 'Linear combination of forecasts with an intercept: a Bayesian approach', *Journal of Forecasting*, vol. 5, pp. 243–9.

Bowerman, B. L. and O'Connell, R. T. (1987), *Time Series Forecasting*, second edition, Boston, Mass.: Duxbury Press.

Box, G. E. P. and Jenkins, G. M. (1976), *Time Series Analysis: Forecasting and Control*, revised edition, San Francisco: Holden-Day.

Box, G. E. P. and Pierce, D. A. (1970), 'Distribution of residual autocorrelations in autoregressive integrated moving average time series models', *Journal of the American Statistical Association*, vol. 65, pp. 1509–26.

Brasse, V. (1983), 'The inaccuracy of exchange rate forecasting agencies in the United Kingdom', *Economic Review (City University Business School)*, vol. 1, pp. 35–44.

Brauers, J. and Weber, M. (1988), 'A new method of scenario analysis for strategic planning', *Journal of Forecasting*, vol. 7, pp. 31–47.

Brock, W. A. (1986), 'Distinguishing random and deterministic systems', *Journal of Economic Theory*, vol. 40, pp. 168–95.

Brock, W. A., Dechert, D. W. and Scheinkman, J. A. (1987), 'A test for independence based on the correlation dimension', *SSRI Working Paper no. 8702*, Department of Economics, University of Wisconsin, Wisconsin.

Brock, W. A. and Sayers, C. L. (1988), 'Is the business cycle characterized by deterministic chaos?', *Journal of Monetary Economics*, vol. 22, pp. 71–9.

Brodie, R. J. and De Kluyver, C. A. (1987), 'A comparison of the short term forecasting accuracy of econometric and naive extrapolation models of market share', *International Journal of Forecasting*, vol. 3, pp. 423–37.

Brown, B. W. and Maital, S. (1981), 'What do economists know? An empirical study of experts' expectations', *Econometrica*, vol. 49, pp. 491–504.

Brown, R. G. (1959), *Statistical Forecasting for Inventory Control*, New York: McGraw-Hill.

Buiter, W. H. and Miller, M. (1981), 'The Thatcher experiment: the first two years', *Brookings Papers on Economic Activity*, no. 2, pp. 315–67.

Burns, A. F. and Mitchell, W. C. (1946), *Measuring Business Cycles*, New York: NBER.

Campbell, J. Y. and Mankiw, N. G. (1987), 'Are output fluctuations transitory?', *The Quarterly Journal of Economics*, vol. 102, pp. 857–80.

Campbell, J. Y. and Shiller, R. J. (1987), 'Cointegrational tests of present value models', *Journal of Political Economy*, vol. 95, pp. 1062–88.

— (1988), 'Interpreting cointegrated models', *Journal of Economic Dynamics and Control*, vol. 12, pp. 505–22.

Canarella, G. and Pollard, S. K. (1988), 'Efficiency in foreign exchange Markets: a vector autoregressive approach', *Journal of International Money and Finance*, vol. 7, pp. 331–46.

Carbone, R. (1984), 'AEP filtering', pp. 201–20 in Makridakis *et al.* (1984).

Carbone, R. and Longini, R. L. (1977), 'A feedback model for automated real estate assessment', *Management Science*, vol. 24, pp. 241–8.

Central Statistical Office (1988), *Input–Output Tables for the United Kingdom 1984*, London: Her Majesty's Stationery Office.

Chatfield, C. (1980), *The Analysis of Time Series: An Introduction*, second edition, London: Chapman and Hall.

— (1988), 'The future of time-series forecasting', *International Journal of Forecasting*, vol. 4, pp. 411–19.

Chisnall, P. M. (1986), *Marketing Research*, third edition, London: McGraw-Hill.

Chow, G. C. (1960), 'Statistical demand functions for automobiles in the U.S.: a study of consumer durables' in A. C. Harberger (editor), *The Demand for Durable Goods*, Chicago: University of Chicago Press.

Clemen, R. T. (1986), 'Linear constraints and the efficiency of combined forecasts', *Journal of Forecasting*, vol. 5, pp. 31–8.

Clemen, R. T. and Winkler, R. L. (1986), 'Combining economic forecasts', *Journal of Business and Economic Statistics*, vol. 4, pp. 39–46.

Coates, J. F. (1985), 'Scenarios part two: alternative futures', pp. 21–46 in Mendell (1985).

Cooper, J. P. and Nelson, C. R. (1975), 'The ex-ante prediction performance of the St. Louis and FRB-MIT-PENN econometric models and some results on composite predictors', *Journal of Money, Credit and Banking*, vol. 7, pp. 1–32.

Cooper, R. L. (1972), 'The predictive performance of quarterly econometric models of the United States' in B. G. Hickman (editor), *Econometric Models of Cyclical Behavior*, New York: Columbia University Press.

Dalrymple, D. J. (1987) 'Sales forecasting practices: results from a United States survey', *International Journal of Forecasting*, vol. 3, pp. 379–91.

Davidson, J. E. H., Hendry, D. F., Srba, F. and Yeo, S. (1978), 'Econometric modelling of the aggregate time series relationship between consumer's expenditure and income in the United Kingdom', *Economic Journal*, vol. 88, pp. 661–92.

194   **References**

Dawes, R. M. (1986), 'Forecasting one's own preference', *International Journal of Forecasting*, vol. 2, pp. 5–14.

Dax, P. (1987), 'Estimation of income elasticities from cross-section data', *Applied Economics*, vol. 19, pp. 1471–82.

De Leeuw, F. and McKelvey, M. J. (1981), 'Price expectations of business firms', *Brookings Papers on Economic Activity*, no. 1, pp. 299–313.

De Pelsmacker, P. (1988), 'Marketing, expenditure and quality adjusted price effects on market share evolution in a segmented Belgian car market (1972–81)', *Applied Economics*, vol. 20, pp. 15–30.

Dickey, T. A. and Fuller, W. A. (1979), 'Distribution of the estimators for autoregressive time series with a unit root', *Journal of the American Statistical Association*, vol. 74, pp. 427–31.

— (1981), 'The likelihood ratio statistics for autoregressive time series with a unit root', *Econometrica*, vol. 49, pp. 1057–72.

Diebold, F. X. (1988), 'Serial correlation and the combination of forecasts', *Journal of Business and Economic Statistics*, vol. 6, pp. 105–11.

Diebold, F. X. and Pauly, P. (1987), 'Structural change and the combination of forecasts', *Journal of Forecasting*, vol. 6, pp. 21–40.

Dimson, E. and Marsh, P. (1984), 'Unpublished forecasts of UK stock returns' *Journal of Finance*, vol. 39, pp. 1257–92.

Dino, R. N. (1985), 'Forecasting the price evolution of new electronic products', *Journal of Forecasting*, vol. 4, pp. 39–60.

Doan, T. A. and Litterman, R. B. (1986), *Users' Manual. RATS Version 2.0*, VAR Econometrics Minneapolis.

Doan, T., Litterman, R. and Sims, C. (1984), 'Forecasting and conditional projection using realistic prior distributions', *Econometric Reviews*, vol. 3, pp. 1–100.

Dodson, J. A. (1981), 'Application and utilization of test-market-based new-product forecasting models', pp. 411–22 of Wind, Mahajan and Cardozo (1981).

Dolado, J. T. and Jenkinson, T. (1987), 'Cointegration: a survey of recent developments', *Applied Economics Discussion Paper No. 39*, Institute of Economics and Statistics Oxford.

Dooley, M. P. and Shafer, J. R. (1976), 'Analysis of short-run exchange rate behaviour: March 1973 to September 1975', *International Finance Discussion Paper no. 76*, Federal Reserve System Washington DC.

Dorfman, R. and Steiner, P. O. (1954), 'Optimal advertising and optimal quality', *American Economic Review*, vol. 44, pp. 826–36.

Dornbusch, R. (1976), 'Expectations and exchange rate dynamics', *Journal of Political Economy*, vol. 84, pp. 1161–76.

Engle, R. F. and Granger, C. W. J. (1987), 'Cointegration and error correction: representation, estimation and testing', *Econometrica*, vol. 55, pp. 251–76.

Engle, R. F., Granger, C. W. J. and Kraft, D. (1984), 'Combining forecasts of inflation using a bivariate ARCH model', *Journal of Economic Dynamics and Control*, vol. 8, pp. 151–65.

Evans, G. B. A. and Savin, N. E. (1984), 'Testing for unit roots II', *Econometrica*, vol. 52, pp. 1241–70.

Fama, E. F. (1970), 'Efficient capital markets: a review of theory and empirical evidence', *Journal of Finance*, vol. 25, pp. 383–417.

— (1984), 'Forward and spot exchange rates', *Journal of Monetary Economics*, vol. 14, pp. 509–28.

Fama, E. F. and Blume, M. E. (1966), 'Filter rules and stock market trading', *Journal of Business*, vol. 39, pp. 226–41.

Fama, E. F. and French, K. R. (1987) 'Commodity futures prices: some evidence on forecast power, premiums and the theory of storage', *Journal of Business*, vol. 60, pp. 55–73.

Feige, E. L. and Pearce, D. K. (1976), 'Economically rational expectations: are innovations in the rate of inflation independent of innovations in measures of monetary and fiscal policy?', *Journal of Political Economy*, vol. 84, pp. 499–522.

Figlewski, S. (1983), 'Optimal price forecasting using survey data', *Review of Economics and Statistics*, vol. 65, pp. 13–21.

Figlewski, S. and Urich, T. (1983), 'Optimal aggregation of money supply forecasts: accuracy, profitability and market efficiency', *Journal of Finance*, vol. 28, pp. 695–710.

Figlewski, S. and Wachtel, P. (1981), 'The formation of inflationary expectations', *Review of Economics and Statistics*, vol. 63, pp. 1–10.

Fildes, R. F. (1984), 'Bayesian forecasting', pp. 221–38 in Makridakis *et al.* (1984).

— (1985), 'Quantitative forecasting – the state of the art: econometric models', *Journal of the Operational Research Society*, vol. 36, pp. 549–80.

Fildes, R. F. and Chrissanthaki, T. (1988), *World Index of Economic Forecasts*, third edition, Aldershot: Gower.

Fischhoff, B. (1988), 'Judgmental aspects of forecasting: needs and possible trends', *International Journal of Forecasting*, vol. 4, pp. 331–9.

Fisher, J. A. (1962), 'An analysis of consumer good expenditure', *Review of Economics and Statistics*, vol. 44, pp. 64–71.

Flores, B. E. (1986), 'Use of the sign test to supplement the percentage better statistic', *International Journal of Forecasting*, vol. 2, pp. 477–90.

Frank, M. and Stengos, T. (1988), 'Chaotic dynamics in economic time series', *Journal of Economic Surveys*, vol. 2, pp. 103–33.

Frankel, J. A. and Froot, K. (1986), 'Using survey data to test some standard propositions regarding exchange rate expectations', *National Bureau of Economic Research*, working paper no. 1773.

Frattiani, M., Hur, H. D. and Kang, H. (1987), 'Random walk and monetary causality in five foreign exchange markets', *Journal of International Money and Finance*, vol. 6, pp. 505–14.

Frenkel, J. A. (1976), 'A monetary approach to the exchange rate: doctrinal aspects and empirical evidence', *Scandinavian Journal of Economics*, vol. 78, pp. 200–24.

Gardner, E. S. (1985), 'Exponential smoothing: the state of the art', *International Journal of Forecasting*, vol. 4, pp. 1–28.

Gardner, E. S. and Makridakis, S. (1988), 'The future of forecasting', *International Journal of Forecasting*, vol. 4, pp. 325–30.

Geweke, J. and Meese, R. (1981), 'Estimating regression models of finite but unknown order', *International Economic Review*, vol. 22, pp. 55–70.

Goldfeld, S. M. and Quandt, R. E. (1965), 'Some tests for homoscedasticity', *Journal of the American Statistical Association*, vol. 60, pp. 539–47.

Goodman, S. J. (1979), 'Foreign exchange forecasting techniques: implications for business and policy', *Journal of Finance*, vol. 34, pp. 415–27.

Gordon, R. A. (1961), *Business Fluctuations*, second edition, New York: Harper and Brothers.

Gordon, R. J. and King, S. R. (1982), 'The output cost of disinflation in traditional and vector autoregressive models', *Brookings Papers on Economic Activity*, pp. 205–4.

Granger, C. W. J. (1969a), 'Prediction with a generalised cost of error function', *Operational Research Quarterly*, vol. 20, pp. 199–207.

— (1969b), 'Investigating causal relations by econometric models and cross-spectral methods', *Econometrica*, vol. 37, pp. 24–36.

— (1983), 'Cointegrated variables and error correction models', *Working Paper 83–13*, University of California San Diego California.

— (1986), 'Developments in the study of cointegrated economic variables', *Oxford Bulletin of Economics and Statistics*, vol. 48, pp. 213–28.

Granger, C. W. J. and Anderson, A. P. (1978), *An Introduction to Bilinear Time Series Models*, Göttingen: Vandenhoeck and Ruprecht.

Granger, C. W. J. and Newbold, P. (1973), 'Some comments on the evaluation of economic forecasts', *Applied Economics*, vol. 5, pp. 35–47.

— (1976), 'Forecasting transformed series', *Journal of the Royal Statistical Society Series B*, vol. 38, pp. 189–203.

— (1977), *Forecasting Economic Time Series*, New York: Academic Press.

Granger, C. W. J. and Ramanathan, R. (1984), 'Improved methods of combining forecasts', *Journal of Forecasting*, vol. 3, pp. 197–204.

Grassberger, P. and Prococcia, I. (1983), 'Measuring the strangeness of strange attractors', *Physica*, vol. 9, pp. 189–208.

Gross, C. W. and Peterson, R. T. (1976), *Business Forecasting*, Boston: Houghton Mifflin Company.

Grossman, S. J. and Stiglitz, J. E. (1976), 'Information and competitive price systems', *American Economic Review*, vol. 66, pp. 246–53.

Gujarati, D. (1988), *Basic Econometrics*, New York: McGraw-Hill.

Gupta, S. and Wilton, P. C. (1987), 'Combination of forecasts: an extension', *Management Science*, vol. 33, pp. 356–72.

Hadley, G. (1965), *Linear Programming*, London: Addison-Wesley.

Hall, S. G. (1988), 'Rationality and Siegel's paradox, the importance of coherency in expectations', *Applied Economics*, vol. 20, pp. 1533–40.

Hanke, J. (1984), 'Forecasting in business schools', *Journal of Forecasting*, vol. 3, pp. 229–34.

Hannan, E. J. and Quinn, B. G. (1979), 'The determination of the order of an autoregression', *Journal of the Royal Statistical Society*, Series B, vol. 41, pp. 190–5.

Hansen, L. P. and Hodrick, R. J. (1980), 'Forward exchange rates as optimal predictors of future spot rates', *Journal of Political Economy*, vol. 88, pp. 829–53.

Harvey, A. C. (1981), *Time Series Models*, Deddington: Philip Allan.

— (1984), 'A unified view of statistical forecasting procedures', *Journal of Forecasting*, vol. 3, pp. 245–75.

Haugh, L. D. and Box, G. E. P. (1977), 'Identification of dynamic regression models connecting two time series', *Journal of the American Statistical Association*, vol. 72, pp. 121–30.

Hebden, J. (1983), *Applications of Econometrics*, Deddington: Philip Allan Publishers.

Hellwig, M. F. (1982), 'Rational expectations equilibrium with conditioning in past prices', *Journal of Economic Theory*, vol. 26, pp. 279–312.

Hewings, G. J. D. (1985), *Regional Input–Output Analysis*, London: Sage.

Hey, J. D. (1983), *Data in Doubt*, Oxford: Martin Robertson.

Hicks, J. (1974), *The Crisis in Keynesian Economics*, Oxford: Basil Blackwell.

Hill, G. and Fildes, R. (1984), 'The accuracy of extrapolation methods', *Journal of Forecasting*, vol. 3, pp. 319–24.

HM Treasury (1987), *Macroeconomic Model: List of Equations and Variable Definitions*, London: HM Treasury.

Hodrick, R. and Srivastava, S. (1984), 'An investigation of risk and return in forward foreign exchange', *Journal of International Money and Finance*, vol. 3, pp. 5–30.

Holden, K. and Pearson, A. W. (1983), *Introductory Mathematics for Economists*, Basingstoke: Macmillan.

Holden, K. and Peel, D. A. (1983), 'Forecasts and expectations: some evidence for the UK', *Journal of Forecasting*, vol. 2, pp. 51–8.

— (1985), 'An evaluation of quarterly National Institute forecasts', *Journal of Forecasting*, vol. 4, pp. 227–34.

— (1986), 'An empirical investigation of combinations of economic forecasts', *Journal of Forecasting*, vol. 5, pp. 229–42.

— (1989), 'Unbiasedness, efficiency and the combination of economic forecasts', *Journal of Forecasting*, vol. 8, pp. 175–88.

— (1990), 'On testing for unbiasedness and efficiency of forecasts', *Manchester School*, vol. 59 (forthcoming).

Holden, K., Peel, D. A. and Thompson, J. L. (1982), *Modelling the UK Economy: An Introduction*, Oxford: Martin Robertson.

— (1985), *Expectations: Theory and Evidence*, Basingstoke: Macmillan.

Holmes, R. A. (1986), 'Leading indicators of industrial employment in British Columbia', *International Journal of Forecasting*, vol. 2, pp. 87–100.

Holt, C. C. (1957), *Forecasting Seasonals and Trends by Exponential Weighted Moving Averages*, Pittsburg: Carnegie Institute of Technology.

Hooper, P. and Morton, J. (1982), 'Fluctuations in the dollar: a model of nominal and real exchange rate determination', *Journal of International Money and Finance*, vol. 1, pp. 39–56.

Houthakker, H. and Taylor, L. D. (1970), *Consumer Demand in the United States 1929–1970*, second edition, Cambridge, Mass.: Harvard University Press.

Howrey, E. P., Klein, L. R. and McCarthy, M. D. (1974), 'Notes on testing the predictive performance of econometric models', *International Economic Review*, vol. 15, pp. 366–83.

Jarrett, J. (1987), *Business Forecasting Methods*, Oxford: Basil Blackwell.

Johansen, S. (1988), 'Statistical analysis of cointegrating vectors', *Journal of Economic Dynamics and Control*, vol. 12, pp. 231–54.

Johnston, J. (1984), *Econometric Methods*, third edition, New York: McGraw-Hill.

Jorgenson, D. E., Hunter, J. and Nadiri, M. I. (1970), 'A comparison of alternative models of quarterly investment behavior', *Econometrica*, vol. 38, pp. 187–212.

Judge, G. C., Carter-Hill, R., Griffiths, W. E., Lutkepohl, H. and Tsoung-Choo Lee (1985), *The Theory and Practice of Econometrics*, 2nd edition, New York: Wiley.

— (1988), *Introduction to the Theory and Practice of Econometrics*, 2nd edition, New York: Wiley.

Kang, H. (1986), 'Unstable weights in the combination of forecasts', *Management Science*, vol. 32, pp. 683–55.

Keating, G. (1985), *The Production and Use of Economic Forecasts*, London: Methuen.

Keenan, D. M. (1985), 'A Tukey non-additivity type test for time series non-linearity', *Biometrika*, vol. 72, pp. 39–44.

Kennedy, P. (1985), *A Guide to Econometrics*, second edition, Oxford: Blackwell.

Ketkar, K. W. and Ketkar, S. L. (1987), 'Population dynamics and consumer demand', *Applied Economics*, vol. 19, pp. 1483–95.

Klein, P. A. (1986), 'Leading indicators of inflation in market economies', *International Journal of Forecasting*, vol. 2, pp. 403–12.

Klein, P. A. and Moore, G. H. (1983), 'The leading indicator approach to economic forecasting – retrospect and prospect', *Journal of Forecasting*, vol. 2, pp. 119–37.

Kmenta, J. (1986), *Elements of Econometrics*, second edition, New York: Macmillan.

Koedijk, K. G. and Ott, M. (1987), 'Risk aversion, efficient markets and the forward exchange rate', *Federal Reserve Bank of St. Louis Review*, vol. 69, pp. 5–13.

Koehler, A. B. and Murphree, E. S. (1988), 'A comparison of results from state space forecasting with forecasts from the Makridakis competition', *International Journal of Forecasting*, vol. 4, pp. 45–56.

Kotler, P. (1988), *Marketing Management*, Englewood Cliffs: Prentice-Hall.

Lambin, J. J. (1976), *Advertising, Competition and Market Conduct in Oligopoly over Time*, Amsterdam: North-Holland.

Landefeld, J. S. and Seskin, E. P. (1986), 'A comparison of anticipatory surveys and econometric models in forecasting US business investment', *Journal of Economic and Social Measurement*, vol. 14, pp. 77–85.

Laumer, H. and Zeigler, M. (eds.) (1982), *International Research on Business Cycle Surveys*, Aldershot: Gower Publishing Co.

Layton, A. P., Defris, L. V. and Zehnwirth, B. (1986), 'An international comparison of economic leading indicators of telecommunications traffic', *International Journal of Forecasting*, vol. 2, pp. 413–25.

Ledolter, J. (1984), 'Comments on "A unified view of statistical forecasting procedures" by A. C. Harvey', *Journal of Forecasting*, vol. 3, pp. 278–82.

Leone, R. P. and Schultz, R. L. (1980), 'A study of marketing generalizations' *Journal of Marketing*, vol. 44, no. 1, pp. 10–18.

Leontief, W. (1986), *Input–Output Economics*, second edition, Oxford University Press.

Levich, R. M. (1979), 'Analyzing the foreign exchange advisory services: theory and evidence' in R. M. Levich and C. Whilbourg (editors), *Exchange Risk and Exposure*, Lexington: D. C. Heath.

Levy, R. A. (1971), 'The predictive significance of five-point chart patterns', *Journal of Business*, vol. 44, pp. 316–23.

Lewandowski, R. (1984), 'Sales forecasting by FORSYS', pp. 255–65 in Makridakis *et al.* (1984).

Libert, G. (1984), 'The M-competition with a fully automatic Box–Jenkins procedure', *Journal of Forecasting*, vol. 3, pp. 325–8.

Liebling, H. I., Bidwell, P. T. and Hall, K. E. (1976), 'The recent performance of anticipations surveys and econometric model projections of investment spending in the United States', *Journal of Business*, vol. 49, pp. 451–77.

Litterman, R. B. (1986a), 'A statistical approach to economic forecasting', *Journal of Business and Economic Statistics*, vol. 4, pp. 1–4.

— (1986b), 'Forecasting with Bayesian vector autoregressions – five years of experience', *Journal of Business and Economic Statistics*, vol. 4, pp. 25–38.

Ljung, G. M. and Box, G. E. P. (1978), 'On a measure of lack of fit in time series models', *Biometrika*, vol. 67, pp. 67–72.

Logue, D. E. and Sweeney, R. J. (1977), 'White noise in imperfect markets: the case of the Franc/dollar exchange rate', *Journal of Finance*, vol. 32, pp. 761–8.

Lucas, R. E. (1976), 'Econometric policy evaluation: a critique' in K. Brunner and A. H. Meltzer (editors), *The Phillips Curve and Labour Markets*, vol. 1, pp. 19–46, Carnegie-Rochester Conferences on Public Policy, supplement to *Journal of Monetary Economics*, Amsterdam: North-Holland.

Luck, D. J. and Rubin, R. S. (1987), *Marketing Research*, seventh edition, Englewood Cliffs: Prentice Hall.

Lupoletti, W. M. and Webb, R. H. (1986), 'Defining and improving the accuracy of macroeconomic forecasts: contributions from a VAR model', *Journal of Business*, vol. 59, pp. 263–85.

Lusk, E. J. and Neves, J. S. (1984), 'A comparative ARIMA analysis of the 111 series of the Makridakis competition', *Journal of Forecasting*, vol. 3, pp. 329–32.

MacDonald, R. and Taylor, M. P. (1988), 'Testing rational expectations and efficiency in the London Metal Exchange', *Oxford Bulletin of Economics and Statistics*, vol. 50, pp. 41–52.

— (1989), 'Rational expectations, risk and efficiency in the London Metal Exchange: an empirical analysis', *Applied Economics*, vol. 21, pp. 143–53.

McCallum, B. T. (1976), 'Rational expectations and the estimation of econometric models', *International Economic Review*, vol. 17, pp. 484–90.

McCulloch, J. H. (1975), 'Operational aspects of the Siegel paradox', *Quarterly Journal of Economics*, vol. 86, pp. 170–2.

McGuiness, T. (1980), 'An econometric analysis of total demand for alcoholic beverages in the UK 1956–75', *Journal of Industrial Economics*, vol. 29, pp. 85–109.

McLaughlin, R. L. (1982), 'A model of an average recession and recovery', *Journal of Forecasting*, vol. 1, pp. 55–65.

McNees, S. K. (1978), 'The rationality of economic forecasts', *American Economic Review*, vol. 68, pp. 301–5.

— (1986), 'Forecasting accuracy of alternative techniques: a comparison of US macroeconomic forecasts', *Journal of Business and Economic Statistics*, vol. 4, pp. 5–15.

— (1988) 'On the future of macroeconomic forecasting', *International Journal of Forecasting*, vol. 4, pp. 359–62.

Mackie, D., Miles, D. and Taylor, C. (1989), 'The impact of monetary policy on inflation: modelling the UK experience 1978–86', in A. Britton (editor), *Policymaking with Macroeconomic Models*, Aldershot: Gower Publishing.

Maddala, G. S. (1988), *Introduction to Econometrics*, New York: Macmillan.

Makridakis, S. (1986), 'The art and science of forecasting: an assessment and future directions', *International Journal of Forecasting*, vol. 2, pp. 15–39.

Makridakis, S., Andersen, A., Carbone, R., Fildes, R., Hibon, M., Lewandowski, R., Newton, S., Parzen, E. and Winkler, R. (1984), 'The accuracy of extrapolation (time series) methods: results of a forecasting competition', *Journal of Forecasting*, vol. 1, pp. 111–53.

Makridakis, S. and Hibon, M. (1979), 'Accuracy and forecasting: an empirical investigation (with discussion)', *Journal of the Royal Statistical Society Series A (General)*, vol. 142, pp. 97–145.

Makridakis, S. and Wheelwright, S. C. (1977), 'Forecasting issues and challenges for marketing management', *Journal of Marketing*, vol. 41, October, pp. 24–38.

Makridakis, S. and Winkler, R. L. (1983), 'Averages of forecasts: some empirical results', *Management Science*, vol. 29, pp. 987–96.

Makridakis, S. (1984), *The Forecasting Accuracy of Major Time Series Methods*, Chichester: John Wiley.

Maravall, A. (1983), 'An application of non-linear time series analysis forecasting', *Journal of Business and Economic Statistics*, vol. 1, pp. 66–74.

Meade, N. (1984), 'The use of growth curves in forecasting market development', *Journal of Forecasting*, vol. 3, pp. 429–51.

Meese, R. A. and Rogoff, K. (1983), 'Empirical exchange rate models of the seventies: do they fit out of sample', *Journal of International Economics*, vol. 14, pp. 3–24.

Mendell, J. S. (1985), *Nonextrapolative Methods in Business Forecasting*, London: Quorum Books.

Mendenhall, W. and Reinmuth, J. E. (1982), *Statistics for Management and Economics*, Boston, Mass.: Duxbury Press.

Mentzer, J. T. and Cox, J. E. (1984), 'Familiarity, application and performance of sales forecasting techniques', *Journal of Forecasting*, vol. 3, pp. 27–36.

Minford, A. P. L., Marwaha, S., Matthews, K. G. P. and Sprague, A. (1984), 'The Liverpool model of the United Kingdom', *Economic Modelling*, vol. 1, pp. 24–62.

Minford, A. P. L. and Peel, D. A. (1983), *Rational Expectations and the New Macroeconomics*, Oxford, Martin Robertson.

Moore, G. H. (1983), *Business Cycles, Inflation and Forecasting*, second edition, Cambridge, Mass.: Ballinger.

Moore, G. H. and Moore, M. H. (1985), *International Economic Indicators*, London: Greenwood Press.

Moriarty, M. M. and Adams, A. J. (1984), 'Management judgement forecasts, composite forecasting models and conditional efficiency', *Journal of Marketing Research*, vol. 21, pp. 239–50.

Muellbauer, J. (1977), 'Testing the Barten model of household composition effects and the cost of children', *Economic Journal*, vol. 87, pp. 460–87.

Nankervis, J. C. and Savin, N. E. (1985), 'Testing the autoregressive parameter with the *t*-statistic', *Journal of Econometrics*, vol. 27, pp. 143–62.

Nelson, C. R. and Kang, H. (1984), 'Pitfalls in the use of time as an explanatory variable in regression', *Journal of Business and Economic Statistics*, vol. 2, pp. 73–82.

Nelson, C. R. and Plosser, C. (1982), 'Trends and random walks in macroeconomic time series', *Journal of Monetary Economics*, vol. 10, pp. 139–62.

Newbold, P. (1984), 'Some recent developments in time series analysis – II', *International Statistical Review*, vol. 52, pp. 183–92.

Newbold, P. and Granger, C. W. J. (1974), 'Experience with forecasting univariate time series and the combination of forecasts', *Journal of the Royal Statistical Society*, Series A, vol. 137, pp. 131–64.

Newton, H. J. and Parzen, E. (1984), 'Forecasting and time series model types of 111 economic time series', pp. 267–87 in Makridakis *et al.* (1984).

Odling-Smee, J. (1989), 'Comment on "The exchange rate and external trade"', in A. Britton (editor), *Policymaking with Macroeconomic Models*, Aldershot: Gower Publishing.

Oppenlander, K. H. and Poser, G. (1984), *Leading Indicators and Business Cycle Surveys*, Aldershot: Gower Publishing Co.

Ord, J. K. (1988), 'Future developments in forecasting', *International Journal of Forecasting*, vol. 4, pp. 389–401.

Ozaki, T. (1980), 'Non-linear time series models for non-linear random vibrations', *Journal of Applied Probability*, vol. 17, pp. 84–93.

Parente, F. J. and Anderson-Parente, J. K. (1987), 'Delphi Inquiry Systems', pp. 129–56 in G. Wright and P. Ayton (editors), *Judgmental Forecasting*, Chichester: John Wiley and Sons.

Peel, M. J., Peel, D. A. and Pope, P. F. (1986), 'Predicting corporate failure: some results for the UK corporate sector', *Omega*, vol. 14, pp. 5–12.

Perron, P. (1988) 'Trends and random walks in macroeconomic time series: further evidence from a new approach', *Journal of Economic Dynamics and Control*, vol. 12, pp. 297–332.

Perron, P. and Phillips, P. C. B. (1987), 'Does GNP have a unit root? A revaluation', *Economic Letters*, vol. 23, pp. 139–45.

Petruccelli, J. D. and Davies, N. (1986), 'A portmanteau test for self-exciting threshold autoregressive-type non-linearity in time series', *Biometrika*, vol. 73, pp. 687–94.

Phillips, P. C. B. (1987a), 'Time series regressions with unit roots', *Econometrica*, vol. 55, pp. 277–302.

— (1987b), 'Towards a unified asymptotic theory for autoregression', *Biometrika*, vol. 74, pp. 535–47.

Pindyck, R. S. and Rubinfeld, D. L. (1981), *Econometric Models and Economic Forecasts*, New York: McGraw-Hill.

Pokorny, M. (1987), *An Introduction to Econometrics*, Oxford: Basil Blackwell.

Polenske, K. R. (1980), *The US Multiregional Input–Output Accounts and Model*, Lexington, Mass.: Lexington Books.

Poulos, L., Kvanli, A. and Pavur, R. (1987), 'A comparison of the accuracy of the Box–Jenkins method with that of automated forecasting methods', *International Journal of Forecasting*, vol. 3, pp. 261–8.

Priestley, M. B. (1980), 'State dependent models: a general approach to non-linear time series analysis', *Journal of Time Series Analysis*, vol. 1, pp. 47–71.

Reid, D. J. (1969), 'A Comparative Study of Time Series Prediction Techniques on Economic Data', Unpublished Ph.D. thesis, University of Nottingham, Department of Mathematics.

Russell, T. D. and Adam, E. A. (1987), 'An empirical evaluation of alternative forecasting combinations', *Management Science*, vol. 33, pp. 1267–76.

Sargan, J. D. (1964), 'Wages and prices in the United Kingdom: a study in econometric methodology', in P. E. Hart, G. Mills and J. K. Whittaker *Econometric Analysis of National Economic Planning*, London: Butterworth.

Sargan, J. D. and Bhargava, A. (1983), 'Testing residuals from least squares regression for being generated by the Gaussian random walk', *Econometrica*, vol. 51, pp. 153–74.

Saunders, P. (1980), 'Price and cost expectations in Australian manufacturing firms', *Australian Economic Papers*, vol 19, pp. 46–67.

— (1983), 'A disaggregated study of the rationality of Australian producers' price expectations', *The Manchester School*, vol. 51, pp. 380–98.

Saville, I. D. and Gardiner, K. L. (1986), 'Stagflation in the UK since 1970: a model-based explanation', *National Institute Economic Review*, no. 117, pp. 52–69.

Scheinkman, J. and LeBaron, B. (1986), 'Non-linear dynamics and stock returns', *Department of Economics*, University of Chicago, Chicago Illinois.

Schmalensee, R. (1972), *The Economics of Advertising*, Amsterdam: North-Holland.

Schnaars, S. P. (1986), 'A comparison of extrapolation models on yearly sales forecasts', *International Journal of Forecasting*, vol. 2, pp. 71–85.

Schnaars, S. P. and Topol, M. T. (1987), 'The use of scenarios in sales forecasting', *International Journal of Forecasting*, vol. 3, pp. 405–19.

Sharpe, W. F. (1964), 'Capital asset prices: a theory of market equilibrium under conditions of risk', *Journal of Finance*, vol. 19, pp. 425–42.

Sims, C. A. (1980), 'Macroeconomics and reality', *Econometrica*, vol. 48, pp. 1–48.

Somanath, V. S. (1986), 'Efficient exchange rate forecasts: lagged models better than the random walk', *Journal of International Money and Finance*, vol. 5 pp. 195–220.

Sparkes, J. R. and McHugh, A. K. (1984), 'Awareness and use of forecasting techniques in British industry', *Journal of Forecasting*, vol. 3, pp. 37–42.

Stavrinos, V. G. (1987), 'The effects of an anti-smoking campaign on cigarette consumption: empirical evidence from Greece', *Applied Economics*, vol. 19, pp. 323–9.

Stone, J. R. N. and Rowe, D. A. (1957), 'The market demand for durable goods', *Econometrica*, vol. 25, pp. 423–43.

Stoney, P. J. M. and Davies, S. (1980), 'Selected bibliography on applications of input–output analysis in industrial marketing and forecasting' in S. J. Gielnik and W. F. Gossling (editors), *Input, Output and Marketing*, London: Input–Output Publishing Company.

Strigel, W. H. and Ziegler, M. (1988), 'Cyclical business and consumer surveys – the current state of the art' in Fildes and Chrissanthaki (1988).

Subba Rao, T. and Gabr, M. M. (1980), 'A test for linearity of stationary time series', *Journal of Time Series Analysis*, vol. 2, pp. 145–58.

Targett, D. (1983), *Coping with Numbers*, Oxford: Martin Robertson.

Taylor, S. (1986), *Modelling Financial Time Series*, Chichester: John Wiley.

Theil, H. (1961), *Economic Forecasts and Policy*, Amsterdam: North–Holland.

— (1966), *Applied Economic Forecating*, Amsterdam: North–Holland.

Thomas, R. L. (1985), *Introductory Econometrics*, Harlow: Longman Group.

— (1987), *Applied Demand Analysis*, London: Longmans.

Tong, H. (1983), 'Threshold models in non-linear time series analysis', *Lecture Notes in Statistics*, 21, Berlin: Springer Verlag.

Townsend, J. L. (1987), 'Cigarette tax, economic welfare and social class patterns of smoking', *Applied Economics*, vol. 19, p. 355–65.

Tsay, R. S. (1988), 'Non-linear time series analysis of blow fly population', *Journal of Time Series Analysis*, vol. 9, pp. 247–63.

Tyebjee, T. T. (1987), 'Behavioral biases in new product forecasting', *International Journal of Forecasting*, vol. 3, pp. 393–404.

US Department of Commerce (1967), 'The X-11 variant of the census method II seasonal adjustment program', Technical Paper no. 15, 1967 version, Washington, DC: US Government Printing Office.

Van der Ploeg, F. (1986), 'Rational expectations, risk and chaos in financial markets', *Economic Journal (Supplement)*, vol. 96, pp. 151–62.

van Helden, G. J., Leeflang, P. S. H. and Sterken, E. (1987), 'Estimation of the demand for electricity', *Applied Economics*, vol. 19, pp. 69–82.

Wallis, K. F. (1986), 'Forecasting with an econometric model: the 'ragged edge' problem', *Journal of Forecasting*, vol. 5, pp. 1–13.

— (1989), 'Macroeconomic forecasting: a survey', *Economic Journal*, vol. 99, pp. 28–61.

Wallis, K. F., Andrews, M. J., Bell, D. N. F., Fisher, P. G. and Whitley, J. D., *et al.* (1984), *Models of the UK Economy: A Review*, Oxford University Press.

Wallis, K. F., Andrews, M. J., Fisher, P. G., Longbottom, J. A. and Whitley, J. D. (1986), *Models of the UK Economy: A Third Review*, Oxford University Press.

Wallis, K. F., Fisher, P. G., Longbottom, J. A., Turner, D. S. and Whitley, J. D. (1987), *Models of the UK Economy: A Fourth Review*, Oxford University Press.

Webb, R. H. (1988), 'Commodity prices as predictors of aggregate price change', *Economic Review Federal Reserve Bank of Richmond*, vol. 74/6.

Wind, Y., Mahajan, V. and Cardozo, R. N. (1981) (editors), *New-Product Forecasting*, Lexington: Lexington Books.

Winkler, R. L. (1984), 'Combining forecasts', pp. 289–95 in Markridakis *et al.* (1984).

Winkler, R. L. and Makridakis, S. (1983), 'The combination of forecasts', *Journal of the Royal Statistical Society*, Series A, vol. 146, pp. 150–7.

Winters, P. R. (1960), 'Forecasting sales by exponentially weighted moving averages', *Management Science*, vol. 6, pp. 324–42.

Wolff, C. (1987), 'Forward foreign exchange rates, expected spot exchange rates and premia: a signal extraction approach', *Centre for Economic Policy Research*, Discussion Paper no. 188.

Zarnowitz, V. (1979), 'An analysis of annual and multiperiod quarterly forecasts of aggregate income, output and the price level', *Journal of Business*, vol. 52, pp. 1–33.

Author index

Subject index